Passion

Passion

An Essay on Personality

Roberto Mangabeira Unger

THE FREE PRESS
A Division of Macmillan, Inc.
NEW YORK

Collier Macmillan Publishers
LONDON

The Free Press
A Division of Macmillan, Inc.
866 Third Avenue, New York, N. Y. 10022

Collier Macmillan Canada, Inc.

First Free Press Paperback Edition 1986

Printed in the United States of America

printing number

1 2 3 4 5 6 7 8 9 10

Library of Congress Cataloging in Publication Data

Unger, Roberto Mangabeira
  Passion: an essay on personality.

  1. Personality—Addresses, essays, lectures.
1. Title.
BF698.U48   1984   155.2   84-1488
ISBN 0-02-933180-3 pbk.

This book presents a speculative and prescriptive view of personality from the standpoint of a single but pervasive aspect of our experience: our desire to be accepted by one another and to become, through this acceptance, freer to reinvent ourselves. The essay on personality is preceded by an Introduction that elucidates and justifies the style of discourse in which the view is expressed, and it is followed by an Appendix that connects the account of the self to the work of scientific psychiatry.

The book has two major concerns: one substantive, the other methodological. The substantive concern is to offer a modernist criticism and restatement of the Christian-romantic image of man, which forms the central tradition of thinking about human nature in the West. The methodological concern is to reconceive and reconstruct the ancient and universal practice of attributing normative force to conceptions of personality or society so that this practice can better withstand the criticisms that philosophy since Hume and Kant has leveled against it.

Some readers who start with the Introduction may lose interest in an abstract discussion of the difficulties that must be faced in the course of attempts to develop prescriptive theories of human identity when they have no detailed example of such a theory before their eyes. These readers are advised to pass directly to the main body of the essay, returning later to the Introduction if they wish to consider the approach to normative thought that the argument about personality implies. Other readers, however, more respectful of the teachings of modern philosophy, will be so repelled by much in the argument of the main essay—the rapid passage from the descriptive to the prescriptive, the willingness to generalize about people without attention to the differences among historically confined societies and cultures, and the appeal to a language of self-reflection neither scientific nor metaphysical—that they would do better to start the book from the beginning.

The view of personality worked out here has its counterpart in a theory of society organized around a small number of principles. Our practical and passionate involvements ordinarily develop within institutional and imaginative settings that we take for granted. We can always act as if these frameworks did not bind us, with the consequence that their history cannot be understood as a foreordained procession of preestablished social worlds. And though, as individual or collective agents, we can never fashion institutional or imaginative contexts that do justice to all our capabilities, we can invent contexts that empower us, not least by the ease with which they can be recognized and reformed in the midst of everyday life.

It might have been better to present the views of self and society as a single, indivisible argument and thereby discourage the misreadings to which, once divided, the two views are more easily subject. I hope that this truncated interpretation and defense of the modernist vision may nevertheless lend credence to a few simple ideas: that we now possess the elements with which to formulate both a more persuasive account of our shared human identity and a better practice of normative argument than have previously been available; that the significance of the insights now within reach stands out all the more clearly when we take care not to exaggerate their differences from certain long-familiar pictures of human nature and prescriptive judgment; that there is fire yet in some of the old and implausible commitments of our civilization—the project of an ethics that sees love rather than altruism as its crowning ideal, the confidence in our ability to think and act beyond the particular forms of life and discourse in which we participate and to recast them in ways that make us more fully their masters, the belief in a link between the emancipation of society from a rigid structure of division and hierarchy and the success of our efforts at practical collaboration, passionate attachment, and self-expression; that to make good on these commitments we must continue to disengage them from unjustifiably restrictive assumptions about the possible forms of personal experience and social life; and that this disengagement supplies one more occasion to rediscover that thought speaks with authority about who we are and how we should live only when it puts our ideals and self-understandings through the skeptic's flame, risking nihilism for the sake of insight.

Introduction

We want to live in the world as people who do not mistake their unique, individual identities. We do not wish to feel—or to be—disconnected from our actions as if they better suited someone else. And whether or not we become fully aware of it we also care about our shared identity as people.

Of course, there might be nothing to which the idea of a fundamental human identity could refer, nothing but the unfinished sum of our circumstances, beliefs, and desires. Whether the conception of a human nature deserves to be taken seriously depends in part on whether it can be developed in ways that illuminate our immediate experience and that survive the surprises of scientific insight, social invention, and personal disappointment or achievement.

Suppose that such a common identity in fact existed and that it could not be reduced to strong but indeterminate biological constraints nor to precise but trivial cultural traits. We still might not be persuaded to give it any weight in choosing for ourselves, or in advocating for society, a way of life. We might just not care and even if we did care we might lack any good reason to do so. A thesis of this essay is that one way or another we do care: the ascription of normative force to conceptions of fundamental human identity is as tenacious as any other practice in our experience. The scruples of modern Western philosophy have managed to put the more aggressive intellectual expressions of this practice on the defensive. But they have not extirpated it from political and moral controversy or from our moments of more reflective self-scrutiny. Though there are no clinching arguments to be made in favor of continuing this practice, neither are there conclusive reasons to repudiate it.

When we begin to formulate a view of our true identity we are inevitably forced to take a stand on two problems about our situation. Though the two issues are irreducible to each other, they turn out to be connected. One problem concerns our relation to the habitual settings of our action—the routinized collective institutions and preconceptions, the personal habits stylized in the form of a character, and the fundamental methods and conceptions employed in the investigation of nature—that we regularly take for granted. We define ourselves in part by our attitude toward these settings: toward their origins, their transformability, and the standards by which they ought to be assessed. This is the problem of contextuality. The other issue on which we must take a stand when we define a conception of identity concerns our relations to one another. In particular, we must deal with the unlimited quality of both our mutual dependence and the jeopardy in which we place one another and with the tendency of these two features of our experience to push us in opposite directions. They do so in every area of practical life, emotion, and thought. This is the problem of solidarity.

The problems of contextuality and solidarity cannot fully emerge until the individual has gained a sense of his own limited selfhood and lost the conviction of occupying the center of the world, a belief that he gives up only slowly, reluctantly, and imperfectly. The elements of this conviction continue to mark all aspects of our conscious life, from the incomparable immediacy of our perceptions to the barely containable egotism of the will. The issues of contextuality and solidarity represent two sides of the same predicament: the predicament of a troubled particularity. Having been beaten out of its early confidence in its own centrality, the self still rightly discerns in that abandoned pretension a distorted element of truth.

This truth has sometimes been described as the idea of an infinite imprisoned within the finite. It may be less contentiously characterized as the belief that the capabilities and the demands of the self are disproportionate to its circumstances. In one way, we discover this disproportion when we recognize the partial and provisional character of social and personal routines. These routines require special justification because they are particular and we, relative to them, are not. We rediscover the same imbalance whenever we see ourselves as beings who, because we make potentially unlimited practical and spiritual claims upon one another, are always in danger of coexisting in the fashion of the proverbial unhappy couple, who cannot live together and cannot live apart.

Consider first the problem of contextuality. Our mental and social life ordinarily has a structured or shaped quality: we move within accepted limits that influence or constrain our habitual ideas and actions while resisting the disturbances that these actions or ideas may produce. This formative context may be social. It then represents a particular set of institutional arrangements and imaginative preconceptions that comes to stand in place of the more indefinite opportunities of human association. Alternatively, the context may consist in an explanatory or argumentative structure—a basic ontology, a research agenda or a series of guiding concerns, and standards of sense, validity, and verification—that an ordinary course of inquiry or discussion takes for granted. The relative strength of a context of activity or inquiry lies in its resistance to being shaken by the non-exceptional actions that it helps shape. The more entrenched a context, the clearer the distinction between the routine and the extraordinary, between the moves within the context and the struggles about it. The distinction always remains precarious: the acts that reproduce these contexts, in changing circumstances, generate an endless stream of petty conflicts that may escalate at any moment into more fundamental, context-threatening disputes.

What is our true relation to the contexts of our action? The simplest, most confident, and perhaps the most durable answer that has been given to this question in the history of our opinions about ourselves is that our mental activities and social relations possess a natural or absolute context. A context of inquiry is natural if it allows those who move within it to discover everything about the world that they can discover. A context of social life is natural if it makes available to those who inhabit it all the forms of practical collaboration or passionate attachment that people might have well-founded reasons to desire.

The point of the natural context is to reveal the terms of a balance between the striving self and the forms of discourse and of association that this self takes up. The exponent of such a context claims to describe the true face of reason or society: the mode of discourse (or the set of such modes) that accommodates all the discoveries we could make, the model of human association (or the set of such models) that allows for all the forms of practical or passionate human connection that we might justifiably want to establish. Though the natural context can undergo corruption and regeneration and though it can be realized more or less fully, it cannot be fundamentally reinvented.

The search for the natural context characterizes, in one version or another, most of the moral, political, and epistemological doctrines that have exercised the widest influence over the civilizations of the past. But the history of modern thought about society and science can be written in large part as an increasingly fierce though rarely all-out rebellion against the naturalistic premise and as a quest for alternatives to it. The repudiation of the naturalistic view has been restrained by the fear that its complete abandonment would leave us without a basis for criticizing forms of life or thought.

Thus, some have denied that there is any absolute context of inquiry or association but they have then qualified their thesis by affirming the existence of higher-order laws or principles. These rules supposedly govern the evolution of society or of thought or specify a list of alternative possible settings for inquiry and association. Others have taken the more relativistic position that we must choose our contexts arbitrarily (or have them chosen for us forcibly) and then play by their rules. But such thinkers have then found it hard to account for how these frameworks are or can be revised. And still others have downplayed the problem of contextuality altogether, emphasizing the vagueness of all contexts and the weakness of their constraining force. But those that take this position have had trouble distinguishing themselves from the adherents to the naturalistic thesis. For to say that you can have a natural context available to you and to deny that there is any special problem about the construction of your context may amount to much the same thing. The abundance of ways to conceive our relation to our contexts is further increased by our ability to adopt different theses for different aspects of our activity. We may, for example, attribute to the explanatory frameworks of science an authority stronger than the one we are willing to grant to the formative settings of social life or even to the presuppositions of non-scientific ways of thinking and conversing.

But, aside from the variations that result from combining different theses or from choosing different accounts for different areas of experience, we have a further option. The development of this additional alternative represents one of the most important achievements of modern thought; in fact I shall call it the modernist position though the precise referent of the term modernism will emerge only later in this Introduction. The following pages discuss this modernist thesis about contexts in detail because it informs, however indirectly, the particular conception of human identity to be worked out in the main body of this essay and because it supplies a crucial link in the argument for the view that conceptions of personality or society can have normative force.

The modernist account of our relation to the contexts of our ideas and actions is defined by the coexistence of three theses. The first is the principle of contextuality itself: the belief that our mental and social life is ordinarily shaped by institutional or imaginative assumptions that it takes as given. There is no unconditional context—no set of frameworks that can do justice to all our opportunities of insight and association—not even in the areas of experience where we might most expect to find such frameworks. Nor, contrary to those who dismiss the seriousness of contextuality, can any activity go forward without selecting from the indefinitely large range of possible frameworks the one that it will tentatively take for granted. This choice of frameworks establishes at least a provisional contrast between context-preserving routines and context-revising transformations.

The second thesis of this modernist view of contextuality is the idea that we can always break through all contexts of practical or conceptual activity. At any moment people may think or associate with one another in ways that overstep the boundaries of the conditional worlds in which they had moved till then. You can see or think in ways that conflict with the established context of thought even before you have deliberately and explicitly revised the context. A discovery of yours may be impossible to verify, validate, or even make sense of within the available forms of explanation and discourse; or it may conflict with the fundamental pictures of reality embodied in these forms. It may nevertheless be true. In the collision between the incongruous insight and the established structure, the structure may go under, and the proponents of the insight may discover retrospectively the terms that justify the forbidden idea.

What is true of different areas of thought, taken one by one, is also true of the work of the mind as a whole. Put together all the forms of discourse in science, philosophy, and art. Define their formative contexts however you like. So long as you define them with enough precision to save them from emptiness, the powers of the mind will never be exhaustively set out by this catalogue of modes of discourse or inquiry. There will continue to be insights that do not fit any member of the catalogue—and not just separate insights accommodated by casual adjustments here and there but whole lines of belief, explanation, or expression. No final balance can be achieved, either in the life of the mind as a whole or in any segment of this life, between what we might discover or communicate and the available ways of doing so; the opportunity for discovery and self-expression outreaches at any given time all the frameworks for thought or conversation that we can make explicit prospectively.

The same principle applies to the contexts of human association. People will always be able to order their relations to one another, from the most practical forms of collective labor to the most disinterested sorts of communal attachment, in ways that conflict with established terms of mutual access. Most of this deviation will be so fragmentary as to seem a mere penumbra of distraction and uncertainty around the fundamentals of social order. But intensify the deviations far enough—either generalize or radicalize the local experiments—and you find yourself fighting about the basics.

What is true for any given society is true as well for all societies put together no matter what our historical vantage point may be. There is no past, existent, or statable catalogue of social worlds that can incorporate all the practical or passionate relationships that people might reasonably, realistically, and rightly want to strike up. So the power to make society always goes beyond all the societies that exist or that have existed, just as the power to discover the truth about the world cannot keep within the forms of discourse that are its vehicles.

The second element in the modernist picture of human activity—the idea that all contexts can be broken—may seem incompatible with the first element—the idea that all activity is contextual. If, having broken the context they are in, people could simply remain outside any context, the thesis that all activity is contextual would be overturned. But the paradox is merely apparent. Context-breaking remains both exceptional and transitory. Either it fails and leaves the pre-established context in place, or it generates another context that can sustain it and the beliefs or relationships allied to it. An insight may enter into conflict with established criteria of validity, verification, and sense, or with a settled conception of fundamental reality. But if it is worth believing at all, then there will be criteria that can be retrospectively constructed with the aim of preserving it. Similarly, a form of practical or passionate association may be incompatible with the established terms of mutual access. But unless it does irremediable violence to a stubborn demand of personal or collective existence, there will be a remade and reimagined social world in which it can figure. In the context of association as in the context of representation, every act of limit-breaking either fails or becomes an incident in a quick movement toward an altered conditional world.

Conditionality is never overcome. But it may be loosened. For contexts of representation or relationship differ in the severity of the limits they impose upon our activity. The acknowledgment of this difference is the third element in the modernist picture of human activity.

A conceptual or social context may remain relatively immunized against activities that bring it into question and that open it up to revision and conflict. To the extent of this immunity, a sharp contrast appears between two kinds of activities: the normal activities that move within the context and the extraordinary transformative acts that change the context. This contrast is both a truth and a lie. Though it describes a reality, it also conceals the provisional quality of the distinction between context-preserving and context-breaking activities. The small-scale adjustments and revisions required by the former can always turn into the more uncontained conflicts that imply the latter. Once you disregard the fragility of the distinction between routine and transformation, the conditionality of contexts becomes easy to forget. You can then mistake the established modes of thought and human association for the natural forms of reason or relationship: that limitless plain where mind and desire and society-making might wander freely without hitting against any obstacle to their further exertions.

But you can also imagine the setting of representation or relationship progressively opened up to opportunities of vision and revision. The context is constantly held up to light and treated for what it is: a context rather than a natural order. To each of its aspects there then corresponds an activity that robs it of its immunity. The more a structure of thought or relationship provides for the occasions and instruments of its own revision, the less you must choose between maintaining it and abandoning it for the sake of the things it excludes. You can just remake or reimagine it.

Suppose, for example, a society whose formative system of powers and rights is continuously on the line, a system neither invisible nor protected against ordinary conflict, a society in which the collective experience of setting the terms of coexistence passes increasingly into the tenor of everyday life, a society that therefore frees itself from the oscillation between modest, aimless bickering and extraordinary revolutionary outbursts, a society in which people do not treat the conditional as unconditional by falling to their knees as idolaters of the social world they inhabit. Imagine a scientific or artistic representation that extends our power to innovate in the day-to-day practice of the scientific or artistic view. Imagine, further, that this extension comes about by making the forms and methods of representation themselves increasingly apparent, controversial, and revisable.

The cumulative change I describe in the conditions of reason or relationship neither hides nor abolishes the conditional quality of our contexts. It recognizes this quality with a vengeance and, in so doing, changes its nature. To live and move in the conditional world is, then, constantly to be reminded of its conditionality. To gain a higher freedom from the context is to make the context available to the transforming will and imagination rather than to bring it to a universal resting point. Thus, the third element in the picture of human activity confirms the complementarity of the other two elements—the theses that everything is contextual and that all contexts can be broken.

The distinctive character of the modernist doctrine of contexts may be brought out by contrasting it to another typically modern conception. This alternative view has found expressions as diverse as Wittgenstein's late philosophy and the theory of hermeneutics. Like the account just outlined it also begins with disbelief in natural contexts and in all the more equivocal surrogates of the naturalistic thesis. It does so, however, in a way that combines cognitive skepticism and social dogmatism.

According to this thesis the condition for sense and value is participation in a shared form of social life or a shared tradition of discourse rather than reference to discrete facts about the world. Thus, we cannot follow a rule without knowing whether we are using words in the same way from one moment to another and we cannot know whether we so use them except by observing group response to individual usage. The appeal to criteria of sameness presupposes consensus rather than making consensus possible. What holds for sense goes in spades for values.

This doctrine may seem the height of skepticism; it rejects any hope of objectivity beyond human communities and their contingent histories. From this brush with nihilism, however, the doctrine easily lapses into complacency because it teaches us that we must take communities of sense and value more or less as we find them. We must choose a social and mental world and play by its rules on pain of having no rules at all and of suffering cognitive or social chaos.

By contrast the modernist doctrine of contexts described earlier holds out the promise that we can change the character of communities of sense and value (a notion that should be taken as loosely equivalent to the idea of contexts of activity). By making them increasingly open to revision we also qualify or transform the force of our commitment to any one of them. But a facility for revision is not necessarily a device for correction. The modernist doctrine of contexts must therefore be supplemented by ideas about the features that make one explanatory or society-making practice better than another. And these ideas must in turn be drawn from a study of the accomplishments and failures of these very practices as they happen to have come into our hands. We have nowhere else to look for help.

When the modernist view of contextuality is combined with certain other beliefs it can be shown to have important implications for the construction of social theories and social ideals as well as for the understanding of our place in nature. These implications in turn demonstrate how much in a view of our fundamental identity ultimately turns upon beliefs about the status of our contexts.

The invention of contexts of social life that are increasingly open to revision is required by a variety of more specific forms of practical, moral, and cognitive empowerment. Thus, we are empowered by the development of practical capabilities that free us from deprivation and thereby allow us to broaden the range and strengthen the effect of our striving. The growth of these practical capabilities requires that the relations among people at work or in exchange not be predetermined by any rigid canon of possible dealings. In this way these relations may increasingly come to embody the restless interaction between problem-definition and problem-solving. To this end, it is not enough that people be free to recombine factors of production; they must also be free to rearrange and renew the practices that define the institutional context of production and exchange.

The heightened plasticity of economic life may be ensured by the traumatic effect of a central, coercive will upon the dense, resistant texture of social relations. Or it may be attained by a multiplication of economic agents whose deals and enterprises generate new relations as well as new techniques and products. From the pitiless standpoint of the development of practical capabilities, the task is not to choose between command and market or to find an ideal mix between them—as an obtuse ideological debate would suggest—but to invent the institutional forms of command economies or market economies that minimize the impediments to plasticity. In one case, the obstacle is the tendency of established power to subordinate its plan to its interest in self-perpetuation. In the other case, it is the tendency of decentralized economic agents to demand that transitory advantages be turned into vested rights, embodied in the absolute and permanent control of divisible portions of social capital. But the more congenial to permanent innovation an institutional form of economic life becomes, the more perfectly it exemplifies the modernist ideal of a context so open to revision that the contrast between routine moves within a framework and revolutionary struggle about it loses its force.

Another mode of empowerment consists in our relative success at diminishing the conflict between the need to participate in social life for the sake of material, emotional, and cognitive sustenance and the impulse to avoid subjection to other people. To the extent that we cannot overcome this conflict, we must choose between the disempowerment of isolation and the disempowerment of submission. Of all the circumstances that aggravate this clash between the requirements of self-assertion, the most influential in society is the entrenchment of mechanisms of dependence and dominion that turn all social involvements into threats of subjugation. To disrupt these mechanisms it is necessary, though it may not be sufficient, to prevent any aspect of the institutional and imaginative order of society from gaining effective immunity to challenge, conflict, and revision: that is to say, it is necessary to enact the modernist ideal as a form of social life.

Finally, we are empowered by freeing our understanding of society from superstition, both because insight itself represents a version of empowerment and because it makes the other varieties of empowerment possible. The characteristic form of superstition about society is the superstition of false necessity: the ease with which we mistake the constraints imposed by a particular formative context of social life for the inherent psychological, organizational, and economic imperatives of society. So deeply does this prejudice go that no sooner do we seem to have rejected it than we reinstate it under a new disguise. Thus, we may deny the necessity of a given form of social life only to redescribe that form as an unavoidable stage in a trajectory of historical evolution or as one of a well-defined list of possible social worlds. The tenacity of the prejudice should hardly cause surprise, for it is bound up with the ways in which we have traditionally understood and practiced theoretical generalization. We are made to see this hypostasis of local constraints into deep-seated law as the unavoidable instrument of general social thought.

The modernist view of contextuality can serve as the basis for a social theory that generalizes without this hypostasis. Such a social theory would neither deny the structured quality of social life—the influence of the formative institutional and imaginative contexts—nor resort to the idea of a set of historical laws that governs the evolution or the range of types of social organization. One of its central themes would be the conditions and consequences of changes in the relation of individual or collective agents to their contexts, especially when the change consists in the assertion of greater mastery over these contexts.

Forms of social life that more fully embody the modernist ideal of heightened plasticity may often be invented for reasons that have nothing to do with a devotion to this ideal or an understanding of its requirements. But the repeated development and successful operation of such social experiments call for an art of ceaseless social recombination. A social theory constructed on modernist lines must be, among other things, the remaking of this art into a systematic discourse.

Even after this theory had been devised it would still lack normative force until we had justified the authority of the ideal of empowerment and established the sense in which substantive conceptions of personality or society can exercise normative authority. But it is important to understand from the outset that the modernist theory of contexts represents less a view of the means toward the achievement of individual and collective self-assertion than a thesis about the very meaning of self-assertion.

What conception of our place in nature is compatible with the modernist thesis about our relation to our contexts? Consider one such conception, presented through a sketch of three types of order that can be found in nature. Though we participate in all three types, the third alone is distinctive to us, and its description amounts to a restatement of the modernist doctrine of contextuality. Thus, this argument serves several purposes. It emphasizes a view of our relation to our contexts. It provides an occasion to reformulate the particular view advanced in the preceding pages. And it suggests how this view may be reconciled with the picture of reality presented by the science of our day.

Imagine, then, a series of superimposed ways in which things may be ordered in nature. Whenever one order dissipates, another emerges to occupy its place. Each of these varieties of natural order requires a different style of explanation. Each supervening order presents explanatory opportunities that compensate for the difficulties created by the loosening of the previous orders. These discontinuities in the types of order and explanation do not coincide in any simple fashion with the boundaries between inanimate and living matter, or between the biological and the social. Nor do the supervenient forms of order and explanation ever entirely displace the preceding and weakened ones.

In the course of this overlaying of forms of order and explanation, there is a waning of the distinction between what must be accepted as given (by way of initial conditions or the value of the variables) and what can be rationally explained. The contrast between order and disorder is softened, together with the contrast between the nature of order in theory and in the phenomena that theory explains. Our conception of intelligible relations becomes increasingly subtle and capacious.

A scientific theory abstracts from phenomena. It focuses on certain aspects of a region of reality. Within the area it singles out for study, it distinguishes what can be determined by explanation from what must be accepted as merely given. It simplifies so as to bring out the structural and functional aspects of a complex, underlying reality. A similar process, at work in nature itself, generates a type of order in the midst of what would otherwise be unorganized and unintelligible phenomena.

The distinctive feature of this first type of order is the appearance of a constraining scheme that simplifies matter and, through this simplification, allows structures to be specified and functions to be coordinated. It thereby also creates opportunities for further transformation. Constraint, coordination, and emancipation (if the term may be used to describe the creation of developmental opportunities) appear linked together. The chemical bond, for example, might be understood as a simplified structure of this sort with respect to the microscopic, quantum description of matter. Whatever the ultimate dynamic reason for the emergence of these constraints, their effect upon the organization and history of nature is unmistakable.

In order to perform a coordinating role at "higher" levels a simplifying structure may require an optimum amount of detail. It cannot specify too many details (like a crystal) or too few (like a gas). As you move toward the realm of living matter, you find that the simplifying traits acquire certain characteristics of which, earlier, they had only traces. These characteristics foreshadow some of the defining features of human symbolism. One of these traits is the arbitrary connection between the physical constitution of the matter picked out to perform a certain role by the coordinating structure (e.g., the amino acid assignments in the genetic mechanism) and the role itself: the link between the signifier and the signified. Another feature is the capacity of the constraining structure to refer to itself, to contain messages about its own order. This capacity is indispensable to the self-replication and the developmental regulation of living matter. Simplifying structures with these two features of arbitrary significance and self-regulation have so many shared properties, and create so many distinctive difficulties and opportunities for explanation, that they can be justifiably considered a second type of order in nature, supervening on the first type.

The emergence of these new structures of constraint-coordination-emancipation runs parallel to the increasing importance of historicity: the quality of being mired in many loosely connected causal sequences that resist reduction to a single master process. This looseness may increase before such coordinating structures have fully emerged. Thus, historicity may in some cases go far, with no more than a modest development of coordinating structures: take, for example, the most history-dependent geological phenomena such as the making and transformation of sedimentary rocks.

This second type of order opens up possibilities of explanation that compensate for the difficulties caused by the march of historicity. Deterministic or probabilistic processes operate on and through these simplifying structures rather than directly. (Remember, for example, the influence of natural selection upon genetic programs.) What appears at first as pure randomness and particularity is partly a consequence of the imposition of an intermediate level of order between the probabilistic or deterministic forces of the physical world and the end results of these forces, such as the organism and its life. In contemporary science the operations of this intermediate level—the coordinating structures or "programs"—have been viewed through suitably adjusted and reinterpreted analogies of purpose and programming, drawn from a human setting. In the study of these self-regulating structures the contrast between what is arbitrarily given, as initial conditions, and what is rationally explained, by lawlike statements, diminishes. Design and accident are brought together, as in the relation of the signified to the signifier. The occasions and devices of limiting structure and developmental opportunity intersect.

It may be tempting to imagine that the second mode of order—and the style of explanation that relies on it—extends to society and history. For our mental and social contexts seem to resemble the second type of natural order in the way they determine conduct, though not in the identity of the determining forces. But there is a basic objection to this analogy. People act both as if their thoughts and actions were governed by constraining-coordinating-liberating structures of the kind just described (as well as by a brute residuum of material influences unassimilated or untamed by these structures) and as if their thought and conduct were ruled by no structure at all. Sometimes one and sometimes the other aspect of their situation seems preeminent.

But neither is ever entirely absent. Moreover, as individual or collective agents we can alter the very character of the structures that form our contexts, inventing varieties of discourse and social life over which we exercise an unprecedented mastery and thereby progressively softening the contrast between routine acts within a structure and revisionary acts about the structure. The power to work both within and beyond a given constraining-coordinating system and to diminish the contrast between being within it and being beyond it defines a third type of order.

The frameworks of thought that are taken for granted in a given line of inquiry or conversation, or the sets of institutional arrangements and imaginative preconceptions that remain relatively undisturbed in the course of the routine activities that they help shape, resemble the second type of order. Indeed, these frameworks of thought and these institutional and imaginative contexts of social life possess to an even greater degree the properties of self-reference and free symbolism that characterize the second variety of order in nature. But the power that such discursive structures or social contexts exercise over human activity is limited in two ways.

One limit arises from the existence of forces that have an independent origin. These forces include the biological endowment of humanity and the facts of material scarcity. They also embrace the totality of events that mankind has been through, whether viewed as a single species or as a collection of separate nations and classes. This half-forgotten history shapes people's dispositions and hopes even when their overt beliefs and practices fail openly to reflect its influence.

There is also another, very different qualification to the influence of explanatory structures or formative contexts of social life. This additional limit is our ability to act in ways that show our capacity to discover and to do more than can be accommodated by any definitive list of possible mental and social systems. This capacity both to suffer and to override the influence of the constraints that represent the social counterparts to the second type of order *is* the third mode of order. The modernist doctrine of our relation to the contexts of our action can now be recognized as a description of this third type of order, the only type that, being unique to us, stands in the closest connection to the issues we must address when we formulate a self-conception.

A special paradox marks our dealings with one another. This paradox is the problem of solidarity. The way we solve this problem represents, alongside the view we take of our relation to the contexts of our activity, a second major element in a conception of our fundamental identity. We present to one another both an unlimited need and an unlimited danger, and the very resources by which we attempt to satisfy the former aggravate the latter.

To obtain the means for our material support we must take a place in the social division of labor. When we do so, the institutional forms of production and exchange risk enmeshing us in the ties of subjugation and dominion. For no scheme of social divisions and hierarchies can be counted secure until it is constantly reproduced and reinforced by the petty transactions of daily life.

To satisfy our longing for acceptance and recognition, to be intimately assured that we have a place in the world, and to be freed by this assurance for a life of action and encounter, we must open ourselves to personal attachments and communal engagements whose terms we cannot predefine and whose course we cannot control. Each of these ventures into a life of longing for other people threatens to create a craven dependence and to submerge our individual selves under group identities and social roles.

We cannot obtain the categories that allow us to describe our situation and to reflect about ourselves unless we share in specific, historically conditioned traditions of discourse that none of us authored individually. Without these categories the imagination cannot work. But with them we cannot easily prevent ourselves from becoming the unwitting reproducers of a shared picture of the world. If we stray too far or too quickly from the collective script we are left without a way to converse.

These experiences present less a conflict between the affirmation of individuality and participation in social life than a clash between the enabling conditions of self-assertion. For our efforts at self-assertion—at marking out a sustainable presence in the world—may be undermined both by the lack of social involvements and by these involvements themselves.

Does the clash between these two sets of enabling conditions have clear implications for social thought and social practice? Or is it so vague in conception and indeterminate in reach that it can support widely different conclusions for the criticism and justification of social arrangements and personal conduct? Is there a rigid inverse relation between these two requirements of self-assertion so that a gain on one score exacts a loss on another? Or are there some forms of personal encounter and social organization that intensify the conflict between those requirements while others efface it? Can we, in other words, create for ourselves situations that do better than others at satisfying both conditions of self-assertion? The implicit or explicit answers we give to these questions define our solution to the problem of solidarity; and the view of solidarity, when combined with a thesis about our relation to the contexts of activity, provides us with a picture of ourselves.

This essay gambles on the idea that we can develop an account of our basic human identity that is neither trivial nor fatally beholden to the preconceptions of a particular culture. It even proceeds on the assumption that we can, to a limited extent, justify the practice of imputing normative consequences to substantive views of society and personality, though only after we have subjected this practice to major revisions.

The conception of a human identity is developed here from the limited and limiting perspective of the problem of solidarity.

Moreover, the discussion focuses on the emotional rather than the practical or cognitive aspects of this problem: the experience of mutual longing rather than that of participation in a division of labor or a tradition of shared discourse. But this aspect of the theme of solidarity is dealt with in a way that implicates the other aspects. And the whole argument of this book presupposes, elaborates, and in a certain measure supports the modernist thesis about the status of our contexts.

We should hardly be surprised to see views of our relation to the settings of action bear so heavily upon our idea of solidarity. For our assumptions about the extent to which and the ways in which the conflicting demands of self-assertion can be reconciled are influenced by how we see our capacity to escape or to revise the social and imaginative frameworks within which we deal with one another. Thus, belief in a natural context for social life is likely to go together with the convictions that there exists a fixed, ideal balance between the claims of engagement and of solitude and that a specific set of social arrangements—almost invariably an idealized version of present society—realizes this balance. The further away we move from this naturalistic thesis toward a modernist view of contextuality the more likely we are to see the relation between the two conditions of self-assertion as itself transformable. No wonder the modernist approach to the contextual quality of experience helps shape, though it cannot fully define, a view of solidarity.

The conception of human identity worked out in the main body of this essay can be read as an interpretation and a development of what are often seen as two different and even antagonistic traditions when they are regarded as coherent traditions at all. One of these elements is the central Christian-romantic tradition of thinking about human nature. The image of man produced by that tradition constituted until recently the central teaching of our civilization. The other immediate source of the view of human identity I shall defend is modernism, the view inaugurated by the revolutionary artists and thinkers of the early twentieth century. The part of the modernist conception that deals with the character of our contexts has already been described.

On the one hand, modernism is a moment in the transformation—I shall even argue, the purification—of the Christian-romantic idea of the self. In this role the modernist picture of personality can best be compared to the feudal-aristocratic ethic of chivalry and the bourgeois-sentimental ethic of devotion to practical work and legitimate domesticity. Like them, it represents a transaction between the indistinct but powerful impulses of the Christian-romantic tradition and the self-justifying and self-defensive concerns of particular classes in particular societies.

But modernism also performs another role. It serves as the bearer of the peculiar brand of skepticism implied by the modernist doctrine of contexts: skepticism about the many evasive devices by which we try to conceal from ourselves the full implications of the non-existence of natural contexts for life and discourse. In this second role modernism puts received conceptions of personality and society to the test, forcing us to purge them of arbitrarily restrictive assumptions about the limits of personal and social experience or about the ways that we may moderate the conflict between the enabling circumstances of self-assertion.

There is a striking correspondence between the quality of the original social base of each of the great movements of feeling and opinion that have successively recast the Christian-romantic view of man and the extent to which the ruling moral vision of each movement has depended upon naturalistic assumptions about society. The footloose and peripheral intelligentsia was less of a clearly defined social rank than the bourgeois class, just as this class had a more indistinct identity and a less institutionalized social role than the landowning and warrior caste of pre-bourgeois

Europe. For a person must see the tyranny that the social categories of division and hierarchy exercise over life weaken before
his very eyes and he must feel in himself an identity that his social
station cannot exhaust before he can enter wholeheartedly into
the modernist attitude toward society.

There are two reasons to treat the modernist and the
Christian-romantic views as continuous: one explanatory, the
other admonitory. By studying these views as complementary
rather than as antagonistic we can discover facts about them that
might otherwise easily escape us. Moreover, when the modernist
and the Christian-romantic ideas of the personality are seen in
this way, both are more readily protected against the mistakes to
which modernism without this foundation or the Christian-
romantic view without this criticism are constitutionally subject.
Of course, the sense in which we can make mistakes about such
matters at all will not become precise until the style of argument
that attributes normative force to understandings of personality
and society has been elucidated and justified.

Two great themes establish the unity of the Christian-
romantic tradition of thought about personality: the primacy of
personal encounter and of love as its redemptive moment, and the
commitment to a social iconoclasm expressive of man's ineradicable homelessness in the world. These obscurely related themes are
first presented here with an emphasis on their specifically Christian form. But it will soon become apparent that they have close
parallels in the kindred vision I shall call romance. Though the
Christian and romantic elements in this tradition overlap they are
not identical.

We advance in self-understanding and goodness by opening ourselves up to the whole life of personal encounter rather
than by seeking communion with an impersonal, non-human reality. Even mankind's dealings with God, in the explicitly theological
versions of this picture, are conceived on the model of a face-off
between individuals. Our relations to one another should take on

the quality described by the concept of love and the related ideas of faith and hope. Love, faith, and hope are distinguished from the pagan virtues of courage, prudence, moderation, and fairness by both a characteristic impulse and an animating idea. The impulse is the willingness to put personal attachments up for grabs and to subject them to extraordinary expectations and risks in much the same way that escalating collective mobilization opens the rigidified terms of social life to experiment and revision. The idea is that through such ventures we may offer and receive acts of mutual acceptance. These acts reconcile the conflicting requirements of self-assertion and thereby broaden the scope of individual action, for they deliver us from solitude without surrendering us to collective opinion. More generally, their claim upon us derives from our inability to find satisfaction anywhere except in the presence of other context-transcending and insatiable beings like ourselves. Our search for an impersonal good diminishes rather than emancipates us because everything impersonal is also contextual, whereas the key fact about a person is that he never completely fits the concrete settings of his existence.

The second great theme in the Christian side of this Christian-romantic image of man is its iconoclastic attitude toward particular social orders. A person's deepest identity is not defined by his membership in social ranks and divisions. The logic of claims that any given set of social categories establishes must be overridden whenever it clashes with an opportunity to extend further into personal expression or social practice the qualities that are most fully realized in faith, hope, and love. Some schemes of social life may do better than others in this respect. But to sanctify a specific version of society is to transfer to a limited secular object—an ideal of civilization—an allegiance that properly belongs only to the human or the divine other and to the principle of personality itself. It is to misunderstand what the language of philosophical idealism and modern theology describes as the disproportion of the infinite to the finite. The more entrenched against revision a social plan becomes, the more it enacts and imposes an intolerably restricted picture of our fundamental identity and our opportunities for practical or passionate connection.

The social iconoclasm of the Christian-romantic tradition can best be understood as a variation on the idea that man is never at home in the world: that nothing but another homeless person can satisfy the unlimited demands of his spirit. The conception of homelessness is simply the reverse side of the fear of idolatry, the fear that man might accept a limited worldly objective as an adequate goal of his striving. This apprehension, however, is balanced in Christian doctrine by the belief that we must respond to our supernatural calling by making our worldly habitation more open to love. The idea of homelessness and the commitment to change the world should not be seen as a specialized set of moral beliefs. They merely draw out the implications, for the domain of personal encounter, of God's intervention in history, culminating in the decisive event of the Incarnation.

The relation between the themes of love and iconoclasm can be clarified by asking how the world must be changed to be made more fully open to love. At a minimum, people must be taken care of in their basic needs. In this circumstance of basic security, they will more readily tolerate the added defenselessness that faith, hope, and love demand. From this point on, however, two different directions may be taken by the understanding of what is required in order to make the world more open to love. These alternatives represent recurrent options within the history of Christian teaching, and they reappear as one of the many distinctions between early and late romance.

On one view the basic requirement is that society cling to its canonical form: a legitimate system of clearly defined hierarchies and stations. By placing himself within this order and by meeting the responsibilities that it assigns to him, the individual frees himself from the hypertrophy of self-obsessed desire and ambition that undermine his capacity to love and to be loved. The alternative line that the transformation of society may follow is the breakup of all fixed social roles, divisions, and hierarchies. The best social order is the one that by making itself more completely accessible to real challenge prevents any scheme of rigid roles, divisions, and hierarchies from hardening. In this way people may more readily deal with one another as concrete individuals rather than as fungible placeholders in the grand system of national, class, communal, or gender contrasts. As a result they may also be preserved against the dangers to human reconciliation that arise whenever personal loyalties become entangled in social dependencies. For such entanglements invariably put the distancing stratagems of control and resistance in place of the search for mutual acceptance.

The choice of one of these two answers to the question—How may society be more fully opened to love?—depends upon factual assumptions about society and history. These assumptions form no intrinsic part of Christian faith. Yet it is only when we work out the second, authority-subverting answer that the theme of social iconoclasm takes on its full dimension and that its relation to the primacy of personal encounter becomes clear.

The role of the Christian element in the Christian-romantic tradition demands a further gloss. The same basic ideas about encounter and iconoclasm can be found in the neighboring religions of Judaism and Islam. Yet, as a matter of historical fact, it was largely in their Christian form that these ideas served first as an inspiration and then as an interlocutor of the secular romance, the other major element in our dominant tradition.

More importantly, adherence to this Christian-romantic view of man exacts no religious faith. To acknowledge that certain beliefs owe much of their original development to the teachings of Christianity and its sister religions is not to assert that the justification of those beliefs includes acceptance of revelation. For the same image of our shared identity may be subject to two readings.

On one reading—call it Feuerbachian—talk about God represents an extended and distorted way of talking about man. The use of theological language may best be explained by the search for metaphors capable of expressing the infinite, unruly, overflowing quality that distinguishes subjectivity and intersubjectivity by contrast to the particular forms of social life in which they become partially embedded. Once the Feuerbachian translation has been accomplished, the religious origin of the belief becomes irrelevant, except as a warning that nothing be left untranslated and that the untranslatable residues be put aside.

On an alternative reading—call it analogical—the psychology of personal encounter prefigures the theology of redemption. Our confrontations with God and other human beings provide both clues to each other's meaning and resources for each other's fulfillment. Within the history of Christianity the idea of an analogical relation between the secular and the supernatural levels of our experience of personality represents the sequel to the Thomistic conception of natural reason as capable of arriving independently at some of the truths of revelation. But this sequel replaces natural reason, as the parallel first step toward higher insight, by personal knowledge—a change that merely extends to epistemology the normative ascendency of the personal over the impersonal.

For the purposes of a secular view of human identity we have no need to choose between the Feuerbachian and the analogous readings of the Christian presence within the Christian-romantic tradition. These readings may make a crucial difference only at the extremes of speculation and conduct, just as two scientific theories may converge in their conclusions so long as their applications remain confined to certain dimensions of magnitude. Even the believer may have no reason to object to this limited equivalence, seeing faith more readily in an orientation of the self than in a profession of belief.

Consider now the romantic element in the Christian-romantic view. The term romantic as used here does not refer to the nineteenth-century Romantic movement except insofar as what I shall describe as late romance played an important role within it. Romantic designates instead the secular romance, perhaps the single most influential mode of moral vision in the history of our culture. With both pagan and Christian roots, it has its own character and cannot adequately be understood as a mere secularization of Christianity. Its affinity to Christian teaching is nevertheless unmistakable.

It may seem strange to speak of literature in the same breath with religion as a source for the definition of existential ideals. Yet there are few other places where we may find so clearly expressed a willingness to treat the mind as a repository of secret knowledge, won in the midst of dense personal encounter, rather than as a conceptual performer that looks in abstract speculation for a reprieve from personal demand.

There is a distinction to be drawn between early and late romance, a distinction qualified by the awareness that the early version has survived, at least in popular culture, long after the appearance of the late one. The most familiar protagonist of early romance is the young adventurer, at once superman and everyman, who tries to remove a specific obstacle to human happiness, usually one that stands in the way of his own happiness and, more specifically, of his marriage to the woman he loves. His self-knowledge and self-transformation are made to depend upon personal confrontations that escape the limits of any instrumental calculus.

The hero (or heroine) may be the victim of a usurpation or a misfortune that throws him into a world of confused identities and dark powers, of force and fraud. He wrestles with the representatives of this world and finally escapes from it. In the more paganized versions of the romance, his escape is won through patience and guile, by which he turns the devices of the lower world against itself, and through a favoring providence, which is the help and opportunity that flow to the people who have the resourcefulness and vibrancy of life. In the more Christianized versions of the romance, the hero's good will collaborates with grace, represented by the divine or human love that responds to his efforts.

The confrontation with the realm of violence leads through a single escape, or through a series of transformative moments, to a higher state of enlightenment and reconciliation. True identities are revealed, marriages celebrated, and new orders of social life established. The hero is able to make a home out of the renewed earth. The ordeal he has undergone, more than a lapse of useless suffering, enables him to accept the world more fully while seeing through that which is evil and illusion in it. He has to stagger through aggravated confusion and conflict in order to cut through false restraints on vision and action. Only then is his wisdom or his love able to accept other people and reality itself, without superstition or subservience.

The characteristic tropes of early romance are the true love and the ennobling quest: the worth of the former confirmed by the dignity of the latter. The protagonist strives and loves within his proper social sphere. If he seems to rise above it, the appearance of a class change may be dissipated by the retrospective discovery that the position he achieved is in fact one to which, unbeknownst to him, he had been born. And this piety toward hierarchical order in society goes along with an unembarrassed confidence in conventional morality and its hierarchies of value. Over this worldly and spiritual order, grace or fate presides. This providence elects the hero, chooses his mate, sets his ordeal, and grants his reward.

Late romance is the transformation undergone by early romance under the pressure of anxiety about the availability of true love and worthy striving. Everything that was assurance now turns into a problem. The concern with the quest and the encounter remain. But the issue now becomes less whether they will succeed in a particular instance than whether they are possible in any instance. (An example: Flaubert.) The source of the controlling anxiety in late romance might be described, in categories mentioned earlier, as the increasing loss of faith in the existence of a natural context for thought and social life.

Late romance represents perhaps the single most important strand in Western prose fiction and poetry from the mid-seventeenth century down through the twentieth century. It has, however, always coexisted with the high and popular expressions of its predecessor. Thus, it is early romance, burdened with an ambivalence toward the principles of nineteenth-century bourgeois society, that we find in great, vulgar, generous artists like Verdi or Victor Hugo, while a poet such as Pushkin may sometimes present a purer, more childlike version of this same tradition, combined or juxtaposed with an ironic anticipation of the themes of late romance.

Like early romance, late romance has both drawn upon and penetrated popular culture. The penetration has been all the more far-reaching because the period when this moral vision emerged was also a time when a relatively independent folk culture ceased to exist, victim to the same jumbling up of social divisions and hierarchies that helped undermine the social assumptions of early romance.

Despite the scope of its antecedents and influence, late romance has specific literary origins. One of its major sources is the pastoral elegy, gradually detached from its classic form and situation. The link between the broader vision and its narrower literary mold becomes apparent in the motif of the loss of an arcadian paradise, an episode typically precipitated or exemplified by the loss of the true companion, whose presence sustained the now-distraught protagonist in his striving. The image of the secular Eden is easily recognizable as a variation on the idea of a natural context. And its disappearance is correctly intuited to usher in a time of painful uncertainty in our relations with one another.

In the circumstance of separation that follows the breakup of the worldly garden the hero is exposed to a long series of mishaps and illusions. One misfortune—which has occupied political thought more than literature—is the temptation to interpret the arcadian myth as the description of a recoverable past rather than as the dreamlike expression of constraint and insufficiency in the present. This misplaced identification encourages the anti-modernist fantasies of communal integration and permanent civic militancy that merely invert a reality they are unable credibly to reimagine or reconstruct. The literary-psychological counterpart to the politics of the would-be return to the natural context is the effort to regain the moment of visionary immediacy. But even when more firmly anchored in biography than its political analogue is in politics, this moment turns out to be either unsustainable or sterile, except as a memory in the tale of its own loss.

Another response to our banishment from the arcadian paradise has played a much more prominent role in literature, for it deals directly with the problems of personal encounter. In his circumstance of estrangement the protagonist looks for a task that would be worthy of him, worthy above all of his context-transcending identity and his context-transforming capabilities. But the search for the justified task—which is also a quest for a credible community—is dogged by a persistent doubt. Each candidate activity may in fact derive its apparent worthiness from the groundless prejudices of a particular culture. Or it may be nothing more than the arbitrary symbol of a felt need for justified action.

In love as in work, the protagonist of late romance seeks an escape from the dangers of solipsism and self-obsession. But at no moment can he know for sure whether the beloved he sees is truly another person or merely a severed part of his own personality, a fragment that stands, as a delusive image, between himself and the apparent subject of his love. The relation between the true love and the worthy quest undergoes here a radical change. No longer do we find the idea of a quest that is undertaken in order to show oneself deserving of love: faith in an impersonal task as an apprenticeship for faith in an individual. Instead, love becomes a struggle for exit from the self and for sustenance from others amid the deceptions and oppressions of society. But the unredeemed social world strikes back, dulling people's faculties and denying them the means with which to imagine one another.

The execution of the worthy task for the sake of the true love is replaced by the willing exposure to an ordeal that consists precisely in uncertainty about whether there do exist a love beyond narcissism and a work beyond illusion that might take the individual out of himself and turn his self-division into empowerment. The moral and epistemological complexity of late romance results from its unwillingness to resolve this issue clearly on one side or the other. But like the modernist outlook that in so many ways it helped shape, late romance suffers the temptation to escape from this search for personal access and transformative activity into a fascination with art and artifacts. The palace of mirrors and illusions is glorified as the authoritative reality in contrast to the unlovely, resistant world we no longer feel able to reconstruct or even to imagine.

Because of the explicit connection that it establishes between the primacy of encounter and the sentiment of homelessness, late romance comes closer than early romance to the distinctively Christian element in the Christian-romantic tradition. It does so, however, in a way that emphasizes the unavailability of a natural context for social life and the lack of the clearcut orderings of value and emotion that accompany such a context. This way of describing the tradition brings out the continuity between the Christian and the modernist visions of solidarity, a continuity to which the polemical concept of secularization cannot do justice.

Consider now modernism and its relation to the Christian-romantic view of man. Modernism and modernist are used here to designate a specific movement of opinion and feeling rather than a vague sense of contemporaneity. The modernism I have in mind was pioneered by the great novelists and poets of the early and mid-twentieth centuries—by writers like Proust, Joyce, and Virginia Woolf, Karl Kraus and Samuel Beckett, Bely, Kafka, Musil, and Céline, Eliot and Montale. The more discursive statements of the modernist vision by philosophers such as Heidegger and Sartre are often less inclusive and more biased toward the extreme version of modernism that I shall soon describe. (A more balanced statement of the modernist vision might be found in Kierkegaard, in Hegel's treatment of the problem of self-division, or even in Pascal.) Modernism may therefore seem even less likely than the Christian-romantic tradition to yield a coherent image of man. For though its historical context may be far more specific, its insights remain largely embedded in works of art from which they seem incapable of being disengaged without being trivialized in the process.

Yet the distinctive character of the modernist vision becomes clear once compared with the traditions of reflection about personality against which it rebelled. One of these traditions was the mechanistic and cynical psychology that, already articulated by Hobbes, found its way into the scientific psychology, the literary naturalism, and the progressive or revolutionary social theories of the nineteenth century. The other perspective against which modernism rebelled was the sentimentalized version of both Christian teaching and secular romance that flaunted its confidence in the possibility of human reconciliation and of knowledge of another person while treating the conventions and arrangements of European bourgeois society as an unobjectionable backdrop to emotional life. In the eyes of the modernists both these tendencies of thought—the mechanistic and the sentimental—failed to recognize that the personality makes and discovers itself through its experience of not fitting into the given settings of its existence and through its failure ever to escape entirely from cognitive and emotional isolation. No wonder the modernists often found their immediate precursors in Romantics like Hölderlin or Stendhal who had probed the ordeal of self-division and defiance to society.

Modernism has long ceased to lead a merely bookish life; instead of reading about it we can find it all around us. It reflected, foreshadowed, and helped form the cultural-revolutionary practice of our day: the politics of personal relations that seeks to recombine the forms of experience traditionally connected with distinct social or gender roles. Thus, the central ideas of modernism have passed into a worldwide popular culture. In this popularized form they have become the ideology of cultural-revolutionary politics.

Neither the high-flown nor the popular varieties of this modernist insight developed a vision of a reconstructed society. Both pay for their lack of political imagination. They easily mistake the deficiencies of a particular social order for the inherent limitations of society. And they repeatedly find that the search for personal experimentation and self-fulfillment ends in disappointment when it is not tied into a wider social solidarity or a larger historical project that can rescue the individual from his obsessional and futile self-concern. Nevertheless, modernist and leftist radicals share at least one basic idea: the belief that every entrenched system of social division and hierarchy represents an unnecessary and unjustifiable constraint upon the possibilities of social life and individual existence.

The first distinctive theme of modernism is little more than an extension of the classical doctrine of personal encounter. The modernists emphasize that our dealings with other individuals have primacy over the search for an impersonal reality or good. And among all encounters they ascribe special importance to those that put in question the relation between the requirements of self-assertion. Their skepticism about the possibility of love and, more generally, about the access that one mind may gain to another results, as will soon be seen, from their relentless pursuit of the iconoclastic theme—the other great concern of the Christian-romantic view of human nature.

A second element in modernism is its view of our relation to the contexts of our action. In its most moderate form, this view is the very doctrine of contextuality outlined earlier. This doctrine gives a secular, precise, and general form to the iconoclastic theme in the Christian-romantic tradition. Its specific social expression is the belief that no institutional order and no imaginative vision of the varieties of possible and desirable human association can fully exhaust the types of practical or passionate human connection that we may have good reason to desire and a good chance to establish. The anomalies of practical or passionate encounter provide starting points for alternative social orders. The inability of institutions and dogma fully to inform the direct dealings between individuals constitutes the basic condition for the remaking of society.

Notice that within this doctrine of contextuality a tension exists between the subversive power of deviant forms of human association and the need to settle upon a specific ordering of social life. Emergent opportunities of practical or passionate human connection cannot be fully exploited unless they find a stable institutional and imaginative setting that acknowledges and sustains them. But though these settings differ in their openness to revision, none can be ensured of satisfying the next emergent opportunity and none can fully shape our direct experience of practical dealing and passionate longing.

The modernists have rarely been content to leave the doctrine of contextuality at that. Their divinization of the self has often led them to pass from the conviction that the person transcends his contexts to the intolerance of all limits, whether the constraints of the body or those of society. At the same time, the modernists' lack of political imagination—a fateful by-product of the parting of the ways between modernism and leftism—has denied them the vision of instituted forms of social life that could in fact be better suited to a context-revising self. The result of these tendencies has often been to turn the modern doctrine of contextuality into the belief that the individual can expect no real progress from the revision of his contexts. He can assert his independence only by a perpetual war against the fact of contextuality, a war that he cannot hope to win but that he must continue to wage.

From the standpoint of the central Christian-romantic tradition, this version of the modernist approach to contextuality represents a heresy: it exaggerates certain elements of the tradition while suppressing others. When the belief in the primacy of the personal that modernism shares with the Christian-humanistic tradition is combined in some instances with the modernist doctrine of contextuality and in others with the extreme, heretical version of this doctrine, it produces the more concrete ideas that we most often associate with modernist thought.

The modernists' attitude toward the contexts of human life leads them to repudiate the authority of any fixed system of social roles, ranks, and collective identities. It provokes them into distrusting any conventional repertory of symbols and ceremonies for expressing the varieties of subjective experience. And it therefore also encourages them to emphasize the fluidity and the ambivalence of the passions and the dangerous partiality of all fixed hierarchies of moral judgment. They see love in hatred and hatred in love and show us how an opportunity for greater human reconcilation may arise from the bitterness of disappointment and antagonism. These insights find encouragement in the view that no particular framework of society and culture can give full expression to the opportunities of practical or passionate connection.

Together with this emphasis upon the ambivalence and the dynamism of the passions, the modernists show a special fascination with the anomalous passions of despair and lust. Though these emotions may begin as events within the normal push and shove of personal interaction, they soon develop into an attack upon the authority and self-sufficiency of the social and cultural order. In one instance this attack is mounted from above—from the faithlessness of reason—and in the other instance from below—from the rebelliousness of desire. It is rarely possible to tell for sure to what extent the assault is directed against particular social worlds and to what degree it means to reject the claim that any social world makes upon our imagination and allegiance. Disbelief in the authority of the larger social context that our lives have taken for granted passes into a more general agnosticism about our ability to give sense to human activity. We despair radically when we believe that criteria of sense and value can come only from particular social worlds and that we have no reason to take one of these worlds more seriously than any other. So too the subjective experience of lust may begin in a localized insurrection against the particular prohibitions upon which the logic of kinship depends. But it ends as an inability to see the other individual as a person with his own resources of secrecy and striving. It therefore amounts to a denial of that imagination of otherness upon which the entire life of society draws. The uncertain effect of lust and despair merely dramatizes as a personal ordeal an ambiguity in the modern doctrine of contextuality.

There is at least one more belief that stands close to the center of modernist thought. But unlike the views previously discussed, it arises from the extreme, heretical doctrine of contexts rather than from the standard version of the doctrine. The modernists often combine an acknowledgment of the supreme importance of personal love with a skepticism about the possibility of achieving it or, more generally, of gaining access to another mind. Disbelief in political or religious redemption and in the teachings of conventional morality intensifies the redemptive expectations placed upon personal love. But both the obsession with the godlike, transcending self and the conviction that all institutionalized forms of social life spell death to our spiritual freedom undermine confidence in our ability to reach the other person in thought and emotion. The heretical variant of modernism teaches us to wage an endless war against all the concrete settings of our existence. But how can the conduct of this war be made compatible with the hope of developing a social medium of conversation and practice that makes us more fully accessible to one another by loosening the hold that predefined collective categories of role, rank, and conventional expression exercise over our experience? We should rather expect love to be recognized in the end as a refined narcissism or as a futile attempt to escape our solitude, and the image of the beloved to convey only the fantastical projections of our inner cravings.

If my characterization of the Christian-romantic and modernist views of personality is defensible, it supports the attempt to treat the latter as a moment in the transformation of the former. The modern doctrine of contexts draws out the social meaning of the iconoclastic theme and, in so doing, clarifies its relation to the Christian-romantic theme of love. Only when they adopt the extreme and heretical view of contextuality do the modernists reach conclusions that defy the central Christian-romantic tradition.

This schematic and polemical analysis already suggests the ambivalent relation of modernist skepticism to our received image of man. The skeptical turn may strengthen this image by freeing it from arbitrarily restrictive assumptions about the possible forms of passionate or practical human connection, assumptions that constantly threaten to degrade the classical view of human nature into an apology for subjugation and fatalism. But we have no guarantee that once the skeptical critique has been allowed to run its course there will be any substantive conception of personality left. Perhaps all views of the self will be shown up as merely the groundless prejudices of particular societies or cultures, and the ultra-modernist approach to contexts will be retrospectively justified as the heroic alternative to a despairing relativism. The real issue for us is not whether this outcome to the history of our moral and political opinions is possible but whether it is unavoidable. We can answer this question only by clarifying the character of the collective practice that has produced different images of man and attributed to each of them a normative force.

The discussion of the preceding pages might seem incapable of leading to anything but a hypothesis about the history of culture: claims about the developmental tendencies of a particular tradition of thinking about human nature. To offer this discussion as a preliminary move in the elaboration of a prescriptive image of our shared identity is to assume rather than to demonstrate the validity of ascribing normative force to conceptions of the self or to the views of society with which those conceptions are bound

up. It is to disregard rather than to disprove the distinction between normative and factual claims that constitutes the starting
point of most modern moral and political philosophy.

Openly to take the governing image of man from a historically specific tradition seems only to aggravate the suspect character of the procedure. For it seems that to proceed in this manner
we must make one of two implausible assumptions. On the one
hand, we may be making a qualified relativistic claim that every
tradition has, and deserves to have, normative authority for those
who belong to it. But this view eviscerates normativity to the
vanishing point and presupposes that we can and should avoid
choosing what tradition to be in. Alternatively, we may be claiming merely that the historically specific tradition we have chosen is
the one that most closely approaches an independently justified
ideal. But then surely this ideal and the arguments that support it
should be our real concerns. Are these the only alternatives?

I propose to defend the practice of attributing normative
force to substantive conceptions of personality or society but to
do so in a way that requires a revision of the practice. This revision
will plainly acknowledge the very fact that, more than anything,
has undermined confidence in this style of normative thought. The
subversive fact is the need to rely upon conceptions generated by
a particular culture or enacted by a particular society. A revised
version of the practice of attributing prescriptive authority to
views of personality or society supports the blend of normative
and factual claims in this essay. It also exemplifies the modern doctrine of our relation to the contexts of our activity, a doctrine that
in turn informs the entire account of human identity presented in
the main body of this work.

Consider first that the method of attributing normative
force to conceptions of personality represents the most wide-
spread and tenacious of all types of normative discourse. It might
well be called the standard or classical style of normative
argument. Characteristically, it presents an image of man as self-

evident or as supported by revealed truth or by a metaphysical picture of non-human reality but, in any event, as a transcendent perspective from which to judge all particular traditions.

We need a conception of our relation to our practices that can help us understand and judge this classical style. Ideally, it should be a view that both instantiates the modernist approach to contexts developed here and lends itself to independent assessment as a description of actual normative argument.

We have recourse to a limited number of basic conceptual and institutional practices. Each of these practices employs distinct categories and assumptions—presuppositions that make sense of it and offer guidance to those who engage in it. To a considerable extent these basic practices represent artifacts with an accidental history. We have no reason to suppose that all the presuppositions of all our fundamental practices fit together into a single cohesive scheme and some reason to suspect that they do not. After all, we developed these practices to deal with particular problems rather than as steps in the execution of a unified theoretical program.

Those who insist that we reject the classical style because it disregards the distinction between normative and factual claims forget that the distinction they invoke is less a fact about the world, or even a property of language and judgment, than an assumption of certain conceptual practices, especially natural science. This assumption is irrelevant to many other practices and incompatible with at least one other. The philosophical critics ask us in effect to abandon one practice—the classical style of normative argument—out of respect for the implicit ideas of another. Why should we?

At any given time we *are* largely the sum of our fundamental practices. But we are also the permanent possibility of revising them. We can change them. Occasionally, we can abandon one and invent another. No sharp distinction exists between altering a practice and repudiating it, because, as historical artifacts, these practices lack essences.

When invited to change or revise a practice like the classical style of normative argument, all we can do is to consult the preponderance of our insights and ambitions, to study the available options, and to reflect upon the lessons of past efforts. We can ask whether something we very much want to do—such as increasing our control of nature—requires this change. We can try to establish whether the practice assumes something about the external world or about our own capabilities that the overwhelming weight of understandings generated by other practices renders implausible, so implausible that we can continue to entertain it only as an almost miraculous exception. And, having done all this, we must still decide whether we *can* either find an alternative practice or dismiss the needs that the present practice in fact satisfies. The complement to William James' remark—"People believe everything they can"—is—"People believe everything they must."

Inevitably, we must accept a conservative presumption. To question the legitimacy of our fundamental practices is somewhat like asking us why we should continue to be ourselves. The reasonable answer often falls somewhere between—Why shouldn't we?—and—We can't help it.

To criticize the classical style of normative argument in this spirit is to examine it in something like the manner of scientists comparing alternative research strategies, though the standards of success and failure are far less certain here than in science. It is to abandon the hope of deducing an answer from first principles or from an analysis of language or judgment or from the patient and conclusive investigation of external reality. It is to consider the available alternatives open-mindedly, to draw lessons from past failures, and to seek untried opportunities.

What can we learn from past attempts to replace the classical style? The single most influential such attempt has been undertaken by the mainstream of modern moral and political philosophy, the very same current of thought that so sedulously upholds the stark contrast between normative and factual claims. Our decision about whether to continue this line in the development of thought or to try something else instead should take into account what we understand to have happened in the history of modern thinking about ideals of personality and society.

The whole course of modern moral and political philosophy can best be understood as an effort not to base prescriptive conclusions upon substantive conceptions of personality and society. The distinct ways that philosophers have tried to do this define the differences among the leading philosophical schools. At times the favored technique of avoidance has been the attempt to discover an inferential method that can teach us how to combine the preferences, or how to generalize from the intuitions, of different individuals when neither the intuitions nor the preferences are thought to compose a distinct image of human nature. At other times the escape route has involved a search for the constraints upon action that are somehow inherent in the moral point of view, defined as the commitment to consider people as free, responsible, and equal agents, subject to maxims that can be impersonally justified and universally applied. And at still other times an attempt has been made to dispense with the need to rely upon a substantive image of human nature by claiming (remember the pragmatists) that there is no distinctive philosophical problem about the justification of normative ideas; you simply give reasons for preferring one position to another. No special basis is possible, much less necessary.

But the results of these alternatives to the classical style have been consistently disappointing. For each of these approaches turns out to be indeterminate except to the extent that it remains subject to a specific confusion. The method for drawing inferences from wants and intuitions, the pure constraints of the impersonal moral standpoint, and the pragmatists' reasons are always either too empty or too contradictory to provide guidance. They achieve determinacy only to the extent that they continue, covertly, to invoke a substantive image of human nature. This image tells you which wants and intuitions to credit, how to put flesh on the bones of impersonal moral constraints, and what to count as an argument in favor of a course of action.

Before drawing a lesson from this continuing disappointment, consider the motives that originally prompted modern philosophy to embark on these techniques of avoidance. One motive was specifically philosophical; the other had to do with the more general history of culture. The specific philosophical reason was the rejection of Aristotle's teleology. Most philosophers of the past believed, as many still believe, that the presuppositions of different human practices must be either true or false and moreover true or false with respect to a single coherent view of the world. (This belief has sometimes been called metaphysical realism.) A metaphysical-realist justification of the classical style of normative argument need not accept the categorical scheme of Aristotelian metaphysics. But it is hard to see how it could keep from resembling Aristotle's philosophy in the crucial respects of asserting that things tend toward a purpose natural to them and that the achievement of this purpose is their good. We have evidence that such a position will occur to whomever desires to justify in metaphysical-realist terms the classical style of normative argument. For this position has been independently formulated, in the most diverse historical circumstances within and outside the West, by philosophers concerned to elucidate the connection between normative and factual claims. Because this connection forms a central part of all religions and religiously based ethics, the effort to establish it has always seemed important.

Aristotelian teleology proved incompatible with a nascent science concerned to explain mechanical forces and blind chance in ways that might yield counterintuitive and mathematically formalizable truths. The rejection of Aristotelian metaphysics in turn seemed to discredit the practice that this philosophy had been traditionally used to clarify. But once we cast off the prejudice that a practice requires the type of justification that satisfies metaphysical realism, we are free to preserve the classical style of normative argument while rejecting its familiar metaphysical support. In place of metaphysical realism we can put the practice conception suggested earlier and developed throughout this Introduction. The practice conception leaves open the possibility that we might have reason to reorient or even to abandon our efforts to seek guidance from images of personality or society. But it denies that this reason could ever be our inability to reconcile the assumptions of this activity with the preconceptions of all our other activities, including the scientific explanation of the world.

The rebellion against Aristotelian teleology is not the only impulse underlying the modern philosophical attempt to avoid commitment to a substantive conception of personality or society. The standard version of normative argument, with its many parallels in jurisprudence and moral theory, flourished in societies whose basic institutional arrangements and imaginative preconceptions remained largely immune to the destabilizing effects of ordinary conflicts. In such societies people continued to entertain a naturalistic view of the contexts of their activity. The actual subjection of ever-broader areas of social life to transformative conflict has been chiefly responsible for discrediting the idea of a canonical model of personality or society. In this altered climate people may continue implicitly to rely upon conceptions of human nature. But to the reflective—to those who criticize this reliance upon views of human identity—every image of man will appear to be little more than the prejudice of a society and a culture. However, just as the classical approach to normative argument can dispense with Aristotelian teleology and metaphysical realism, so too it can outlast the rejection of the naturalistic view of contexts, though perhaps only through a major shift in method and meaning.

Given the disappointing consequences of the modern philosophical attempt to dispense with a view of the self or of society as a basis for normative vision, it seems reasonable to change course. We can try to alter the standard version of normative argument from within by submitting it to a thoroughgoing criticism. In so doing, we must reckon with the possibility that once criticism pushes far enough nothing will be left.

It is nevertheless salutary to consider that the worst that could happen to us by pursuing this alternative to the mainstream of modern moral and political philosophy is to be left where we already are. For a radically skeptical outcome to such a change of course is less likely to affect the way we really think and act than a transformation of the classical style. Though we may be told that our established practices of inquiry and invention make arbitrary and unjustifiable assumptions about the world, and that no version of these practices could be any less defective, we shall not easily give up on the requirements of life. Having taken note of the destructive skeptical result, we are likely to continue doing what we did before, with the only means available to us, the means provided by our current ways of doing things. Precisely because of its extremism, the scorched-earth campaign of radical skepticism is also ineffective: it allows us to tack an agnostic reservation onto an unreformed practice. (Hume's treatment of causation provides, in a different area, the most familiar example of this conservative irony.)

A criticism of the classical style must include both a critique of the practice of attributing prescriptive force to substantive conceptions of personality and society (or of the sense in which we ascribe this force) and a critique of the substantive conceptions themselves. The result of this twofold criticism is to offer a way of proceeding (a revised version of the classical style) as well as a substantive point of departure (the modernist moment of the Christian-romantic view). The argument for these proposals puts a theory of our relation to our fundamental practices in the place of metaphysical realism. It also frankly acknowledges that the materials initially available for criticism consist in the views of human nature produced by particular cultural traditions and that much in these views is tacitly presupposed rather than explicitly articulated.

A social world does not become stable until its legal or customary rules can be understood and elaborated as fragmentary and imperfect expressions of an imaginative scheme of human coexistence rather than just as provisional truce lines in a brutal and amoral conflict. Such a scheme describes the desirable and realistic forms of human association—of practical collaboration or passionate attachment—that deserve to be realized in different areas of social life. This imaginative vision of social life implies, and is implied by, a developed image of man: a conception of our relation to our contexts and to one another.

A fundamental image of man generates existential projects as well as imaginative schemes of social life. By an existential project I mean an individual's view of how he can live in a way that gives a measure of sense, unity, and value to the course of his life. An existential project puts an image of man to work by offering guidance to an individual lifetime rather than to a set of social relations. This Introduction and the essay that follows deal with images of man less as social visions than as existential projects.

The most important repositories of enacted social visions are the actual normative orders—especially the legal systems and the traditions of legal doctrine—that make a social world into something more than an arena of violent and unlimited struggle. The most significant articulation of existential projects can be found in the major religions and religiously inspired ethics of world history. Far more than the abstract doctrines of moral and political philosophers, these legal and religious traditions embody visions and projects that have withstood the test of experience, enabling large numbers of people over long periods of time to make sense of their experience.

Once we see how conceptions of personality or society support social visions and existential projects, we can also understand what it means to credit these conceptions with normative force. The term normative judgment can only be a shorthand designation of a specific historical practice, not the name for an inherent, distinct, and unchanging human faculty. Our view of the nature as well as the basis of normativity must therefore change according to our beliefs about this practice, whether we acknowledge the connection or not. Thus, a person who thinks of normative judgment as largely a matter of general principles used to criticize or justify particular acts, or one who sees it merely as a fancy way to redescribe a devotion to a desire, has a conception of the practice different from the theory developed here. He therefore also has a somewhat different view of what it means to say: you should. The *should* of the existential project or the social vision means: execute this project and enact this vision, or find a better vision and a better project, or else fail at self-affirmation. In Kantian language this *ought* is hypothetical rather than categorical. But the rejection of its hypothesis—the effort at self-assertion—involves something far more drastic than the repudiation of a discrete goal of striving. It is more like the repudiation of striving itself.

The modernist doctrine of contextuality suggests a standard of empowerment—economic, moral, and cognitive—for preferring some social visions or existential projects to others. But this standard can be supplemented by many others. One of the most important of these additional considerations has to do with stability. A social scheme is unstable if it fails to reckon with behavioral predispositions or material constraints that work to disrupt it. The instability is especially serious when the scheme is itself responsible for the severity of these subversive constraints and predispositions. An existential project may suffer from psychological instability if it disregards or understates a recurrent feature of our experience. Characteristically, the fact played down is an aspect of our dependence—upon our circumstances and our bodies and above all upon other people. The dependence or the engagement that the person denies gives his actions a direction he had not expected or desired, confronting him with longings that he cannot acknowledge and with obstacles that he cannot overcome. These embarrassments eventually force themselves into his awareness and sap his confidence in the existential project to which he had adhered. Yet the unstable project is incorrigible: it cannot make room for the denied dependence without losing its specific characteristics or abandoning its distinctive concerns.

When we criticize by these standards a set of historically unique social visions or existential projects, two different results may occur. One of the results suggests a greater and the other a lesser degree of power to justify our choices among images of man and among the social visions and the existential projects that embody these images. Call them the more skeptical and the less skeptical conclusions. Each of these two possible outcomes conveys a different message about the sense in which conceptions of fundamental human identity have prescriptive force. The difference between these messages describes the maximum tightness or looseness of the link between the factual and the normative within a suitably corrected version of the classical style of normative argument.

On the more skeptical picture, successive doses of criticism of historically given conceptions of human identity will either discredit all such conceptions or produce conceptions that increasingly diverge from one another. Everything will depend upon our point of departure; we shall not be able to justify our starting point on the basis of the success with which it has withstood skeptical attack. On the alternative, more rationalist picture, existential criticism will show up some existential projects (or the conceptions of human identity that inspire them) as unstable. But when it does not undermine these visions, criticism will purify and strengthen them. The surviving, chastened views will converge, though never perhaps to a single cohesive position. Consequently, our need to begin with a historically specific view of personality becomes relatively less important. Any start can be justified retrospectively by its relative success in surviving critical assault. To be sure, the final result will remain anthropocentric—the truth from our point of view rather than from a standpoint that transcends us. But we have much less reason to care about this speculative hedge than about an inability to reach, through argument and experience, even a modest measure of agreement.

We cannot know in advance whether the more skeptical picture or the less skeptical one is correct. For one thing, they represent distant, idealized limits of current processes. For another thing, no localized facts about the world or about our capabilities tell us which of the two pictures is accurate. We hardly have an alternative to gambling on the decision to revise the classical style of normative argument rather than to abandon it: the more skeptical outcome of the revision still improves on the false and broken promises of modern philosophy.

The contrast between the two possible conclusions may seem feigned; the less skeptical result appears to be both improbable and incompatible with the modernist thesis about contexts. Nevertheless, I shall argue that we have reason to take seriously the possibility of a specific version of the more rationalist outcome. This version would be realized by the satisfaction of three conditions. The first is the existence of a limited number of fundamental conceptions of human identity, or existential projects, that deserve to be taken as the major candidates for criticism. These candidates are primarily conceptions and projects supported by the major world religions and by the moral doctrines associated with them. The second condition for the less skeptical outcome is that these images of man be divided between those that criticism destroys and those that it strengthens. Some views, for example, turn out to be psychologically unstable, while others do not. The third condition is that the views that do survive the critical attack come closer together. Modernism represents not the hypothetical focus of this convergence but an approach toward it from the particular direction of the Christian-romantic conception of human identity.

These conditions are connected. If, for example, there were an indefinitely large number of accounts of our shared identity that deserved to be seriously considered, we could never be sure whether the next conception of our shared identity to be studied might not turn out to be both corrigible and non-convergent. Of course, even if the number of past and present contenders is small we cannot exclude the possible emergence of a corrigible and non-convergent view, not unless we appeal to a doctrine of *a priori* constraints upon the possibilities of moral experience. But such a doctrine could never be reconciled with the theory of our relation to our contexts and practices that is defended and developed here. This theory not only must acknowledge that such a surprising possibility might emerge but must also insist that its emergence would change who we are. The difference between the situations of a short though open-ended list of alternatives and of a list that is just plain open-ended amounts to no more than a distinction in degrees of assurance.

Notice that even on the more skeptical account of the impact of criticism upon given views of human nature we still have standards with which to criticize these views. We can still ask to what extent a particular conception succeeds in helping us make sense of our experience. The tests of success are varied and their outcomes uncertain. But the tests need not for that reason be arbitrary. All our forms of self-knowledge, from scientific psychology and psychiatry to sustained introspection, enter into this assessment. (That there can in principle be no clear break between ordinary self-reflection and a scientific study of the mind is a thesis taken up in the Appendix to this book.)

The inconclusiveness of our self-knowledge is aggravated by a difficulty that a distinctively modern form of skepticism has underlined. We change our situation in the course of trying to understand it. We make ourselves into what we think we are and then interpret success in transformation as if it were success in discovery. Now, though this problem puts a joker in the pack of normative argument, its significance should not be exaggerated. Despite their influence upon the experience that they interpret, conceptions of human identity may differ in their ability to withstand criticism and to survive the recombinations of experience that actual social conflict produces. This difference is the main point of the distinction between corrigible and incorrigible views. The significance of convergence is not to signal an underlying moral order that somehow exists out there but to give content to the seemingly empty idea of forms of human connection that depend on no arbitrarily restrictive assumptions about personal or collective possibility.

At this point someone may object that even the less skeptical outcome offers only meager hope of justified choice among conceptions of human identity. We could never know for sure how far we had traveled along the path of criticism and convergence. But someone who presses such an objection is like a man who debates the fine points of high cuisine in the presence of the starving. The issue is not whether we can establish moral claims on a secure metaphysical basis but whether we can escape the most devastating skepticism.

The following pages exemplify the less skeptical picture of the effect of criticism upon some of the most influential images of man, conceived as existential projects. Though nothing entitles us to choose this view over its more skeptical rival, much can be learned by using it as a vantage point from which to consider those prestigious images of personality. The traditions to be discussed should not be taken as members in a list of moral options for mankind that has been awaiting slow discovery from the start of history. They are merely among the most seductive and fertile conceptions of human nature that have in fact arisen. Each resulted from a relatively accidental history. Each, driven by the pressure to help people make sense of all their experience, sacrificed coherence to plausibility and suffered the imprint of irreconcilable ideas; makeshift compromises are more easily tolerated than painful exclusions.

These traditions are nevertheless presented here with an eye to their most distinctive and general characteristics: the tenets that suggest a unique direction for our thinking about human identity. My aim is not to offer a fragmentary outline of the history of moral opinions but to emphasize the breadth of the points of departure at our disposal. To that end I disregard the tendency of each tradition to incorporate the characteristics of all the others (without undergoing the self-revision that would make these additions defensible) and thereby to present itself as all-seeing synthesis in the face of fanatical partiality.

The attention devoted to this criticism of received views of human identity may seem excessive as an illustration of a controversial methodological point or as an argument for an image of man that has not yet been presented. But its overriding purpose is to learn how and where we fail in our efforts to think prescriptively about ourselves.

The first family of existential projects and images of man to be described is the heroic ethic. Though it has appeared most prominently in the barbarous and military moments of world history, it is a position that repeatedly attracts, in every culture, those who combine devotion to a collective task with skepticism about the possibility of moral insight.

The defining focus of the heroic ethic is the hero's relationship to the community that he serves but from which he stands apart. As an existential project the heroic ethic offers the hero a task—but to the non-heroic society it provides only a benefit. It has no message for the common man, and for the hero himself it has a message of apartness. The consequences of these limitations will soon become apparent.

The conceptual background to the heroic ethic is the ironic view of human existence: the individual rises in a period of moral and physical vitality, and then he begins to fall. This decline makes a mockery of his never entirely abandoned claim to be at the center of the world and to exist forever. Along the way he suffers the interaction between his own petty flaws—the inevitable result of his embodied and discordant nature—and the great forces of necessity and chance that act upon him and accelerate his decline.

But the ironic view of existence and the commitment to break limits are not enough to define the heroic ethic. For the hero must know which limits to break; he must have a job. He and the non-heroic society he serves must strike a deal. The hero receives from the non-heroes the specific mission that gives content to the otherwise empty idea of limit-breaking. Often it is a work that must be performed at the edge of established society and in violation of its norms. Thus, the isolation of the hero, while emphasizing his proud disengagement from the texture of normal social interdependencies, also insulates society from the polluting effect of his activities. The soldier kills to protect a civil order founded upon the prohibition of violence. And the adversary intellectuals and artists typically try to rescue something from the suspicion that our experience is senseless and our ideals groundless and that everything is therefore permitted. To do this they must live close to a subversive skepticism from which people want their societies and cultures to be defended.

The hero receives from this transaction a task that enables him to reenact the ritual of limit-breaking and thereby to revenge himself against the belittling constraints upon the self. His election for this task by society and by fate sets him apart from other people. This acknowledged superiority over common humanity provides him with additional reasons to believe that he is not the small, frail, accidental man that the elementary circumstances of life seem to indicate we all are.

Non-heroic society also stands to gain from its dealings with the hero. In the first place, it benefits by the performance of a task that the non-heroes regard as useful or vital but that they cannot carry out themselves, not at least without relinquishing cherished aspects of their social life. The non-heroes also win another, less tangible advantage. Like the spectators of heroic action in a tragic drama, they find that the routines of everyday life are energized and ennobled when felt to take place at the very edge of the extreme efforts that the hero undertakes and of the violent conflicts that he confronts. The story of the hero tells the spectator, in the theater or in society, that life is not as mean as it may appear, because its petty trials pass readily into a superhuman ordeal. Not only that, but the spectators have presented to them a broader image of human possibilities, which is to say, a picture of something within their own selves. These material and spiritual benefits may persuade the non-heroic to tolerate the hero's arrogance.

As an existential project the heroic vision suffers from two crucial defects. Both shortcomings result from the same blindness to the true character of people's cognitive and emotional dependence upon one another.

The first defect is the inability of the hero to deal with the specific social character and origin of his task. The heroic mission does not descend from heaven. Its content reflects ideals and arrangements that were themselves produced by particular practical or imaginative conflicts. Yet the hero expects his job to confer upon him an unquestionable dignity as if this job were not infected by its limited, relatively haphazard origins.

So long as the hero remains unaware of the messy, historically determined quality of his mission, he is the pathetic victim of a delusion, assigning unconditional value to a conditional ideal and providing a transitory service that he imagines to be an eternal example. But as soon as he becomes conscious of the equivocal, earthly nature of his task—and to some extent he always will be aware of it—he finds himself burdened with an ironic relation to his endeavor. This relation shows him that he has not after all escaped the situation described by the ironic view of man's rise and fall. For the hero to improve his task, to make it worthier of his efforts, he would have to transform society and culture. He would therefore also need to throw himself into the give and take of social life and not allow himself to be entirely ruled by the pretense of disengagement.

As the hero becomes more fully sensitive to the accidental and controversial nature of his undertaking, the other defect of the heroic vision becomes apparent. He finds that he has lost the advantages and discoveries of personal encounter for sake of a task that if not unworthy can never be worthy enough to justify this sacrifice. So long as the hero continues to cultivate the heroic posture, he knows the life of personal interdependence in a peculiarly unhappy form. Just as he is enslaved to a contingent social ideal on which he inappropriately confers a transcendent value, he craves the approval of the very people over whom he claims an absolute superiority; if they refuse to renew his certificate, his doubts and resentments can only increase. To accept his longing for another person, to admit that the other person may fail to reveal or to bestow himself, and to recognize his own dependence upon fragile, historically founded communities of sense and affect—this the hero cannot easily reconcile with his self-conception or his pose.

Because the non-heroic spectators cannot give the hero what they implicitly promised, he too cannot keep his part of the deal. The hero's work may be useful, and it may be jolting. But the non-heroes fool themselves when they mistake their own artifact—the hero and his task—for the representation of ultimate human empowerment. They would have done better to seek this empowerment through the criticism and revision of their ordinary experience, beliefs, and institutions.

The deficiencies of the heroic ethic are incorrigible because they can be corrected only by a vision that would negate the distinctive features of this ethic. Such a vision—the heroism of the ordinary man and of ordinary life—would affirm the overriding importance of personal attachments. Its inspiration would be faith rather than pride, and it would see the faith we place in our tasks and in the defense of particular forms of life as an always dubious extension of the faith we have in one another as living individuals whom no tasks or forms of life can fully satisfy. The intellectual basis of this reorientation is the thesis that schemes of human association represent only better or worse versions of the more inchoate field of possibilities that we can always rediscover in our direct practical or passionate dealings. A heroism inspired by such a belief cannot be reconciled with unreserved confidence in an impersonal task nor can it see itself as an alternative to the dangers and disappointments of actual human solidarity.

A second family of moral ideas might be called the ethic of fusion with the impersonal absolute. It has received its clearest intellectual statement within Hinduism and Buddhism although the countervailing tendencies within both these religions have been so numerous and powerful that neither religion can justifiably be identified with this view. Because this existential project has benefited (or suffered) from such elaborate speculative defense, it pays to begin with a description of its ordinary conceptual background. This background is the contrast between the illusory, though perhaps only ultimately illusory, phenomenal world, where the principle of individuation is in command, and a plane of absolute reality, where the distinctions among individuals and among things vanish.

Thus, monism is the most familiar philosophical expression

of this contrast. But the monistic view can readily be replaced, as in the Samkhya brand of Hinduism, by a belief in the irreducible multiplicity of individual souls, each of which is regarded as an absolute. For the speculative issue of the unity or diversity of the absolute matters less to this existential orientation than the loose contrast between the ordinary world of human action or interaction and a reality that towers above it. From the standpoint of this reality the concerns of our ordinary world seem unimportant, corrupting, or absurd.

The heart of the ethic of fusion with the absolute is the commitment to gain release from the bonds of common suffering, unrest, ambition, and distraction and to merge the self-conscious individual into the principle of absolute reality, whether the unified spirit or the individual soul. History is demoted to a spectacle of violence and confusion that obscures the true vocation of the individual, except insofar as acts of compassion or dutifulness may help him escape, in this life or in another, from the constraints of his phenomenal self.

In the purest versions of this existential project the search for the absolute takes one of two seemingly opposite though in fact complementary forms. The individual may wrench himself out of society, treading the path of the recluse. Or he may obediently accept his social lot while cultivating his inner aloofness. He sings in his chains, as they say, and the very lack of ultimate importance that he confers upon his worldly attachments enables him to accept them with increasingly less embarrassment. The escapist and the resigned response share the premise that social life cannot be reformed to mirror more fully the absolute reality: no reconstruction of the social world can overcome the facts of individuality and encounter and the myriad of earthly cravings to which they give rise.

Whenever it has emerged as a major element in religious beliefs the effort at fusion with the absolute has been counterbalanced by ideas and commitments that qualify and even reverse its practical sense while maintaining (though not always) its conceptual background. Nowhere can the presence of these contrasting tendencies be seen more dramatically than in the history of Hinduism and Buddhism. On the one hand, a central role may be given to compassionate action in the process through which the individual frees himself from the realm of illusory cares and distinctions. The devotee may even personalize the absolute and conceive his confrontation with the personal deity by analogy to his personal attachments, seeing both as marked by the same insatiable longing for acceptance. (Remember, for example, the *Saiva Siddhanta* and the later great surge of personal devotion within Hinduism that goes under the name of *bhakti*.) On the other hand, as soon as the search for fusion with the absolute becomes central to a dominant creed it meets with the pressure to adapt to actual society: to the basic institutional arrangements and imaginative preconceptions on which a social order is founded and to the divisions and hierarchies that this formative structure generates. The system of social ranks (e.g., the caste system) may even be seen as divinely mandated. And if present social positions are believed to be largely rewards or punishments for adherence to the duties of one's social station in a previous existence, the result may be to lend the entire order a fearsome authority. The lackadaisical and aloof acceptance of a social role turns into a prostrate, worried, and even obsessional observance of social proprieties.

So the metaphysical contrast of phenomenal and absolute reality may be made to coexist with concerns that cannot be reduced to the moral options of the recluse or of the inwardly aloof role-performer. Conversely, these existential attitudes may be entertained against the backdrop of metaphysical or religious conceptions that may point conduct in a different direction. Thus, the ethic of escape and resignation has often proved attractive as a morality for the sensitive and the privileged in a society of superficially held Christian beliefs.

Though the connection between morality and metaphysics implied by this characterization of the quest for fusion with the absolute may be loose, it is real. For the metaphysic of the phenomenal and the absolute teaches the individual that his salvation lies in his ability to make contact with a reality—impersonal spirit or the inward disembodied soul—that promises a way to bypass the world of ordinary human encounters, longings, and conflicts. No wonder the mystical strands within Judaism, Christianity, and Islam combine a tendency toward speculative monism with a susceptibility to the attitudes of escape and resignation.

Like the heroic ethic, the effort at fusion with the absolute is psychologically unstable, and the sources of its instability closely resemble those that account for the self-subversion of that other existential endeavor. The individual must continue to live in the world. He must find within the world a partial and imperfect manifestation of the absolute reality to which he orients his striving. Without such a prefigurement he could not even begin to comprehend this absolute or to feel the force of its authority; it would lack a connection with familiar human life. He must find something in his present experience that embodies in part the decisive quality of the longed-for absolute reality, the context of all contexts. This quality is the ability not to be confined to an arbitrarily limited or rigid state of affairs or to its constitutive rules and distinctions.

The element in our experience that most closely answers to this description is personality itself: the indefinite range of forms of inquiry and argument that override particular frameworks for explanation or conversation, the open-ended possibilities of subjective experience that go beyond the routinized version of the self that is a character, and the opportunities for new forms of practical or passionate attachment that cannot be assimilated to the established institutions and the ruling dogmas of society. Yet the votary of the impersonal absolute (or of the isolated, disembodied soul that seeks to withdraw from the school of encounter) does not understand the central importance of the real, incarnate personality and of his practical or passionate transactions. He is drawn away from the very concerns that might impart to his experience more of the quality that he attributes to the context of all contexts. He devalues and avoids the personal or collective experiments that might move inquiry, character, and social life toward the ideal of accelerated self-revision that the modernist doctrine of contextuality describes. As the gap between ordinary life and the imagined absolute widens, the individual may find himself increasingly less able to grasp the unconditioned and to experience its power. Or he may respond in the opposite manner and treat paltry rituals, established social arrangements, or blank and evanescent states of mind as epiphanies of the absolute, thereby turning a sublime hope into a comedy of misperception and servility.

Just when the self-defeating character of the attempt at identification with the impersonal absolute becomes apparent, the other destabilizing obstacle to this existential project gains prominence. The devotee of the impersonal absolute finds himself constantly nagged or threatened by the irrepressible demands of the real, embodied person, the person who has an unlimited craving for other people's help and acceptance and even for their bodies. To be sure, he may achieve a measure of success in his attempt to find serenity through disengagement. But he can do so only by maintaining a distance from others that deprives him of the chief means with which to experiment with his own character. His imprisonment within a rigidified version of his self is confirmed by his need constantly to rekindle studied apathy through cranky obsession.

These failures of vision cannot be corrected without prejudice to the defining features of this existential endeavor. The distinction between an impersonal absolute and a phenomenal realm of incarnate individuals who stumble through an illusory material and historical world must be replaced by the distinction between the context-revising person and the contexts of discourse, character, or social life within which he habitually moves. For the believer this secular contrast will prepare rather than displace the contrast between God and his creatures. Believers and unbelievers alike will act on the conviction that the approach to the less contextual passes through, though it may not be exhausted by, the effort to change the quality of our contexts. They will treat the domain of personal dealings and historical conflicts as decisive for their spiritual fate. A quest for the absolute that has taken this turn is on the road to convergence with a modernist version of the Christian-romantic idea.

The ethic of heroic devotion and the ethic of fusion with the absolute fail for the same reasons. They represent similar responses to the individual's discovery that he is not at the center. In both instances the core of the response is the search for disengagement. This search encompasses both an affirmative and a negative aspect. The affirmative element is the attempt to make contact with a significant and authoritative principle that rises above the ordinary, equivocal realm of human interaction: the uncontroversial task of the hero or the distinction-overriding reality of the speculative monist. The negative element in this quest is the effort to become invulnerable to others and to the disappointments that may result from not being in charge.

Once you appreciate this shared theme of the two main incorrigible projects, you can also grasp more clearly the special, ambivalent position of modernism. Many, perhaps the most important, elements in the modernist view can be seen as a criticism and a deepening of the Christian-romantic image of man. But modernism has also often flirted with the view I earlier described as the extreme, heretical version of the modernist doctrine of contexts. This heresy asserts that the self cannot hope to change the quality of its contexts in order that they may provide it with a more congenial environment in which to develop and deploy its context-making and context-transcending capabilities. Repeating a characteristic tenet of the mystics within the Semitic salvation religions of

Judaism, Christianity, and Islam—the principle of the *via nega-tiva*—this modernism teaches that the individual can assert his true nature only by a permanent labor of denial: denial of any stable mode of subjectivity, intersubjectivity, or social life.

The consequence of this attitude for politics is a relentless utopianism that denounces all institutional arrangements and systems of rights by reference to an unattainable standard of complete freedom from any instituted form of social life. The consequence of the secular *via negativa* for the approach to personal relations is the view that emotion survives only in opposition to real human communities. For these communities, from marriage to large groups, require a social presence, a provisional order, and even a daily routine.

This misguided variant of modernism differs from the incorrigible existential projects discussed in the preceding sections by its resolute identification of the unconditional source of sense and authority with personality and personal encounter rather than with an impersonal reality or task. It nevertheless resembles those projects in its failure to accept the actual world of history and personality. In this world every defiant vision must either die away or find a new sustaining context of ideas, habits, or institutions. The extreme modernist responds to this fact by becoming a spirit on the run. He cannot enter with a willing heart into continuing loyalties, and he cannot therefore experience fully the dangers and opportunities of accepted vulnerability. He cannot even completely imagine the otherness of other people. He tends to see them as he sees himself—as a disembodied individual rather than as a person largely though not entirely defined by his membership in particular communities of sense and affect, communities that in turn depend upon the institutional and imaginative structures through which they reproduce themselves.

But worst of all for this modernist is his inability to repeat the act of context-smashing often enough, or to make each such act last long enough, to purge social life of its shaped and repetitious quality. His program pushes him to ever greater extremes in the attempt to destroy and deny context. But although this fanaticism of denial may consume all his energies it cannot in the end liberate him from the real society in which he lives.

There are at least two other families of ideas that have performed a major role in the history of moral opinions. They, too, exclude or downplay certain important aspects of experience and, as a result, risk the same psychological instability that characterizes the two sets of moral ideas just described. This time, however, the failures of vision can be corrected without depriving the existential projects, or the image of man that underlies them, of their distinctive features.

To be sure, the difference between correcting a view and abandoning its distinctive characteristics will always be unclear and controversial. After all, these positions represent a series of contingent historical traditions rather than a well-ordered system of the possible normative options open to mankind. But unless all general moral and political ideas are to be dismissed as freely manipulable slogans, we must be able to assess the degree to which a given idea lends itself to being developed in a certain direction.

The relatively less skeptical picture of the effect of criticism upon our received views of human identity presupposes the contrast between corrigible and incorrigible projects. It also depends on the beliefs that more than one corrigible project exists and that as many as do exist will be found to converge toward the position that the modernist version of the Christian-romantic idea also seeks. These claims are implausible if not counterintuitive. So it is all the more pleasing to discover that we have reason to take them seriously, although we can never hope to exclude the possibility that the more skeptical picture might after all turn out to be true.

There is at least one major historical example of a vision of man that, like the Christian-romantic image itself, suffers from no fatal psychological instability. This example is the conception of human identity worked out in Confucianism. The Confucianist tradition can be taken as simply the clearest and best developed instance of all those views that combine a central emphasis on the problem of human solidarity with what I earlier called a naturalistic approach to the contexts of our action. (The Christian-romantic view, by contrast, joins the emphasis on solidarity to an iconoclastic attitude toward society and history.) It preaches adherence to a particular canonical list of exemplary social relations as well as to both the intimate ordering of the emotions and the great ordering of society that sustain those exemplary forms of human association and receive sustenance from them. Characteristically, the canonical social relations that connect the macrocosm of social organization to the microcosm of the human passions require that unequal power, practical exchange, and reciprocal allegiance be combined in the same human relations.

The order of emotions and the arrangements of society, the doctrine teaches, depend on each other. When these two orders converge toward the same regulative scheme they moderate the antagonism between the opposing conditions of self-assertion and they generate prosperous and happy communities. But once the public arrangements of society or the intimate emotions of its members depart from this ideal, a vicious cycle of self-seeking, distrust, and conflict may begin that only acts of exceptional statesmanship in the public life or of self-denial in the private life may be able to reverse.

Though the proponents of this teaching may denounce the current state of society, their faithfulness to the naturalistic thesis requires them to believe that even the worst social situation represents a corrupt version of the true model of civilized life. The forms of society and subjectivity cannot be reinvented.

The Confucianism I have in mind is the classical teaching of Confucius himself and his early followers rather than the neo-Confucianism that emerged during the Sung and that subordinated this conception of solidarity on some occasions to a speculative metaphysics or cosmology and at other times to a detailed program of social reform. The vision that Confucianism exemplifies represents the most common theme in the history of moral and political opinions. The variations that this theme has undergone can be understood largely as the consequence of relaxing the naturalistic premise. The most familiar representative of this vision in the history of normative controversies is the commitment to mutual responsibility in small groups and to the institutional arrangements and psychological predispositions that support these reciprocal engagements. The closest modern political example of the doctrine is a program that combines a commitment to social welfare with an acceptance of political demobilization. According to this program, people's basic needs should be taken care of—if possible by their own communities and enterprises, if necessary by central government. But the way of caring for them should minimize the occasions for conflict over the fundamentals of social life and prevent the contest of ideologies from interfering with the search for improved efficiency and harmony.

Classical Confucianism offers insights into the problem of solidarity that have never been surpassed by any other tradition of comparable influence. First, there is the sureness of its focus on the relationship between the social and the personal. Confucianism recognizes that models of direct relations between people form the elements of whole schemes of social life. These schemes are not realized and cannot be judged until they have been changed into the small coin of personal encounter and experience.

Second, the Confucianist precept underlines the affirmative or destructive valency of the other person as the ground on which the whole life of passion develops. The self-reflecting individual in the presence of another person is like a man officiating at a sacrifice. The deeper his moral insight and perfection, the less he understands or experiences personal encounter in purely instrumental terms.

Third, the teaching acknowledges the dynamism of the life of passion. It emphasizes the readiness with which apparently different passions change into one another and the rightful subordination of all of them to a central constructive impulse. In Confucianist doctrine this relativizing and guiding force is *jen:* the quality of self-expression and self-formation that manifests itself in both sympathy and detachment. *Jen* enables you to perfect the ideal forms of social relationships through mastery over the conflicts and desires that might unsettle you and tear you apart.

On their way to becoming concrete moral and political teachings, however, these early Confucianist insights are combined and contaminated with the implications of the naturalistic view. For this reason, Confucianism suffers from a defective conception of society and subjectivity.

As an approach to society it mistakes a specific system of social division and hierarchy for the scheme of social life that can best reconcile the conflicting conditions of self-assertion. It disregards the constraints that such a system imposes upon the development of alternative forms of production and exchange and alternative modes of subjectivity and solidarity. Its tolerance for these constraints shows in the advocacy of personal relations that soften naked dominion by infusing them with elements of exchange and allegiance. This advocacy is a prescription for squandering opportunities of practical progress and human reconciliation. Confucianism fails to recognize the many-sided productive, emotional, and cognitive empowerment that may result when established or emergent privilege faces ever-renewed challenge, when the contrast between routine moves within the social order and revolutionary conflicts about it loses its force, and when the tyranny of collective categories of gender, class, or nationality over individual circumstance is overthrown.

As a view of selfhood the weak point of the classical Con-

fucianist doctrine is its naive and impoverished conception of subjectivity and personal encounter. To the canon of social roles and
conventions there corresponds, according to this doctrine, an ordering of the emotions. And the combination of the collective and
psychological orders sets the terms on which society can cohere
and prosper and individuals can be secure and happy, each in his
separate station.

With the abandonment of belief in a canonical form of
social life that provides a transparent medium of mutual access, all
varieties of self-reflection and communication must come to be
seen as having an uncertain, troubled relation to received conventions and established arrangements. Our membership in historically given and flawed human communities provides us with the
only standards of sense and value we have. These standards form
the unavoidable basis of communication and self-reflection. But
unless we constantly push our experiments in self-reflection and in
practical collaboration or passionate attachment beyond what established society or available discourse can countenance we incur
a double loss. Not only do we fail to make many discoveries about
ourselves and about the world and to find more successful ways to
reconcile the conflicting conditions of self-assertion, but we may
find ourselves increasingly reduced to an unconscious servitude.
We may begin to act and to think as if all our thoughts and actions
could indeed be governed by a lawlike structure we were powerless to escape or to revise.

The defiance of these constraints exacts, however, a price
of its own. Part of this price consists in a confusion about the assessment of emergent forms of subjectivity and intersubjectivity.
And another part of the price lies in the antagonisms that may be
excited and the betrayals that may be committed in the course of
the attempt to find a better solution to the problem of solidarity.

Though the defects in the Confucianist vision that result
from its association with the naturalistic idea are serious, they can
be remedied. The view of solidarity that lies at the heart of this
conception can be cumulatively transformed by loosening the nat-

uralistic thesis about contexts. The early stages of the revision may rely upon diluted versions of this thesis. But the correction would not be complete until it had concluded the rebellion against naturalism by embracing the modernist account of our relation to the contexts of our activity. My summary criticism of the implications of classical Confucianism for the view of society and personality has already suggested the direction in which this reformed Confucianism would move.

Long before the classical Confucianist teaching had been reformulated along such lines, many of its adherents might reject it, saying: This is not what we meant. But nothing in the reformed doctrine would be incompatible with the central Confucianist insights into personality and personal encounter that I earlier enumerated. And nothing in it would be anathema to a modernist restatement of the Christian-romantic view of human identity.

The Christian-romantic image of man represents still another corrigible vision. Its distinctive tenets have already been defined.

Where does its weak point lie? Previous discussion suggested a tentative answer. The Christian-romantic view has frequently been joined if not to the naturalistic attitude then to a weakened variant of that attitude. The result has been to encourage the identification of this conception of human identity with the characteristic outlook of the social classes positioned to produce the moral ideas with the greatest influence in the society of their time, ideas such as the aristocratic ethic of chivalry or the bourgeois ethic of controlled though sentimentalized domesticity and punctilious devotion to work. But if this facility for practical equivocation were the sum of the defects to which our central Western conception of personality is prone, this conception would be in a far better position than classical Confucianism. The theme of social and historical iconoclasm that, together with the theme of love, lies close to its core already predisposes it to deny the absolute claims of particular forms of social life.

In fact, however, my earlier account of how the Christian-romantic view is likely to go wrong remains so incomplete as to be misleading. For there is a related but more subtle respect in which a failure to appreciate the insights that modernism has propagated makes itself felt within this tradition. This further weakness of insight is an ambivalence toward simple human vitality in all its forms, from the dim tenacity that gets people from one chore to another to the proud magnificence, the joy in exorbitant capability, that the adventurer or the transformer may display.

The Christian-romantic view is marked by two commitments whose relation to each other usually remains uncertain and even paradoxical. The view suggests that the constant return of the self into its customary ways represents a major form and cause of failure in the moral life. The salvation religions fear that this vast spiritual sloth will prevent us from making contact with human and divine personality: the human self, which always transcends its world, and the divine creator, who transcends the world. Similarly, the secular romance—the other strand in this central Western tradition—sees in this acceptance of dazed repetition the failure to take possession of oneself by transforming the facts around one. Whether portrayed in religious or secular terms, the surrender to habit is recognized to be closely linked to the defeat of the imagination: the diehard commitment to a particular way of dividing up the world that closes itself off to perceptions and arguments that this classification may exclude. Frozen into a set of delusively self-evident categories, we lose our hold upon reality. Our self-satisfied common sense becomes a hallucination, as we congratulate one another upon its mendacious transparency and fixity.

But the campaign against quiescence is balanced by a militant suspicion of the pleasure in capability and self-affirmation. The

more exaggerated the brio of empowerment, the more determined the hostility with which it is met. The religious strand in the
tradition is quick to see the display of magnificence as a denial of
finitude, a rebellion against the Creator, and a refusal of self-
sacrifice for the sake of other people. Though the hostility of the
secular romance to this glory in life may be less obvious, it is no
less real. For delight in the development and exercise of a power
threatens to deflect the protagonist of the secular romance from
the sacrificial quest for self-knowledge and service that represents
his true calling.

Antagonism toward pride in self-affirmation and hostility to
the dogged, repetitious quality of our ordinary life seem to
conflict. The escape from the routines of existence or of the imagination appears to lead to the celebration of capability that our
mainstream tradition so intensely suspects. To say merely that the
quest for empowerment deserves credit when it serves outward-
looking or benevolent ends is to put a conclusory moral distinction in the place of a persuasive psychological account.

At the root of this ambivalence lies an unsureness about
what to think and what to do about everything in our nature that
expresses the attachment to life and the happiness of empowerment. So long as this uncertainty persists, our conception of personality will remain prey to the most outlandish conclusions. At
times it will enlist the moralistic obsession with rules or with fixed
catalogues of the virtues and vices in order to wage war against all
the simple, life-affirming, and frivolous inclinations of the heart. At
other times it will go to the opposite extreme and hold up the fabulous example of the empowered superman who defies all obstacles to the development of his faculties and the assertion of his
will. The theoretical commitment to accept the real embodied person has rarely been matched in our central tradition by the ability
to show just what place the search for empowerment should occupy in our social visions and existential projects. Because this
search has so important a role in the modernist vision, the mod-

ernist restatement of the Christian-romantic image of man can provide the occasion to close this dangerous gap in our thinking about ourselves.

To this end we must accomplish two connected tasks: the development of a psychology of empowerment and the analysis of the social conditions on which empowerment depends. A psychology of empowerment must do justice to the ambivalent relation between the lure of highly developed faculties and the banal sluggishness of ordinary existence. The reach for the large endeavor and the surprising action signifies a heightening of the same acceptance of life that appears less grandly in the dumb, determined movement through the activities of the day and in the plain man's willingness to press forward in the midst of pain, bungling, repetition, and exhaustion. Empowerment represents the movement of vitality toward joy; though it may involve a painful wrenching out from the habitual objects of our longing, it can also generate desires and fulfillments that are increasingly less susceptible to the deadliness of rapid satiation. The entire spectrum of forms of vitality from the modest to the magnificent must be given a position at the center of a more defensible version of the Christian-romantic view of human identity if we are to take seriously the commitment to accept the real embodied person.

A psychology of empowerment must also reckon with the ambivalent relation of empowerment to the transforming experiences of love, faith, and hope that play so large a part in our classical conception of the self. The search for empowerment can result in spiritual pride, a flaunting of the will, a narcissistic delight in self-assertion that excludes sacrifice and self-bestowal. Nevertheless, the heroism of everyday life also renders a service to the sacrificial and self-transforming passions. It can save them from confusion with the resentful and hypocritical moralism of the weak. That the lessening of dominion and dependence avoids the equivocal identification of attachment with submission is a claim repeatedly argued here. The same process that encourages the heartless cult of an unsacrificing magnificence of self-assertion also helps eradicate the sources of the confusion between the most slavish and the most exalted forms of moral experience.

People may establish the best attachments in the midst of the most absolute tranquility of circumstance. They may, on the contrary, be pushed by uncertainty into the meanness of distrust, despair, and disbelief. But the growth of the transforming and ennobling passions that constitute the opposite of those moral failures and the ability of these passions to penetrate the crust of everyday perception and habit seem to depend upon loss and sacrifice. This much has always been recognized by the very teachings that present faith, hope, and love as the summit of the moral life. Now, the primary form of loss and sacrifice is the sacrifice and the loss of your settled place in a settled world. This is the event that allows you to distinguish the gold from the tinsel: the opportunities of human connection from the forms of established society, and the disclosures of incongruous insight or disobedient desire from the distraction and the narcosis of habit.

The contribution that empowerment makes to faith, hope, and love can be described in another way. Trust is the climate in which these passions flourish. Forgiveness is the antecedent and the preserver of trust. In the course of social life people shoot at each other an endless flurry of poisoned arrows: all the voluntary and involuntary harms they do one another. The accumulation of these real or imagined wrongs progressively reduces the area of free movement in social life; each person feels drastically limited in the initiatives he can take by his earlier history of animosities and resentments. By the same token, he is prevented from running the risks of vulnerability that render faith, hope, and love possible. The experience of empowerment makes it easier to tear the poisoned arrows out. It weakens the force of mean-minded concerns founded upon fear and self-contempt. It enables the person to imagine himself connected in untried ways to other people, even to those who harmed him or whom he harmed. The flawed,

fragile, reversible transfiguration of ordinary vitality by empowerment and of empowerment by sacrificial love is the highest secular
redemption for which we are entitled to hope.

The understanding and the achievement of empowerment
help sustain an existential project that treats love, faith, and hope
as aspects of the culminating ideal in the domain of the intimate
and the non-instrumental. So too the ideas and attitudes that underlie such a project prevent the aim of empowerment from suffering a perversion to which it is peculiarly subject in the conditions of modern life and culture. The movement toward a fuller
reconciliation between the enabling conditions of self-assertion—a movement whose interpersonal form the Christian-
romantic tradition describes as love and whose hierarchy-subvert-
ing effects concern emancipatory ideologies like liberalism and
socialism—represents our core experience of freedom. Conversely, the sense of our inability to change the relation between these
conditions of self-assertion provides our basic experience of constraint upon will and imagination. This sense begins as disappointment and ends as despair.

A familiar response to this despair is a particular self-
defeating version of the ideal of empowerment. The version at
issue might be studied as one of the many latter-day transformations of the heroic ethic if it did not so deliberately try to sever
even the tenuous links between the would-be hero and the non-
heroic society. As the bad conscience of the Christian-romantic
tradition it has come to mark much of high and popular culture. In
high culture it appears as the cult of a vibrant and exalted self-sufficiency. The self-reliant individual supposedly shakes loose his
dependencies and achieves a radiance of assertion that combines
an almost god-like overcoming of constraints with a very human
richness of individuality. We find this conception of empowerment stated, with mounting extravagance, in the *Emile,* in Emer-
son, and in Nietzsche. In contemporary popular culture a similar
ideal reemerges as the search for adventures that can compensate

the individual for the belittling routines of his humdrum existence.

But whatever its specific form, this vision of empowerment cannot deliver the happiness that it promises. It does not teach forgiveness of others because it is blind to the imperative of self-forgiveness. It fails to recognize and accept the real, exposed, tottering individual, housed in a dying body and dependent upon uncontrollable others for all the tangible and intangible supports that enable him to sustain a presence. The pursuit of empowerment that arises from a despair about our ability to change the quality of our personal and social relations is likely to end in a reversal of its objective. The individual wakes up to discover that he is still the same precarious, embodied person and that in chasing a mirage of self-sufficiency he has foregone the forms of action and encounter that might have strengthened his freedom in fact.

A psychologically realistic and stable variant of the ideal of empowerment must look to the cumulative transformation of personal and social relations. Its enemies are those who either despair of such changes or view them with a dreamy shallowness that is bound to end in disenchantment. Its champions are those who seek to uncover the twofold root of empowerment in the revision of our intimate life of relation and in the reconstruction of institutional arrangements.

The indispensable counterpart to a psychology of empowerment is a social theory capable of describing the forms of social life that advance the practical, passionate, and cognitive forms of empowerment. Such a theory would show how this advance takes place through a softening of the contrast between conflicts about the social order and conflicts within it and through a weakening of the influence that an individual's place within the categories of social division and hierarchy exercises over his experience and opportunities. This theory would also teach us how to imagine and explain change in the institutional and imaginative contexts of social life without supposing that such change is governed by a system of pre-established laws. For if we were so governed we could have no hope of winning greater mastery over the contexts of our activity; at the moment of our greatest apparent freedom we would remain in the thrall of unseen compulsions.

The design of such a social theory lies beyond the scope of the present essay. Without its help, however, the correction of the Christian-romantic image of man must remain incomplete. Unable to tell just what set of social relations could best reconcile the ideal of empowerment with the forms of cooperation and attachment that a driving concern with empowerment seems to jeopardize, we cannot carry the ideal of personality to its conclusion. We continue to risk the identification of this unfinished ideal with a form of social life that slights our freedom, turns us into its puppets, and makes practical cooperation and passionate attachment hostage to the practices of dominion and dependence.

The preceding parts of this Introduction suggest a substantive and a methodological point of departure for developing a normative conception of our fundamental human identity. The substantive starting point is the modernist restatement and reconstruction of the Christian-romantic view of man. This restatement results, in large part, from the application of a modernist conception of contextuality to an older doctrine of solidarity. The methodological point of departure is a revised version of the standard form of normative argument, which attributes prescriptive force to substantive conceptions of human identity. This reformed practice fixes the sense in which images of the self—or the social visions and existential projects that they animate—can guide the conduct of life or the organization of society.

We have to acknowledge a range of possible measures of

prescriptive authority, from the stronger to the weaker, without being able to tell for sure which of these measures our fundamental conceptions of human identity can in fact possess. If the relatively more skeptical view prevails we can claim for the modernist moment of the Christian-romantic view only that it represents a statement of our central tradition of thinking about human nature that is less dependent than its predecessors upon unjustifiably confined assumptions about the possible forms of personal experience and social organization. If the relatively less skeptical picture is correct we may hope for something more: that the existential implications of the Christian-romantic view suffer from no fatal psychological instability and that, once chastened by modernist skepticism and complemented by modernist concerns with empowerment, they converge toward the lessons of other traditions that benefit from a similar reformation. Not even on the most confident view, however, may we present the Christian-romantic tradition as the sole legitimate perspective on human nature.

Even after the substantive and the methodological starting points have been chosen we must still settle on a way of talking and a genre of writing. No available genre entirely suits the purpose. Some of the traditional modes of discourse fit the classical, pre-modernist approach to normative argument, while others reflect the modern philosophical attempt to circumvent conceptions of human identity altogether as a basis for normative arguments. I propose to adopt a stylistic counterpart to the methodological strategy pursued in the preceding pages. Just as the classical practice of normative argument can be revised by a sustained exposure to modernist criticism, the stylistic parallel to this practice can profit from a similar chastening.

The last major genre to serve as the vehicle for a theoretically and morally ambitious account of our fundamental identity was the speculative treatise on human nature. This genre retained its popularity well into the earlier part of the nineteenth century, when the rise of scientific psychology and of the idealist precursors to modernism began to undermine its premises. And though it took forms as diverse as the systematic works of Hume and Adam Smith and the fragmentary reflections of Pascal, it could always be identified by the coexistence of three characteristics. Each of these characteristics revealed a distinct set of assumptions. A mode of speculative writing capable of expressing the modernist moment of the Christian-romantic view and the revised version of the classical normative style must reshape these characteristics and assumptions.

A first distinguishing trait of the genre was simply the confidence with which it attributed normative consequences to conceptions of the self and, especially, to portrayals of emotional life. The confidence came so easily that it affected even Hume, the very writer to whom we most owe the polemical contrast between factual and prescriptive claims. It accounts for the continuous passage between moral or political teaching and social or political analysis that we find throughout this tradition of writing about human nature. This Introduction has already suggested the specific blend of skepticism and hope that should replace the earlier attitude.

A second mark of the speculative treatise on human nature was its willingness to treat our fundamental identity as something that could be thought about apart from the version of humanity that each culture articulates and each society establishes. The authors of those treatises felt sure they could say things about personality that were neither trivial nor false. The historical consciousness so important to modernism has robbed us of this assurance. It has made us recognize that even the most intimate experiences of, say, jealousy or love differ in each historical situation. It has taught us to abandon as futile the essentialist hope of distinguishing in human nature a significant, unchanging core and a variable periphery.

How can a speculative essay on personality absorb the modernist insight into the historical specificity of all our forms of consciousness and sensibility? The vocabulary of self-scrutiny and evaluation set out here develops a recognizable tradition, and its proximate aim is to enable us to make sense of our experience of immediate attachment or isolation in a particular historical circumstance. But this circumstance is one in which social life has been subjected, in an unprecedented measure, to the instruction of conflict. Society has witnessed a loosening of the established plan of social division and hierarchy and a jumbling of the varieties of activity and awareness that may be possessed by any particular nation, class, community, or individual.

Modernists advocate a relentless recombination of the experiences traditionally identified with distinct roles, genders, classes, or nations, and denounce their societies for continued submission to the constraints of false necessity. But the modernist message would not be persuasive or even intelligible unless a great deal of jumbling had already taken place—enough to suggest how much could be gained, in opportunities for self-assertion, by overcoming the constraints that remain. Insofar as modernism is the theory of a jumbled experience, of an experience of association projected beyond the limits of a highly defined society and culture, it represents more than the extended self-image of a particular social world. For one of the traits that makes particular the social life with which modernism deals is precisely the diminished place that it gives to particularizing limitations upon production and exchange or upon subjectivity and attachment. And this relative freedom from particularity, the gift of cumulative conflict, may be further strengthened by the imagination, which anticipates the work of conflicts that have not yet been fought out.

The servile dogma of a certain historicism insists that the sole discourse we can have about our subjective experience of social life is a particularizing discourse: the attempt to explicate and elaborate the assumptions that distinguish a given culture from all others. This style of thought wants to outlaw any less self-referential talk about social life as the naive and illegitimate identification of a particular society with universal laws of social organization. But this prohibition imposes an arbitrary constraint upon the principle of historicity because it fails to recognize that the extent to which our contexts imprison us and reduce us to a compulsive passivity is itself one of the things up for grabs in history. This unhistorical limit upon historical variability illustrates the indefensible version of the modernist view of our relation to our contexts: the version that combines skepticism with surrender, by teaching that all we can do is to choose a social world or a tradition of discourse and to play by its rules.

The variant of the modernist doctrine of contextuality outlined at the start of this Introduction supports both a particularizing and a universalizing discourse about our experience of life with other people. The point is not to choose one over the other but to change the way we understand and practice both.

The particularizing discourse that is validated by a modernist approach to contexts shows how a tradition of self-reflection is remade in the very process of being applied by particular classes and communities as their members attempt to make sense of their experience. This particularizing discourse gains its modernist flavor both from its belief that understanding is possession and possession reinvention and from its attentiveness to the dialectic between the pieties of a prestigious culture and the undercurrent experiments in association that these pieties simultaneously suggest, forbid, and conceal.

The universalizing discourse consists in the attempt to seize on the parts of our tradition of individual and collective self-reflection that are comparatively less tainted by the illusions of false necessity. We try to correct our conception of possible and desirable association by submitting it, in thought and in practice, to a negative and an affirmative exercise. The negative exercise is the attempt to recast our ideas about sociability by diminishing their dependence upon a historically confined sense of associative possibility. The affirmative exercise is the effort to imagine the ordering of social life that empowers us more fully by giving freer play to the two great dynamics of empowerment—the dynamics of passion and of practical problem-solving, each of which requires that our relations to one another be kept in a state of heightened plasticity. The universalizing discourse that practices this negative and affirmative exercise is the revised sense given by modernism to the antique ambition of universality in prescriptive theories of human nature.

To adopt a universalizing discourse on modernist assumptions is not to deny that the categories and commitments of a normative tradition have a historically located origin. Thus, a modernist view of contextuality fails to generate an image of man unless it interacts with a solution to the problem of solidarity. Though this solution may be corrected by the negative and affirmative devices just mentioned, it will probably always bear the marks of its specific historical genesis. We cannot tell how much in the composite result should be attributed to the particularity-destroying discoveries and inventions of modernism and how much to the distinctive Christian-romantic treatment of solidarity. We cannot say: up to this point the revised view of our shared identity rests upon a particular experience, beyond this point it speaks with the authority of universal experience. To claim the power to draw such a distinction would be to presuppose a place beyond history from which we could assess the influence of historical specificity.

The modernist practice of a universalizing discourse implies a gamble. We bet that something will be left over after we have pushed the skeptical assault as far as we can and that this residue of more reliable insight can emerge step by step from experiences and ideas we already possess. Our only alternatives to this gamble are a radical skepticism on which we cannot act or a cultural fatalism that subverts the seriousness of our actions and that mistakes their relation to the contexts in which they occur.

A third characteristic of the speculative treatise on human nature, alongside its prescriptive and its universalistic claims, was the unabashed appeal to a natural language of reason in which educated men and women could converse about their experience. It was a language that neither met the standards of empirical science (though many dreamt of turning it into a science) nor pretended to derive its conclusions from a metaphysical picture of reality as a whole (though some attempted to extend it into a meta-physic). From the highly self-conscious perspective of our time, this pure language of self-reflection may seem a fantasy. It lacks grounding in a scientific study of behavior. It does not even claim to exemplify general truths about the world.

Yet there may be strength in these apparent weaknesses. Any behavioral science brings a limited and limiting perspective to bear upon its subject matter and is invariably tempted to study only what it can hope to elucidate with its present methods. And a metaphysic, while pretending to derive conclusions about human nature from allegedly fundamental truths about the world, typically does the very opposite: it projects a view of subjectivity and intersubjectivity into a picture of ultimate reality and then pretends to derive from this projection the very image of man that had originally inspired the metaphysical account. Thus, the modernist metaphysicians of the twentieth century (e.g., Heidegger, Sartre) sometimes tried to re-deduce a modernist anthropology from an ultra-metaphysical story about the nature of being.

Moreover, the image of man developed in this essay, and the social vision with which this image is connected, suggest a special reason to fight for a defensible version of the old language of cultivated self-reflection. Remember that a central theme of this image is the concern with empowerment, defined to include both growing mastery over the contexts of activity and success in diminishing the conflict between the conditions of self-assertion. Only by incorporating an ideal of empowerment can the Christian-romantic image of man be rescued from the failures of vision and the perversities of emphasis to which it is peculiarly exposed. But empowerment in personal experience, as in the life of society, requires that people be able to speak about what is closest and most urgent to them. Apart from the pressure of material needs, nothing can be more important to people than their understanding of their own identities. To be able to speak only about what is less significant, to feel that the most weighty concerns are inexpressible—this itself amounts to another definition of disempowerment.

Art may rescue us from this condition by giving precise expression to what we mutely feel. But art would be enough only if it had turned into the medium of everyday conversation and self-probing. To be sure, identity will only exceptionally be articulated as systematic theory. Even discursive thought may be unnecessary. At a minimum, however, the empowered individual must be able to tell stories about his experience. Through these stories he may imagine the things that have happened to him in his life of encounter as part of a wider range of relational opportunities and the things he has felt as intimations of yet unexperienced forms of subjectivity. He must also be able to pass, by steps, from this storytelling to discursive self-reflection and deliberation. Only then can the language of self-knowledge become a modality of everyday experience rather than a fabulous exception to the quotidian and a mythical compensation for the limitations of insight.

What can this general language consist in? It cannot be merely the extension of particular scientific or interpretive methods drawn from specific disciplines. The received versions of social theory have watered down rather than abandoned the idea of a deep logic, a meta-structure, or a context of all contexts that determines the character and evolution of forms of social organization or sets the outer limits to possible social worlds. And the major traditions of psychology attach psychological generalization to methods that emphasize the same two varieties of lawlike constraint. A mode of discourse based upon such premises could never serve to develop an image of the self that accepts the modernist view of contexts and therefore abandons the idea of a meta-structure. Perhaps no alternative social theory or psychology will ever completely overcome these limitations; the would-be alternatives may forever be tempted to emphasize what they can most easily grasp, to project routines into laws, and to seek generality through the vindication of necessity. All the devices by which social thought steels itself against these temptations may renew them in novel disguises.

A stand-in for the social theory and the psychology we do not yet and may never fully possess is a simplified version of storytelling: a storytelling with the austerity of discursive thought rather than the lush particularism of literary art, a storytelling about the exemplary individual caught in the mesh of personal dependencies and encounters, a storytelling that draws its chief inspiration from the experiences of context-breaking—of violation of the institutional and imaginative order of social life or of the routines of character and imagination—that current social theory and psychology are least successful in explaining, a storytelling that therefore feeds on the leftovers and the rejects of the would-be sciences of man. This storytelling describes the revised, qualified sense I want to give to the archaic idea of a universal language of self-reflection.

How can you know that one such story is better than another? The difficulty lies in the overabundance of reasons for preference rather than in their absence. These reasons may be broadly divided into those that focus upon the truthfulness of an underlying conception of the self and those that address the existential project that such a conception inspires.

The revised version of the classical style of normative argument gives prescriptive force to ideas of personality or society. I have already described the spectrum of views about the sense of this force—from the stronger or more rationalist to the weaker or more skeptical—that are compatible with modernist assumptions. But whatever the measure and mode of normative authority that an account of our shared human identity may possess, this account can be evaluated with the full panoply of empirical arguments that are relevant to the assessment of more specific social or psychological ideas.

First, you can judge the explanatory fecundity of such an account: the extent to which it suggests more readily verifiable or falsifiable ideas in particular disciplines. Thus, the Appendix to this book shows how this theory of the passions can inspire an approach to the explanatory and therapeutic problems of psychiatry.

Second, a conception of our identity may be assessed by its compatibility with a powerful social theory. Though we cannot hope to deduce views of the self and of society from each other, they are so closely connected that a position on one of these scores severely limits our options on the other. We know that a view of the self is indefensible if no defensible social theory can deploy or presuppose it. I claim for the story about selfhood developed in this essay an affinity with a particular social-theoretical program. The theory envisaged by this program carries to its ultimate conclusions the idea that society is made and imagined rather than given. It disengages the attempt to generalize about society and history from the appeal to psychological, economic, and organizational constraints that supposedly underlie the surface of social and historical life. And it combines a recognition of the shaped quality of social life—the importance of the contrast between routine activities inside an imaginative or institutional context and struggle about this context—with disbelief in a higher order that generates a necessary history of contexts or a list of possible contexts. In all these ways such a theory shows how to imagine society and history in the spirit of the modernist doctrine of our relation to the settings of our activity. It thereby frees us from the need to choose between an eviscerated and half-hearted variant of the Procrustean evolutionary or functionalist social theories of yesteryear and a positivist social science whose theoretical reticence disguises its attempt to treat routines, which depend upon the containment of conflict, as if they embodied general laws of social organization. The story about the self presented here can be judged by the results of the social-theoretical program with which it is allied.

A third empirical test of an account of our shared human identity is a qualified introspection. You can consult your own experience, reader, and gauge the extent to which the story hits home. But not all subjective experience counts with the same weight. Having judged the faithfulness of the story to your recollected knowledge of personal encounter and collective association, you must also consider the authority of this knowledge. You must do so by evaluating both the extent to which your experience resists the given order of society and culture and the extent to which this culture and society have overcome the sharp contrast between context-preserving routine and context-revising reinvention. Thus, an informed introspection draws out the lessons of accumulated conflict, which enlarge the realm of recognized possibility, and calls on the help of the imagination, which anticipates as vision what conflict has not yet produced as fact.

A story about our human identity embodies an existential project as well as an empirical view of personality. It can therefore also be subjected to a practical test that focuses upon its implications for conduct. One form of this test has already been illustrated in the course of my comparison between corrigible and incorrigible projects. A story may turn out to be psychologically unstable in just the sense indicated earlier. The evaluative relevance of psychological stability can be generalized into a more basic point about self-assertion.

An existential project defines the meaning of self-assertion; it does not merely offer a hypothesis about the means to achieve an independently defined empowerment. But though our opinions about empowerment inform our experience of it they do not inform it completely. The recalcitrance of this experience instructs. To act out an existential project is to run the risk that we shall in fact be and feel diminished rather than empowered by its execution: in many ways it may turn out to block our efforts to affirm, individually and collectively, a sustainable presence in the world. We may find countless excuses for our disappointments and attribute them to deficiencies in ourselves or to flaws in the human condition. The excuses, however, do not always persuade.

There is no foreordained reason why all these standards for evaluating a story about ourselves should point in the same direction. But the fact that they may not represents a methodological strength precisely because it is so likely a source of embarrassment. If we were to discover that the reasons for preference do repeatedly conflict, we would have to conclude that the type of conception of a shared human identity described here cannot bear the weight that we want it to carry. Just as the variety of standards for judging a given conception of the self offers many chances to criticize or justify the particular conception, so the very real possibility that these standards may regularly yield discordant conclusions puts the usefulness of any such conception to the test.

———————

A single strategy of inquiry and argument inspires this Introduction. At each turn I take an inherited, relatively unreflective and therefore deficient certainty and attempt to correct it by submitting it to a particular style of skeptical criticism. The certainties put through this treatment provide points of departure for the development of a morally ambitious conception of personality: the Christian-romantic tradition (a substantive perspective), the ancient and universal practice of imputing normative force to images of man (a method of thought), and the speculative treatise on human nature (a genre of writing). The skepticism brought to bear on these assurances has its core in the modernist view of our relation to the contexts of our action. This skepticism sees concrete human communities and their histories rather than a supra-human order as the sole possible source of sense and value.

When we subject those certainties to this skeptical discipline, they may be completely annihilated. The impression that something in them survives may be due merely to a failure to push critical analysis as far as it can go. But if the beliefs can emerge transformed rather than destroyed from their bout with modernist skepticism they will come out less arbitrary and dogmatic than before, less likely to serve as a fancy apology for privileges and preconceptions. (Nietzsche: What does not kill me makes me stronger.)

But this account of the strategy may still give a misleading impression of the stakes and opportunities in the effort. The apparently more subversive conclusion—the alternative of total skepticism—ordinarily turns out to be the more conservative result. Having announced that criteria of sense and value depend upon particular historical communities and their accidental histories and having denied that any other foundation could exist, the critic finds in this groundlessness a new reason to reaffirm his allegiance to those historical communities as they currently exist. For what else—he tells us—is there? Thus, he turns a historicizing skepticism on its head and uses it to justify the authority of existing institutional arrangements or of reigning modes of discourse. He perverts the modernist message into a new way to carry on the ancient alliance of skepticism and surrender.

So it is the other, seemingly less skeptical outcome of the confrontation between certainty and criticism that has the more subversive implications because it holds out the promise that our practices might be changed, not merely reasserted with a self-depreciating proviso. We discover the possibility of this more transformative option in a view that emphasizes our ability to change the quality as well as the content of our contexts: the sense in which they exclude what they exclude and the degree to which they are available to us for revision. This view is illustrated here with respect to one of our most fundamental practices: the practice of drawing existential guidance from images of our shared identity.

Philosophy conceived in this spirit is simply context-smashing continued beyond the point where it is normally prudent to carry it, continued, as it sometimes is in poetry or politics, for the sake of the future, which means for the sake of a certain way of living in the present, as people not wholly defined by the current forms of their existence. If someone were to ask us why we want to live in the present in this way, we should answer: first, because this is the kind of being we really are and, second, because by living in this fashion we empower ourselves individually and collectively. Through a study of the fine texture of our subjective experience of encounter, the following essay defends the truth and the pertinence of these two answers and argues that they state the same thesis under different names.

Passion

I

The world is real and dense and dark. But each person is a reality on the verge of shrinking into itself: the other things, the other people are there for desire, memory, and imagination to feed on.

In unspeakable horror, a man is beaten out of this vision. He must go out into a nature and a society that are not his to understand more than a little or to control hardly at all. He has to learn that he is not the center and that he will soon be nothing.

Now it happens that, when he staggers out into a world that is not his own, he discovers that the people in it live in mutual longing and jeopardy. This discovery is the beginning of passion, and it seems both a testimonial, and the promise of an antidote, to the necessity that drives him out of himself.

There is no end to what people want of one another. They not only want to use one another's labor and win one another's loyalties but also to possess one another, and the presence of this want extends from the force of lust and the jealousy of exclusive allegiance to the craving for self-surrender and self-disclosure on the part of another person. When, as in love, this desire for possession is loosened, transformed, or replaced by a radical acceptance of the other person, the nature of the acceptance remains one of imperative need: the existence of the other person is experienced as somehow necessary to your own, and nothing he can do fully satisfies this need.

Even in the purest instances of personal love, this insatiable quality of the longing that a person has for another suffers from a characteristic tension. The desire for the tangible expression of mutual acceptance—from sexual union to the elaborate development of a life in common—repeatedly conflicts with acquiescence in the distinctive selfhood of the other person. For such acquiescence requires much more than forebearance from jealousy and dominion; it must come to terms with the essential secrecy of another personality, and prove itself able to hold firm, across time and self-transformation, to mutual ties, claims, and understandings.

The boundlessness of our need for the other person comes down to this: that everything we get from other people, or that they give to us, or that they represent for us by the mere fact of their present or past existence seems like an advance on a spiritual transaction that we are unable to complete. The unrestricted character of the need is confirmed by our inability to specify just what it would take to fulfill it: as soon as this need seems, on one definition of its character, to have been fulfilled, we find that, under a slightly different definition, it remains to be satisfied. To grasp why all definitions of our longing for one another turn out to be incomplete you must approach the experience of unlimited mutual need from the opposite and complementary angle of unlimited mutual fear.

Inherent in social life is the danger that all forms of exchange and community will be used to entrench the exercise of ongoing, unaccountable, and unreciprocal power. The devices for exchanging labor and the products of labor may help fashion and perpetuate an entrenched hierarchy of power and wealth. The terms on which men and women can secure recognition as members of groups that allow for heightened (though unequal) vulnerability and for common allegiance enmesh them in power relations. Engagement in shared forms of life threatens us with depersonalization as well as with bondage. The individual may vanish—to a greater or lesser extent, he will vanish—into a ready-made social station and find himself recast as a helpless placeholder in the grinding contrast of genders, classes, communities, and nations.

The turning of engagement into subjection finds its clearest expression in the constant reappearance of patron-client relationships and of the moral visions that seek to police and justify them. The patron-client relationship is precisely a point of convergence among exchange, community, and domination, and the doctrines that seek to purify and ennoble clientship treat this convergence as the very basis of civilization. But even believers in such an ideal fear that contract and community will end up subordinate to domination, as its frills and excuses rather than as elements that can be used by the weak to dispossess or even to tame the strong.

The risk that reliance and interdependence will breed domination and dependence is not confined to the settings of economic exchange and tangible community. In a diluted but nevertheless recognizable form the danger reappears in the most elementary facts of participation in a universe of common discourse. Each such universe—a national culture, a literary tradition, an accepted science—contains a hint of exchange (a context for trading information and argument) and a hint of community (an offer of joint membership in a valued realm of civilization). Accordingly, it also gives rise to a problem of power. Wherever people accept certain shared criteria of persuasion and sense, the conventions of discourse may be construed so as to hinder the emergence of perceptions and reasonings that would undermine the received picture of things and shake the powers and the routines that this picture had taken for granted.

The recurrent confusion of contract, community, and domination fails, however, to explain the unlimited quality of people's fear of one another. That confusion represents only the most obvious cause of this fear just as the dependence upon economic exchange provides the most visible expression of mutual need. To take account of all the varieties of this reciprocal fear would require generalizing the conceptions of exchange and community until they had lost every trace of their standard meanings.

People fear one another, in a way that goes beyond the horror of subjection and depersonalization, because they require not simply an exchange of particular advantages and a recognition of their membership in well-defined communities but also a more radical acceptance of their own selves. They want a sign that there is a place for them in the world, a place where they can undertake certain limited experiments in self-knowledge and self-reconstruction without risking material and moral disaster.

The deepest demand for acceptance is one that says: accept

me for what I am no matter what my titles to membership in particular communities and no matter what I can offer you by way of material or moral exchange. To receive a sign of such an acceptance a person must in some way lift his guard or have it lifted for him; he must involve himself in relationships that impose a measure of vulnerability even greater than the measure exacted in preexisting communities—greater because more experimental and less dependent upon established claims and expectations of mutual support and recognition. This gesture of self-exposure lacks a predetermined outcome. It may fail completely: the heightened vulnerability may be met by rejection or, having been accepted, lead nevertheless to disappointment.

The problem of your ability to gain an acceptance that is not reducible to a position within a public system of exchanges and allegiances, and that therefore touches more directly upon your own self, parallels the problem of your capacity to free yourself, whatever your circumstances, from total determination by your own character. The power to treat a character as more than a fate, to open it to revision, counts for much in determining what you can hope for in life. Your character, left undisturbed, ties you to a limited repertory of dealings with others as well as with yourself; if your character is indeed an irrevocable fate, then you can hope for no breakthrough in coming to terms with other people and with your material and moral vulnerability to them.

But this revision of character must in turn be brought about by a subjection of the self to situations and encounters that shake the routines of your outward life and the routinized expression of your passions. If the reinterpretation and the reconstruction of character is possible at all, then it is possible by laying your self open to the surprise and pressure of circumstances in which your habits of personal connection and of self-presentation are at stake—whether these circumstances be lived out in actual episodes of conflict and reconciliation or played out in memory and imagination. The movement of character toward an acknowledgment of enlarged possibility in self-expression and reconciliation depends upon the results of these deliberate or involuntary experiments in accepted and heightened vulnerability: both responses of other people and the lessons we draw from these responses make the difference.

Whenever the transformative experiences of faith, hope, and love take a strictly secular form, their common ground becomes this expanded sense of opportunity in association. Nobody rescues himself; the path to those experiences necessarily passes through situations of aggravated risk in the life of the passions, and success in this pursuit requires that others not attack you at your moment of increased defenselessness; that is to say, it requires acts of grace by other people. If these acts are lacking or deficient, another grace would be needed to make up for their absence.

So both the attempt to gain from others a radical acceptance and the effort to free himself, if only partially, from the tyranny of character force a person to undergo circumstances in which others may do him a harm greater than any he may expect in the usual course of social life. This fact adds another level of depth and indefiniteness to mutual fear. For by its very nature the risk that accompanies the search for radical acceptance and moral invention includes the possibility of failure. The failure would disturb the things that ultimately matter most to people—at least to people able to extend their view beyond the minimal imperatives of survival and security.

Moreover, the answers that the course of relations among people gives to these questions of mutual acceptance are always inconclusive, as much so in the granting of acceptance as in the denial of it. For one thing, the next experience that occurs may cast doubt on all the previous ones. For another, an incurable disproportion exists between the weight of the question and the nature of whatever answers could be given to it in the span of a lifetime. The acceptance that can be offered by another individual is still the act of a being, like yourself, only imperfectly capable of reconciliation and self-disclosure. The help that makes the reconstruction of character possible is only partly subject to deliberation and understanding: no one—neither those who offer the help nor those who receive it—can fully grasp or control the relation of character to achievement, or to disappointment, in the life of passion.

The visible drama of oppression and depersonalization takes place against the background of the shadowy dangers that accompany the effort to have others assure you in the possession of your own being while freeing you from enslavement to your own character. Both the forefront and the background threats arise from the need to enter society in search of things that are indispensable: the means of survival and identity, in one case; the assurance of selfhood, above and beyond station and even character, in the other case. In both instances the specific form of the peril is that these means may be denied you or that they may be given to you in ways that cast you down into a weakness from which you have little hope of escape. Even when they do offer the means, the offer is provisional, and its value uncertain.

In these matters you can never have enough security. No defense against exploitation and no hoarding of acquired advantage can guarantee you against a later defeat and decline in your experiments with the uses of contract, community, and domination. No endured vulnerability to others can give you unbreakable promises of reconciliation in society and of corrigibility in character. You fear the others both for what they can deny you and for what, even under the best of circumstances, they cannot give you, and your fear of them knows no bounds.

The problem of our mutual fear and our mutual need is worked out in the life of the passions, which ring the changes on the relations between our reciprocal and infinite longing for one another and our reciprocal and infinite terror. The doctrine of the passions presented here takes these changes as its subject.

A conception of passion may be developed through a criticism of two familiar but misleading views of its nature. Each of these views implies an inadequate conception of madness. The first approach sees passion as a threat to reason; the second, as a risk to society. Both conceptions, however, also understand passion as a force that complements and sustains the very object—reason or society—that it jeopardizes.

From one standpoint passion is defined by its ambivalence toward reason. Passion is seen as both the great destroyer and the sustaining impulse of our understanding of reality.

The passions lead people to act in ways that they themselves in more reflective moments would reject as unrealistic or too risky. They prompt people to violate their own standards of self-interest and disturb the criteria that define what these interests are. They involve us in relationships that go far beyond what our everyday assumptions about the world take to be possible. For all their capacity to surprise, however, the passions can rarely be defended as devices of a utopian project—the outward signs and instruments of a deliberate effort to change the established world. They are more like a recurrent darkening of sight than an alternative vision.

The other side of passion, on this view, is its service as an elementary energy without which reason would be impotent and aimless. Though reason gives us knowledge of the world, it does not tell us in the final instance what to want and what to do. It cannot provide the quality of sustained commitment that must underlie even, or especially, the most disinterested activities of the mind. Nevertheless, passion, according to this conception, constantly threatens to overload the mind machine whose operation it makes possible.

For those who embrace this image, madness is the condition in which the sense of reality succumbs to passion. Every episode that sees emotion get out of hand and injure our ability to grasp the facts of our situation is a prenunciation of madness or, at least, a sign of the precariousness of sanity.

The element of irreducible truth in this conception of passion, sanity, and madness is its acknowledgment of the susceptibility of the individual's sense of reality to disruption by strong internal experiences of impulse as well as by the resistance and transformation of the environment in which he acts. There are, however, several decisive objections to this account of the emotions.

First, passion, even as understood by those who contrast it to reason, never blocks a single, unified, and transparent picture of reality—not, at least, of social reality. It temporarily suspends and sometimes even permanently disorganizes particular arrangements of more or less conventional, untested, and stubbornly held ideas about self and society. It is often hard to know what to marvel at more: whether the tenacity with which such assumptions are sometimes upheld or the alacrity with which they are at other times abandoned under the prodding of impulses that have not yet, or never will, become ideas. We may be unable to tell whether a dominant picture of personal or social reality gives better insight into the facts and possibilities of a historical situation than the emotions that disrupt this picture.

A second objection to the view of passion as the denial of reason is that it fails to emphasize the variety of ways in which emotion may obey reason or rebel against it. We treat a person as more or less human, sane, and virtuous not just by reference to his mastery of blind impulse but because his impulses take certain forms and directions rather than others. Both across societies, cultures, and historical periods, and in our own introspective experience, we recognize that our predispositions and longings may be as misguided as our ideas. A theory of passion must either make sense of this widely shared belief or refute it.

A third difficulty with the view of passion as the rebellious serf of reason is that it denies by implication what we all commonly experience: that there are some revelations into our own and other people's humanity that we achieve only through experiences of passion. Moreover, the emotional life of an individual is informed by his beliefs; even the way he loves, for example, is influenced by what he thinks he can expect from himself and from others. A doctrine of emotion that treats the passions as if they merely obeyed or disturbed reason must show that these intimations of a richer interdependence between insight and impulse are illusory.

An alternative conception of passion focuses upon its ambivalent relationship to the acceptance of social conventions and of the preeminence of group interests over individual desires. In one sense passion is the experience of an impulse that leads the individual to defy these conventions, subordinating them to his immediate wants. In another sense, however, it is the routinization of deference to these social norms.

At its best, passion represents, on this view, the transmutation of recognized duty into sacrificial impulse. Our deeds of passion may demand sacrifices that reach all the way from the narrowest interests to the very life of the individual. From this perspective the work of the passions is to supplement, at the level of habit, the effort of much moral teaching: to efface the sharpness of the contrast between individual wants and social needs through an emphasis upon the mediating category of moral interests. On such a view, the passions are variants on the major themes of selfishness and altruism rather than on those of illusion and reality.

The essence of madness is then defined as a failure of submission to the constraints of social life. This definition resembles and amplifies the interpretation of passion as the adversary of understanding, insofar as conventions about human realities, possibilities, and probabilities are among those to which a sane person will defer. But it differs from that other account because it does not take for granted the availability of objective truth as a corrective to illusion. It is willing to treat every proposition of fact about social relations as open to question, except the need of the individual to submit in the end to a collective authority that surpasses him. Its final appeal is to social adaptation rather than personal enlightenment.

The true element in this vision is the inescapable dependence of the individual's criteria of sense and nonsense upon participation in a consensus. The words and ideas with which he scrutinizes himself draw their force and meaning from traditions of collective life and discourse; every shift of sense works by analogy and contrast to other senses, whose stability is unchallenged and even fantastically exaggerated. Similarly, the individual's assurance of personal worth and identity can never be entirely disengaged from his success in earning acceptance and approval from other people, a success that partly depends in turn upon his not violating the established routines of behavior too seriously or without special justification.

Nevertheless, it is equally central to an individual's experience of selfhood and sanity that he be able occasionally to cast aside some of the shared forms of conduct and expression, so that even when he does not in fact do this, the possibility that he might is never very far from his awareness. Indeed—even though he may not be able to articulate this knowledge—in the very act of using the canonical forms of discourse and behavior, he must use them in his own unique way. He has access to them less as a system of clear-cut norms than as a mass of ambiguous, incoherent instances of possible existence and communication.

Given this necessary overlap, permanent incongruity, and potential conflict between self and society, the role of passion cannot be sensibly forced into the twin molds of sound deference or unsound challenge to collective order. The practice and the possibility of dissidence are also a condition of selfhood and a mode of communal participation. Moreover, the personal events we describe as passions often confirm collective norms by redirecting them. It is just because personality and society have such paradoxical links of antagonism and confirmation that these interpersonal encounters can have the variety and subtlety that they in fact possess.

The fundamental similarity of the two approaches to passion and madness that I have discussed should now be apparent. They both see passion as occurring in one of two modes. Passion may be the denial of a necessary or exemplary reality, whether reason or collective authority. Or it may be the force that leads people to accept and obey this authoritative reality all the more effectively. Madness is then defined as the situation where the first mode of passion prevails over the second.

The choice passion makes when it comes up against the facts of personal existence and social life is at best: take it or leave it. For passion, according to both views, can neither discover anything (except by providing the mind with its guiding concerns) nor create anything (except by temporary and ultimately futile disruptions of rational or social order).

A different approach to the passions would redress the defects of these two conceptions. It would have to be judged both by its fidelity to our ordinary acquaintance with the moral life and by the services it might render as the basis for an entire account of the defining experiences of personality.

The concept of passion, to be sure, has no fixed referent in the external world. Our conflicting views of passion can never be merely alternative interpretations of the same thing; they are also, inevitably, conceptions of somewhat different things. We start out with an unexamined term, bandied about more or less loosely in ordinary discourse, and then we try to make it part of a general understanding. In the course of this process the idea must be given new and more precise boundaries. Yet it must also continue to embrace the facts of ordinary experience that originally interested and baffled us.

The first step toward the redefinition of passion on which the argument of this essay relies is to view passion as the whole range of interpersonal encounters in which people do not treat

one another as means to one another's ends. The purely instrumental relationship is the only one that reduces the other
personality to the condition of an object—whether an aid or an
obstacle. (Hatred itself and all its satellite emotions refuse to
treat the hated person as a mere means.)

To the extent that a personal encounter approaches this
pole of instrumentality, it loses the elements that all other interpersonal dealings have in common. It yields to the same strategic
analysis that may be effectively applied to a broad range of processes in the non-human animal world. A distinctively human understanding of human affairs must, however, give priority to a study of
the ways people treat one another in the peculiarly personal—passionate or non-instrumental—way. But such an understanding
must also grasp the conditions and the devices that enable people
to divest one another of this transforming aura of personality.

In fact, many of the most crucial relationships in a social order—like those of domination and submission—have both an instrumental and a non-instrumental character. Their strength
depends upon their success in stitching calculation and passion so
closely together that the seams are hardly visible. There would be
an incurable fragility in a power relationship between masters who
saw their slaves as lifeless objects and slaves whose sole reason for
obedience was to fear the punishment of rebellion more than the
burden of slavery. The slaves could not square their submission
with their never completely repressible sense of personality, and
they would be on the constant lookout for every chance to undermine or escape their bondage. The masters would need to exercise
an unrelenting surveillance and coercion that would end up
dominating the entire pattern of their lives. If, however, a power
relationship is wholly parasitic upon passion—love and hatred, admiration and contempt—it must perform the miracle of perennially rekindling among different individuals the emotions upon
which it rests. Hence, the eternal dream of power is to rule by a
reverential fear that systematically confuses prudence and piety
as motives for obedience.

The central sphere for the operation of the passions is the realm of face-to-face relationships. This thesis has two corollaries. The first is that the more continuous and lasting a direct interpersonal encounter, the harder will it be for the encounter to assume a purely instrumental quality. Instrumentalism can survive under such conditions only by a sustained effort of the parties to the relation or, more probably, through the influence of a special background of social practices and beliefs. The other corollary is that non-instrumental relations with concrete people, in the here and now, have a deep priority over non-instrumental relations with social groups or non-instrumental commitments to impersonal ideals. This priority is a matter of both causal fact and normative weight; its sense will emerge as the argument develops. For the moment it is enough to remark that the experiences of intense involvement, seduction, or repugnance that we have in these more remote contexts are always grounded, if only by opposition and denial, in a prior acquaintance with the opportunities and disappointments of face-to-face association. The more articulate symbols and meanings that are ordinarily connected with these larger involvements overlay and infuse a more basic level of concern rooted in the elementary facts of direct encounters.

In the setting of our non-instrumental relations to one another, we come to terms with our unlimited mutual need and fear. This coming to terms is a search. It is a quest for freedom—for the basic freedom that includes an assurance of being at home in the world. To define the search for such a freedom is to formulate a conception of passion that offers an alternative to the doctrines that contrast passion to rational understanding or social convention.

The most radical freedom is the freedom to be, to be a

unique person in the world as it is. The following pages discuss an idyll of moral success that suggests the meaning of this freedom. The entire life of the passions can be seen, here, as a matter of the ways by which men and women participate in this idyll or despair of it.

You involve yourself in a world of encounters that open you up to other people: that acknowledge your basic vulnerability and allow it to take on a wealth of concrete forms. Yet this heightened state of vulnerability with all its surprises and disappointments, this deeper exposure to other people in ways that make you run through countless combinations of longing and fear, does not lead toward your worldly failure and loss of self-possession. You prosper in the world. And your material prosperity is part and parcel of a larger flourishing of your life among other people.

The particular ordeals of conflict that you undergo all deepen your sense of active participation in the social life around you. You neither fall into a state of helpless passivity toward the collective order nor try to hold it at bay and somehow to take charge of it. On the contrary, your sense of not being in charge accompanies your assurance that you can react and that the failure of control is not the imminence of annihilation. People appear to you less as a threatening collective unit than as a society of concrete individuals with whom it is possible to have all manner of relations—only a few of which may be practicable at any given time.

Each foray out into this world of dealings with other people is also a probing into the self; each variation upon our mutual jeopardy and dependence becomes the occasion for a refinement of the capacity to understand, to sustain, and to change what you are as an individual. The consequence of all this endured vulnerability is therefore not the annihilation of your self—your enslavement to the powers and opinions of other people—but rather the discovery that you can exist uniquely and, at some ultimate level, safely in a world of increasingly dense relations with other people.

This last idea suggests that there is another aspect of the idyll besides your coming to terms with other people in a way that gives you social place and self-possession. It is your capacity to live

your own life, and to master the effects of your deeds upon your
character, so that you can change without ceasing to be, in your
own eyes, your self. You go out into the world to seek your ordinary aims of survival and success. The world is full of force and
fraud, of mistaken identities and of advantages valued for more or
for less than they are really worth. Things can happen to you—the
bolder your actions, the more likely they will happen to you—that
change who you are. In fact, no aspect of your character—both as
it is and as you perceive it—is safe from being transformed in just
this way, until finally you are deprived of any sense that there
exists a resistant core of your personality that can survive all trials.

What with all this danger—from the perils of material failure to those of the disintegration of the self—it is natural that
most people should play for low risks. Through a suitable combination of work and domesticity they retreat into the most secure
material haven they can find. They make neither their livelihoods
nor their characters hostage to fortune.

You, however, have great expectations and driving commitments. For their sake, you run the risks that other people avoid.
Through the back and forth of will and fortune the circumstances
of your life change; so do your self-image and your character. But
you do not lose the sense of continuity in your striving and your
identity. On the contrary, you are freed from a shallow and constraining view of who you are: you do not mistake yourself for a
particular social station or even for the set of habits and humors
that is your character. You learn to experience yourself as an identity that is never wholly contained by a character and that grows to
greater self-knowledge and self-possession by the willed acts of
vulnerability or the accepted accidents of fortune that put a character under pressure. To have seen and suffered a great deal and to
have been delivered by all this from a rigidified state of perception, feeling, and conduct is part of the quintessential dream of
moral success. You accept jeopardy as a condition of insight and
emancipation in your dealings with yourself as well as in
your dealings with others.

The sentimental and mendacious touch in this romance of

triumph is the implied parallelism between worldly achievement and self-possession, as if one always accompanied the other. Yet even this aspect of the idyll presents obliquely a human truth. For the qualities that this story emphasizes have a deep kinship to the prudence and patience that enable people to change the world and to do well within it. The readiness to experiment with different kinds of encounters, and with their distinctive styles of vulnerability, is akin to central features of the practical, transformative political imagination: its refusal to take any established set of alliances and antagonisms for granted, its effort to mobilize people in ways that are not predefined by the existing social order, and its capacity to make these essays in mobilization the means for building new varieties of collaboration and community in the practical affairs of society.

The willingness to subject the character to the chances of transformation is directly tied up with the escape from obsession—from arrested perceptions, feelings, and dispositions. This exit from the compulsiveness of the automaton is a condition of patience and prudence. It allows people to identify opportunities but to resist the temptations of importunate action. It helps them see things without mechanically analogizing new events to a limited stock of past experiences. It encourages them to wait when the moment is not yet, both because it liberates them from the *idée fixe* of a single objective and because it enables them to live the present as an experience of renewed surprise about people and situations rather than as a desperate turning of the wheel of routine. So though the fable of moral success is unjustified when it holds out an assurance of material blessing, the qualities it invokes lie close to the heart of practical wisdom. They are a simplified lesson about finding your way, and having fun, in a world in which you are not in charge. They become pertinent when a minimum of material welfare is already available, and they then shade into the practical qualities by which this welfare can be safeguarded and developed.

The decisive theme in the romance of moral success is the

idea of an ordeal of vulnerability to hurt by others and to transformation by your own deeds, an ordeal from which you emerge triumphant. It is a triumph of the ability to throw yourself into an uncontrolled world in a way that, instead of annihilating you, allows you to exist more freely: freer from the compulsions of your character and from the quest for an illusory preemptive security against everyone else; freer to experiment with forms of action, collaboration, and vision.

You lose the world that you hoped vainly to control, the world in which you would be invulnerable to hurt, misfortune, and loss of identity, and you regain it as the world that the mind and the will can grasp because they have stopped trying to hold it still or to hold it away. The world you can make a home in is a world that you no longer hope to control from the distance of immunity, and the character you can accept as your own is a character that you can at last see as but a partial, provisional, and pliable version of your own self. Renunciation and loss, risk and endurance, renewal and reconciliation: these are the ancient incidents in the search to make yourself into a person during the course of a life.

A counter-tale of failure completes this view of the passions. Faced with the prospect of subjecting yourself to the trials of confusion and jeopardy, you are tempted to pull back to routinized dealing with other people: your exchange of material goods and your exposure of intangible vulnerabilities then follow a set pattern. When you do not look upon this pattern as immutable, you view any change in it with the apprehension of disaster. Your habits of sociability exhibit basic predispositions and perceptions regarding others and yourself, perceptions and predispositions that might take altered form in changed circumstances without themselves undergoing fundamental transformation. They are your character. The withdrawal into the routinization of your encounters with others has its counterpart in resignation to your character.

The retreat behind the compulsions of habit and character is all the more attractive because it seems to be the path of common sense. The alternative road, the path described by the idyll of moral success, may be the wiser, but it is a wisdom that, even at its most resourceful, looks like foolhardiness.

In this state of frozen character and routine you experience boredom. Boredom is in fact the weight of unused capacity, an intimation of the freedom from which the self has hidden. Yet it seems to be just the opposite: boredom seems to vindicate routine by its suggestion that there is nothing really worth doing in the world—nothing that could make up for abandoning the safety of habit.

From boredom you periodically escape into diversion: the search for novelty without peril. Diversion is a temporary release from routine and character that never threatens to unravel them because it never occupies their home ground of everyday vision, community, and work. It is a fantasy that hovers around prosaic reality rather than penetrating it. Like boredom it is not what it seems. It seems to be a partial way out from boredom that saves you from the unlimited vulnerability to hurt by others and to loss of identity that the breakdown of habit and character might otherwise bring. But the real human meaning of diversion as a response to boredom is just the opposite. It reaffirms the need for routine while appearing to put routine aside. In the very act of would-be escape it offers a presage of lost identity and defenselessness: in diversion the self drifts aimlessly, just as in routine, made self-conscious by boredom, it stares mutely. The restlessness that leads from one diversion to another and the daydreaming that marks each diversion subtly represent a state of being in which your guard toward others is down and your experiences of play and fantasy outreach your character without giving you the elements of another. Your self begins to disintegrate.

To the extent that an ordinary life is not entirely preoccupied with short-run calculations about how to survive and to the extent that it fails to participate in the idyll of moral success, to that extent it is lived out as an oscillation between routine reflected in boredom and routine denied but reaffirmed in diversion. The failed life is the life that alternates between the stagnation of routinized conduct and vision and the restless craving for momentary release. The alternation denies you the means to transform character, to recast the relationship between your longing and your fear, and in both ways to enlarge your freedom to be. This denial becomes apparent in the moment of boredom. Yet the withering of the self, endured for the sake of immunity to hurt and to the loss of identity, is taunted by a mock deliverance: a foretaste of the collapse of self-defense and the disintegration of self-identity. This fake rescue is the moment of diversion.

The passage, back and forth, between rigidity and diversion is paralleled on a larger and more terrible scale in some of the most characteristic instances of madness. Thus, the schizophrenic suffers from both a runaway compulsiveness and a radical subjection to other people. His automatisms, in speech, desire, and movement, are an ironic exaggeration of the ordinary experience of having a character. Yet he also feels the lack of clear boundaries between himself and other people. His condition shows, blown up, the deep link between the hardening of the self and its submersion in other people. This link gets carefully hidden in ordinary life, where it is taken as the only safeguard against the disintegration of the self.

In the absence of a breakthrough of insight, the parallelism between madness and normal life has the perverse effect of confirming you in withdrawal. Any more far-reaching experiment with the revision of character and of the terms of vulnerability seems to threaten a further descent into the cycle of compulsion and diversion. This threat is the inverted lesson of the idyll.

Still, this characterization of failure can never tell us for sure how to interpret, in ourselves or in others, any given routine of sociability or character. The routine may disregard and limit possible freedom, by standing in the way of an advance toward a greater mutual reinforcement of self-possession and accepted vulnerability. But it may also be a resting place in this advance, a temporary base from which exploration can take place. Its ambiguity is like that of form in art: freedom's constraint and, with luck, its condition. Which of the two meanings is the more accurate turns on how much the agent in fact treats the routine as enabling and provisional.

The passions are the moves in the story I have retold or in our many attempts to opt out of it. Each episode of passion represents a distinctive measure of failure or success, and a distinctive way of failing or succeeding, in the approach to the freedom and the acceptance whose winning the story describes. The moves are lived out at a depth of experience that precedes the distinction between will and knowledge. They are rooted in the most basic of strivings: the striving to be someone, with an assured place in the world. This effort reappears even in the most mundane areas of existence, giving non-instrumental meanings to personal relations that at first seem merely instrumental. The passions are experiments to discover the kind and degree of freedom that a person can hope for. These experiments, however, are also gambles whose outcomes in a concrete life no one can foresee.

The definition of an experience of passion as an episode in the romance of freedom and acceptance, or in the counter-romance that accompanies it, is fully equivalent to the conception that sees each passion as a specific way of coming to terms with the relation between mutual fear and longing among people; one way of talking translates into another. The equivalence is obvious for the part of the fable that speaks of the triumphant acceptance of vulnerability to other people. But it is no less real for the part of the story that tells of the way self-knowledge and self-possession advance by means of the very acts of large ambition or reflective endurance through which a person puts his character at risk.

To throw yourself into the world in a way that endangers not only your welfare but your habits and preconceptions, to gain the liberty from the fixed elements in your behavior that enables you to free yourself still more from compulsion, you must be able to distinguish in practice your character from your self. You must learn to treat your character, with its near-automatic dispositions, as no more than a variation on an indefinitely larger range of conditions of existence. To achieve the assurance that your present character does not exhaust your self you must know how to see in what other people already are the signs of what, for better or worse, you might become.

Sympathy, as a detached identification with the other, is still not enough. Your sense of other characters, of their possible transformability into your own, must be won in a give-and-take of reciprocal involvement. You see—if not in practice then in imagination—the fate and transformations of the other person crisscrossing your own. In your actual encounters with other people you confront the resistance, hardening, or crumbling of their characters and of yours that results from the encounters themselves. This discovery reveals to you the analogy of characters, their ability to pass beyond themselves and into one another, and their corresponding inability to expose, once and for all, the full depth of individuality. The willingness to acknowledge these facts is the meaning of sympathy.

The preceding pages have described the nature of passion and the area of existence where passion can be found. Rather than defining passion by contrast to rational understanding or social convention, I propose to redefine it as the living out of a specific aspect of the problem of solidarity, the problem posed by the relation between the enabling conditions of self-assertion. Remember that these conditions are the imperative of engagement with other people and the need to prevent this engagement from turning into subjugation and depersonalization. Both isolation from other people and submission to their wills and opinions threaten to weaken and annihilate the self. Our success at diminishing the interference between the supports of self-assertion frees us;

indeed, together with the achievement of greater mastery over the contexts of our actions, it represents our exemplary acquaintance with freedom. The life of passion plays out our confrontations with the problem of solidarity. It does so in the domain of our non-instrumental face-to-face relations and in the form of a conflict between our longing to be accepted by other people and our fear of the intangible dangers that both the longing and the acceptance create for our self-possession.

The following pages show how the nature of passion can be analyzed in greater detail and how this analysis tightens the link between the idea of passion and the view of the domain in which passion exists. Imagine, for this purpose, a generative polarity of the passions that reappears at several levels of increasing complexity.

At a first level the unifying polarity is the very coexistence of indefinite need and indefinite fear, manifest in the elementary impulses of attraction and repulsion. You find the other person possessed of a significance that keeps you from treating him merely as an obstacle or a means to the achievement of independently defined ends. The conviction underlying this valency is the belief that the existence of the other is both incompatible with your own and necessary to it—that it both threatens and confirms your self-possession. You are drawn to others in the belief that their existence has some crucial bearing on your own. You are repelled by them out of a sense that their seductive power must be resisted for your individuality to be upheld. Such primitive seduction and repulsion do not yet make for an experience of love and hatred nor do they imply anything about the nature and range of possible reconciliation among people.

The second level of the unifying polarity of the passions describes hatred and love as two responses to the elementary problem of need and fear. Imagine, here, that your impulses of attraction and jeopardy seem to stand in flat and insoluble conflict with respect to another person. As long as he exists he cannot be ignored. Yet his mere presence seems to threaten you, not because he endangers your physical survival but because he brings to a focus your general experience of the radical incompatibility of your existence with the existence of other people. The one apparent solution to this impasse would be the non-existence of the other person and, after his death, the destruction of the memory that he had once lived, for then and only then would his threatening and seductive powers vanish at a single stroke. The desire for such a solution is pure hatred. That hatred never does, and never can, appear in an unadulterated fashion is a point that will be made soon enough.

Now, you can also see this mutual longing and peril as capable of resolution. Under the terms of this resolution the other person's existence is experienced as confirming you in yours; your relation to him exemplifies the experience of freedom that comes from engagements or attachments achieved without dependence or depersonalization, the reconciliation of the enabling circumstances of self-assertion. The experience of such a relation should not be misunderstood as the mere triumph of the element of seduction over the element of repulsion that jointly mark the basic experience of passion. You recognize the bearing of the other person's existence on your own but your longing to approach the source of this significance does not take the form of a desired submergence of your self in the other or of the other in your self. He remains a person apart, only partly accessible and intelligible. In his apartness and hiddenness he nevertheless reassures you both in what you are and in your power to discover or assert forms of reconciliation or self-expression that escape the constraints of your present existence. Your longing for the other person therefore culminates in an experience of mutual confirmation in self-possession. Your primitive horror of the other person becomes your strengthened acknowledgment of apartness. And it is only because of its core of independence that his acceptance of you could ever persuade you to accept yourself and encourage in you the measure of self-forgiveness that makes self-transformation possible. Through these changes the elementary impulses of longing and jeopardy are so recast that rather than being endured as flatly contradictory they converge in a unified experience of vulnerability and confirmation; rather than tending toward a denial of the other's existence or his memory they seize on this memory or this existence as something that sustains your presence in this world.

Alongside the primitive ambivalence of seduction and jeopardy and its recasting in the alternative modes of pure love and pure hatred, there is a third level of the unifying polarity of the passions. It consists in the alternation between a reach toward such an unmixed love and a fall back into a more complicated, equivocal version of the same passion, or, again, in the oscillation between a purer and a more attenuated hatred. The systematic analysis of the passions shows that all our experiences of virtue are variations on love and that all our experiences of vice are variations on hatred. But even the clearest instances of hatred and love turn out to be marked by an internal instability of their own, which this third level describes. Indeed, the transmutations of hate and love worked out by the particular vices and virtues already presuppose this shuttling between a concentrated and a distracted experience of love or hate.

You are able to strive toward absolute love or hate through your capacity to desire single-mindedly: to take a particular encounter as the occasion to make an inclusive commitment of the personality. In this case the desire is a commitment to a particular experience of radical reconciliation or antagonism with respect to another person. Such an experience is radical in several senses. It seizes upon one of two clear-cut, extreme solutions to the problem of our mutual longing and jeopardy. It involves an engagement of your person—in all its thoughts and deeds—with the matter at hand. It resolves the issue of reconciliation or antagonism in regard to every aspect of the other person's being.

But the traits that pull us away from these definitive experiences of love and hatred are equally basic to our nature. These traits are of two kinds.

First, there is our embodiment, which makes our desires

multifarious and resistant to a single, focused act of commitment. Suppose, for instance, that you are moved by hatred for someone. You can nevertheless experience sexual longing for him—and this longing will never be solely either an extension of your hatred or something indifferent to it; it will also amount to a denial of your hatred. For this sexual longing will deny the premise of an incompatibility that encompasses every aspect of your own person and of the person you hate, and it will oppose the desire that the other not exist and that his memory be abolished. More generally, your inability to govern your encounters with others by an unequivocal commitment of your entire person to a single course of action sets up an obstacle to the extremes of love and hatred. You come face to face with this truth whenever the inconstancy and the partiality of your desires are brought home to you. Its basis is the resistance of your real embodied self to any unified or stable direction, even the direction imposed by an overmastering desire that you do not believe yourself to control.

The second natural circumstance that stands as an obstacle to radical love and hate has to do with the relation between reality and possibility, between limit and transcendence, between our thoughts and feelings at any given time and our preconceptions about what relations among people can be like. This impediment demands a more extended analysis that further develops the central idea of passion.

Our experiences of love and hatred are never exclusively concentrated upon the loved or hated person. As these experiences intensify they broaden into a hateful or loving orientation toward people (and in some sense toward the world as a whole). This broadening does not prevent hate and love, addressed to different individuals, from coexisting in the same agent. Nevertheless, the orientation involved in any given moment of love or hatred does not remain focused solely on the loved or hated person; it is rather like a beam of light that extends vaguely beyond the object to which it is directed.

Each experience of passion is an experiment in the resolution of our mutual jeopardy and longing. It takes its place within a previous ordering of predispositions toward others. This ordering is located at one of the many points of convergence between unreflective impulse and reflective thought. Such an ordering is more than a system of ideas about the possible forms of association, and a particular experience of love and hatred is not placed within this ordering in the fashion of an interpreted observation within a scientific theory. But neither is it just a set of conditioned responses to the things that other people do. It is rather a group of orientations that have attained a measure of concreteness and rigidity, both by becoming habits and by enacting certain assumptions about the relations that are possible among people and about the ways these relations can change. This enactment helps form a character—the frozen version of a self.

The development by an individual of these lived-out sets of hypotheses about personal relations is marked by the same dynamic of limit and of achieved or failed breakthrough that we find in so many areas of experience. The enormous weight of a given structure—in this instance, the orientations of an individual to other individuals, mixtures of habit and preconception—coexists with the concealed fragility of this structure—its inability to exhaust the measure of our mutual longing and jeopardy or to accommodate everything we can discover about ourselves and one another. The breakthroughs here seem less frequent than in the collective history of society only because they must be telescoped into a single lifetime and because they may leave no tangible and public vestige.

The content of this element in character consists in a view of how much we can reasonably hope for by way of reconciliation between the conditions of self-assertion. Or, again, it amounts to treating a particular place along the spectrum of love and hatred as a prototype of what the non-instrumental dealings between people can be like when they go as well as they ordinarily can. Among the most important turning points in a life are those in which we recast our views of what this prototype is and alter simultaneously our conceptions of psychological realism and our standards of moral aspiration.

When, therefore, one person hates another, this hatred always has a double reference. Though it refers to the other person, it also recalls the agent's basic ordering of experience—his own images of human possibility, elucidated by beliefs and embodied by habits. There is no pure hatred in the life of passion, just as there are no uninterpreted observations in science and no once-and-for-all solutions to the problems of social organization in history. This fact is the meaning of the ambivalence between hating another and having a hateful view of the world.

It takes an angel to love and hate unreservedly. For pure hate and love require emancipation from embodiment and contextuality. They say angels are incorporeal and ahistorical. People, however, must move between the drive toward unconditionality in their loves and hatreds and the retreat into more compromised commitments. This alternation imparts to all our encounters a characteristic probing not only of the other individual but of our overall chances of reconciliation or antagonism. So this third level of the unifying polarity refers back to the first level—our elementary experiences of mutual longing and jeopardy—and shows how these experiences become the objects of a testing in the course of a life.

The three levels of the generative polarity of the passions are the circumstance of mutual need and fear, the contrasting responses to this predicament offered by love and hatred, and the oscillation in our hatreds and loves between focus and distraction. In life these levels fuse.

The polarity of the passions operates in an area of experience loosely delimited by two boundaries that the life of passion constantly crosses. One of these frontiers separates the concerns of passion from our strictly material need for the products of other people's work and power. The other frontier separates concerns with personal relations, which dominate the realm of passion, from our quest for larger meaning: the attempt to make intelligible both our place in the world (or, indeed, the world itself) and our elementary experiences of personality. The problems that arise beyond these two borders—the problems of wealth and power beyond the first and those of religion beyond the second—are not clearly separable from the ones that emerge in the central area of passion. Our repeated crossings of these dividing lines show how the master polarity of the passions changes into something else.

Others appear to us not only as the protagonists of our infinite longing and jeopardy but also as the sources of concrete material benefits or threats, aids or obstacles to the achievement of well-defined goals of survival, security, or aggrandizement. There is always the question of the degree to which any given encounter, or sphere of life, will be handed over to this instrumental calculation and the degree to which the other person will remain an object of passion and therefore also the focal point for all the concerns described by the three levels of the central polarity.

Some conceptions of society—such as the gift-exchange ideas of many tribal peoples or the characteristic idealizations of the patron-client relationship, with their deliberate confusion of contract, community, and domination—try to efface the distinction between these two ways people can view and treat one another. Some approaches—like those that assign divergent ideals of association to distinct areas of life—attempt, on the contrary, to segregate these two orientations toward the relations of self and other. But neither attempt ever succeeds entirely, because each denies a recurrent possibility of life.

Even in the purest forms of love and hate, people easily find themselves drawn into the calculus of power and exchange. They never know for sure how much they are being made the objects of such a calculus or how much they are engaging in it themselves. Even in their most cold-hearted dealings in wealth and power, people discover that the continuance of a relationship produces, if its stability does not require, the partial remaking of collaboration or dominion into communal attachment. The other person becomes the object of a fascination, the beneficiary of an allegiance or an antagonism, that cannot be adequately accounted for by the help or hindrance he offers to the realization of your goals.

Because no aspect of a person's life is so profane as to be sealed off from his experience of longing and jeopardy, this double confusion becomes an unavoidable and frequent event. Apart from the most elemental clutching at survival, our desires gain all of their sense and much of their force from our membership in a collective world full of other bodies, minds, and wills, a world whose law is that we risk unlimited fear and yearning in one another's presence.

Passion also touches upon the effort to make intelligible the basic circumstances of our existence. We seek in others more than an opportunity to live out our sense of longing and jeopardy; we seek an answer to the enigma of our existence or a way to forget this enigma altogether and to find the consolations of forgetfulness in the trance-like activities of a busy life. At any moment it may suddenly become unclear whether the issue raised by an episode of passion is the constraint upon our reconciliation with others or the constraint upon our insight into reality.

The characteristic pattern of limit and breakthrough, of partial structures and things that do not fit within them, that we discover in so much of the world around us is nowhere more strikingly displayed than in the life of passion itself. Both that which we can and that which we cannot find out about ultimate reality and possibility seem to confront us, in concentrated and proximate form, in our own experiences of selfhood and relation. Each event of passion therefore seems to raise anew the question of our relation to the contexts of our action.

At all three convergent levels of their polarity, the passions dissolve: at one end, into the attempt to reduce other people to objects of calculation and dominion and, at the other end, into the effort to find an answer, or the epitaph of an answer, to the puzzle of existence. This twofold dissolution constantly occurs and is constantly reversed. Both its occurrence and its reversal arise from the most basic features of selfhood: embodiment, contextuality, and the grasping for the supra-contextual.

Each episode of passion has a place along the unifying

polarity just described. Each represents a moment in your coming to terms with the otherness of other people. These events recur, and they fall into groups. Some of the episodes move toward acceptance of a flat conflict between your longing for other people and your inconformity with the existence of others: that is to say, toward acquiescence in the irreconcilability of the conditions of self-assertion. Other such events come closer to offering an experience of confirmation in your own being through another person's existence, and thereby exemplify, in the specific domain of passion, a partial reconciliation between the enabling circumstances of self-assertion. To the former belong the vices, derivatives of hatred, and to the latter the higher virtues of faith, hope, and love, though to call them virtues and vices is to impose the conclusory slogans of evaluation upon your experiments with selfhood in society. And then there are certain other events—I shall call them the proto-social passions—that do not fit at all along the central polarity of the passions and that reflect its incompleteness.

Together, these episodes make up a picture of the characteristic risks and opportunities, beyond those of material harm and benefit, with which the otherness of other people confronts us. To be sure, the picture is unavoidably sketchy and provisional: there is no passion so basic that its sense remains immune to changes in the conditions of social life, and there is no map of moral experience that describes, once and for all, anyone's possible discoveries about selfhood and otherness. The surprise is that the picture can be drawn at all.

Every aspect of the threefold polarity of the passions confirms our inability fully to reconcile our need to be accepted by others, and to join with them in common forms of discourse and life, with our struggle to avoid the many forms of material or intangible jeopardy in which other people place us. Our failure ever to reconcile these demands completely, even in the best of personal and social circumstances, may be seen as a token of the conflict between the conditions of self-assertion and those of attachment to other people. With greater accuracy, it may also be understood as a disharmony between the requirements of self-assertion themselves. The more a person indulges a concern for defense, distancing, and disinvolvement, the more he denies himself the resources for self-construction and self-transformation; he becomes the master of an empty citadel. The analysis of particular passions will show that this paradoxical relation of the self to others holds as much for our ideas and inquiries as it does for our desires and devotions and that it colors every episode of understanding or emotion.

The earlier arguments about the character of passion have placed a countervailing theme alongside the idea of an irremediable tension in the project of self-assertion. This complementary theme is the thesis that passions differ in the extent to which they resolve the conflict within self-assertion, though they can never resolve it completely. Social arrangements in turn differ in the degree to which they encourage this resolution and impart to our ordinary social experiences something of the quality that marks its most intimate and complete manifestations.

Trust and distrust bear on both the disharmony in the passions and its possible, partial correction. Though particular passions, trust and distrust also enjoy a special status. They show more clearly than anything else how the conflict that the polarity of the passions discloses may be aggravated or diminished. Love and hate have been described as the most extreme resolutions of the elementary conflict between longing and jeopardy in our dealings with other people. Trust is the ordinary ground of any advance toward this reconciliation, the basis on which love and the passions connected with it can take hold and endure.

Yet by virtue of their ambiguity trust and distrust also illustrate and illuminate our incapacity to settle this conflict once and for all. Trust requires a partial relinquishment of the demand for immediate and tangible reciprocity. This relinquishment in turn creates anew the opportunity to entrench power under the shadow of trust, even when dependence and dominion do not already mark a personal relation. But wherever there is established, emergent, or even possible power, and whatever forms this power may take, trust and distrust become ambiguous. Each demonstration of trust may be a self-deceptive surrender; each gesture of distrust, a sign of enlightenment and emancipation. The nature of relations in society and of our understanding of them are such that in any concrete instance we can never be sure of the right way to read this ambiguity. The unavoidable lack of assurance confirms the fragility of any resolution of the polarity of the passions and of the central conflict that this polarity reveals.

Trust is, at the core, a simple idea. It is a willingness to accept vulnerability. It is marked by a distinctive motive and response. In a variety of situations where other people might do me harm, the response consists in not trying to escape the situation or in not attempting to create arrangements that diminish other people's capacity to do me in. The motive to trust is my confidence that, whatever the temporary disappointments and misunderstandings, the others will not abandon me in the long run—at least not voluntarily. More precisely, trust is a loyalty, to the community or the joint venture, that is relatively impervious to a calculus of the immediate costs and benefits of participation in the collective enterprise. Participation is viewed as something of an end in itself—an attitude that presupposes neither an act of love toward relative strangers nor a perceived identity over a wide range of values and interests.

The inner nature of trust may be brought out by considering its paradoxical connection with the norm of reciprocity. One of the features that mark relationships of trust is a refusal to insist on a tit-for-tat accounting of gains and losses. You may be bearing the major burden at a particular moment and your collaborators may be doing better than you. Nevertheless, you do not protest. You more or less put aside a concern with your immediate disadvantage. You more or less expect that things will straighten out soon. You are more or less confident that no one in particular is to blame for your present misfortunes. At a minimum you feel sure that the others will not gang up against you and that in fact they will watch out for you.

Though the ideal of reciprocity is repressed and restricted in associations of trust, it is not forgotten. It is as if the parties had agreed to remove this ideal from the forefront of concern so that it might be realized all the more smoothly and effectively; as if—because no such bargain occurs in fact. The participants attach the demand of reciprocity to the ongoing experience of communal life rather than to particular exchanges in the course of the enterprise.

This redirection may be likely to work best if the communal venture benefits from a measure of loyalty that exceeds what even a farsighted reciprocity would warrant. Otherwise, each participant may hold himself aloof from the joint endeavor. He may ask himself whether long-term reciprocity has in fact been maintained and show a greater concern with the short-term balance of advantages than the community can safely allow. Once the attitude of suspicion appears, it spreads: each participant begins to suspect that his colleagues do not themselves characterize their common activity as a shared undertaking. His whole view of it and them changes. Thus, the success of a collaborative style that directs the demand for reciprocity to the whole of the communal venture rather than to any of its parts depends on the ability to go beyond reciprocity as a motive for conduct within the venture. Several more special consequences follow from this view of reciprocity and trust.

First, a relation of trust is not ordinarily focused on a specific, transitory goal. It requires a continuing collaboration, and it provides much of its own aim and reward.

Second, the parties to a relation of trust tend not to think about their dealings with each other in the terms of well-defined entitlements and duties; obligations are defined diffusely. Each participant cares more about the attitudes toward the group and himself that his partners' words and deeds reveal than about conformity to a rigid plan of rights and responsibilities.

Third, when a participant in a relation of trust violates the expectations of his colleagues about how he ought to behave, they prefer to interpret his deviation as an occasional misunderstanding or weakness. They do not jump to the conclusion that he is out only for himself and that the whole association is merely a tool of arm's-length self-interest. Only when a consistent pattern of shirking develops does the relation enter into crisis.

The paradoxical connection between reciprocity and trust is complicated, and even disrupted, when the problem of trust arises in the context of power. For a subordinate to trust his superior means ordinarily that the former accepts as justified the unequal distribution of power in favor of the latter. He views this inequality as the expression of a moral order (e.g., the Hindu *karma* doctrine, which teaches that a person's place in the social order results from his behavior in prior incarnations) or as the price to be paid for a collective advantage (e.g., obedience ensuring, in the best interests of all, the success of the common venture). Both types of justification invoke a value greater than reciprocity, to which reciprocity should be sacrificed. For the higher-up to trust his underling in an unequal relation means that he grants the subaltern broad discretion in carrying out the latter's assigned tasks. Conversely, distrust requires hemming in the subordinate with detailed rules, close personal supervision, or both. Thus, the effect of hierarchy upon the tie between trust and reciprocity shows in a disparity of the measure of trust for the two parties to the relation.

Given the seductive force that the ideal of reciprocity exercises in all encounters, you can already guess that the effort to establish and perpetuate non-reciprocal relations of power requires a systematic dissociation of trust from reciprocity. This uncoupling is much harder to bring about than the establishment of trust in a setting of long-term reciprocity. Yet it is done all the time, and the repetition of this feat colors much of history.

A power relation may, nevertheless, be reconciled with an ideal of reciprocity. One way of ensuring this compatibility is to adopt a system of rotation in which power is exercised for limited periods: I rule over you today, and you over me tomorrow. Another way is to have plural hierarchies: I rule over you in some respects, and you over me in others.

Every political movement and institution, indeed every form of collaboration or exchange, must wrestle with two demons. One is the tendency of the individual to sacrifice everyone else's wants to his own. The other is his inclination to view the arrangements of collective life, in whatever setting or at whatever level of generality, as unfair attempts to put something over on him. The two problems connect because the force of self-interest makes people suspect every social arrangement as the triumph of others over themselves. When self-interest becomes paramount, distrust flourishes.

Both self-interest and distrust are two-sided: viewed in one light they are terms of condemnation; seen in another they are terms of praise. This ambiguity of their moral significance takes us straight to the heart of some of the most perplexing features of social life.

The self-interest that an individual is inclined to set above the desires of other people is necessarily his interest as he himself perceives it. It is never separable from his conceptions of the possible and the desirable. But the views of the desirable and the possible that count are rarely the ones most loudly proclaimed; they typically exist in a twilight of awareness that darkens the perception of hypocrisy.

The causes for equivocation multiply in the way the individual views his relation to other people and to their conceptions of their interests. Two extremes of moral clarity can be distinguished. At one extreme a person may entertain beliefs about his interests that encompass or imply ideas about what benefits others. (These ideas may include the notion that the interests of an individual are whatever he defines them to be.) He may then act in a manner that, on his own admission, selfishly subordinates their wants to his own. At the other extreme the individual may hold a view of the real interests of other people that differs from theirs. He may further believe himself entitled to act in accordance with their real needs as distinct from the needs they think they have. What appears as selfishness to others, he may understand as an enlightened altruism.

Actual moral deeds and self-understanding rarely reach the simplicity of these two limiting cases—either in people's own perception of what is going on or in our ability, as observers, critics, and politicians, to distinguish selfishness from altruism. The selfish act is cloaked more often than not in a half-transparent garb of justification. Those who appeal to these self-serving apologies do not themselves know how seriously to take them. To dismiss such justifications is easy only if you accept the radical thesis that everyone is, by definition, the best judge of his own interests. (Note that this thesis differs from another classical liberal idea: that whether or not an individual is the best judge of his interest, one must respect absolutely the sphere of his self-determination and allow its limits to be set by independent criteria.) The obscurity of the distinction between selfishness and altruism in human conduct is thus directly traceable to the dependence of interests upon opinions: any given association among people can be analyzed from an indefinite number of conceptual standpoints.

An equally pervasive ambiguity accompanies distrust. The individual's suspicion that a social practice in which he is engaged works systematically, but covertly, to the advantage of another group of people may result from his unwillingness to trust other people's good faith. This unwillingness may, in turn, be a consequence of self-centeredness, of obsessive preoccupation with his own concerns as opposed to the well-being of the collaborative ventures in which he participates. But it may also represent a stripping away of false justifications, which is an indispensable preliminary to critical self-consciousness and political transformation. The danger, then, is simply that the spirit of suspicion, having revealed an institution for what it is, will preclude or sabotage the alliances necessary to subvert present institutions and the allegiances needed to sustain the reformed arrangements.

The experience of coming to terms with non-reciprocal power, in a situation of ambiguous distrust, is one of the most common and intriguing in history. Its internal complexity is aggravated by the contradictory relations of reason to resentment, ideal standards to real-world choices, and reciprocity to community.

No matter how careful the criticism of justifications for the non-reciprocal exercise of power may be, it cannot become a collective force unless it is associated in the minds of large numbers of people with resentment at being treated unfairly. But resentment may be easier to excite than to control: it may discourage people from running the risks involved in establishing new social relationships. As a result they will be torn between a despairing acquiescence in established forms of social life and a paralyzing suspicion of alternatives. Indeed, even with the clearest of intellects and the purest of hearts, it may be nearly impossible to tell at any given time when resentment is the motor and when it is the master of one's actions.

Even when non-reciprocal arrangements for the exercise of power within a community can be a justified constituent of a social ideal, they may play a historically progressive role. Non-reciprocity in the exercise of power within particular institutions can help the cause of reciprocity in history. Such, at least, is the claim made by all doctrines of revolutionary inequality and discipline. But this claim itself has uncertain weight. The ideal vision of social relations cannot be merely postponed to a distant future, or it will never come about; it must already be prefigured in the political practice meant to bring the ideal into existence. How much or in what ways the practice ought to anticipate the program is simply not a question to which there can be any general answer.

A final factor of obscurity lies in the threat that even otherwise justified departures from reciprocity may pose to communal life. There comes a point when the suppression of reciprocity begins drastically to poison the experiences of personality and community. People who stand in a relationship of inalterable superiority and subordination can hardly deal with each other as joint participants in community. Their affection for each other across hierarchical lines will be marred by condescension or pity on the part of the superior and self-abasement or shameful yearning on the part of the underling. It can escape these flaws only by an extraordinary effort of transcendence over loveless circumstance.

The preceding discussion has dealt with the ambiguity of distrust as selfishness and enlightenment in the circumstance of non-reciprocal power. This ambiguity takes a still more basic form when the exercise of power is largely reciprocal. The central question for a participant in the community then becomes when to see specific or momentary deviations from reciprocity as indicative of a breakdown in the overall reciprocity of the group. For all the reasons stated earlier, the vitality of communal life demands a willingness to overlook particular hardships and to count on the good faith of one's co-venturers. But the integrity of the group also requires a measure of vigilance to ensure that this trust not be abused; otherwise, the reality of domination will insinuate itself under cover of the claims of community. Over a broad range of social experience it is never easy to distinguish the distrust that strives to exercise this vigilance from the distrust that shows the intromission of defensive self-protection into an order of mutual vulnerability. Success in keeping hold of the distinction depends upon both generosity of judgment and clarity of understanding. Whether you protest against the current communal arrangements or break with the community altogether, you must do so in the spirit of one who keeps alive the hope of reinstating the communal ideal in the existing group or in another.

The problem of rules brings out most clearly this aspect of

the ambiguity of distrust. Rules may help establish, define, and protect the framework of reciprocity. They must, however, still be applied or developed in particular instances; the dilemmas of distrust reappear when people have to decide whether a deviation from reciprocity has in fact taken place. The more clear-cut we try to make the rules in order to avoid interpretive doubt, the greater the risk that they will freeze the spontaneity of communal life. The rule-boundedness may reflect and encourage the decline of an open-ended commitment to a joint enterprise and promote a concern with limited claims and obligations. It focuses attention on what each person is getting or giving. It imposes on collaborative effort a fixity that can hinder its further development.

There is still another sense in which distrust may stand for enlightenment even under conditions of reciprocity. No community can represent a complete or final expression of the ideal: a passionate commitment to particular communities need not be incompatible with the recognition that each of these groups and all of them together are partial and temporary manifestations of humanity. This fact has two moral consequences that perpetuate the ambiguous significance of distrust for the claims of communal solidarity.

One consequence relates to the quality of the subjective experience of participation in community. No matter how noble the aims of communal effort and how just the arrangements of communal life, the love of moral truth and the defense of our powers of criticism and transcendence require that we affirm the necessary imperfection of the group in the very act of devoting ourselves to our fellows within it. There must be an attitude of holding back—a margin of skepticism, secrecy, and withdrawal—that coexists with even the most intense participation. Indeed, this inner resistance to the exclusive and invasive claims that the best and most vital communities make upon our affects and imagination is ultimately the only way to moderate the stultifying, despotic tendencies of group existence. Nonetheless, we can never tell for

sure whether this reaction to the demands of community represents an awareness of social imperfection or a selfish refusal of vulnerability.

The other consequence of the partiality of groups goes to
the willingness to leave the community and, if necessary, to turn
against it. If our loyalties to different communities conflict, we may
try to resolve the conflict as best we can. But if an entire style of
communal life becomes incompatible with the progress of our efforts at individual or collective self-assertion, as defined by an existential project or a social vision, a much more decisive act of
opposition to the community may be required. The need for
such a defiance may result less from changes that have taken
place within the group itself than from the relationship of the
group to emerging possibilities of social life. The awareness that
we may be bound to betray the communities to which we belong
can give communal involvement an urgency it would otherwise
lack. But it cannot solve the problem of determining when such
betrayal represents the assertion of a selfish interest against a
public good and when it is a duty of reluctant rebellion. We may
hope to formulate principles that help guide us in determining
when an individual ought to affirm the sense of group partiality
or become an enemy of the communities he loves. But to treat
such principles as self-sufficient codifications rather than as
allusions to particular existential projects or social visions is to
mistake the relation between the forms of life whose prescriptive
self-understanding these principles represent and the untried, un-
codifiable possibilities of human connection.

———————————————

The premise of my discussion of distrust and enlightenment has been the impossibility of a complete reconciliation between mutual longing and reciprocal fear. And this impossibility

is simply the most intimate form of the irresolvable conflict between
the requirements of self-assertion: between the need to sustain
and develop a self through involvement in shared forms of life
and the need to avoid the dependence and depersonalization
with which all such involvements threaten us. The enabling conditions of self-assertion both interfere with each other and reinforce each other. One aim of our efforts to reinvent ourselves
and our societies is to increase the margin of reinforcement and
to narrow the margin of interference.

We know that the ruling polarity of the passions can
achieve no quietus just as the conflict between the conditions of
self-assertion cannot be definitely settled by any existential project or social order. We know it by a series of experiences that
gloss the meaning and the depth of our apartness.

Remember the ambiguity of distrust as selfishness and
enlightenment. The very facts that establish an order of justified
trust threaten to undo it: we are often unable to tell whether trust
is being upheld or abused, because we know that its vindication is
constantly passing into its abuse. Moreover, even in the presence
of the most successful examples of trusting association we may
feel an apprehension of danger that makes us pull back and remain
aloof from the group. This inner sense seems to be more than an
intimation that the experience of trust may go sour. It also
expresses a dissatisfaction, somewhere between boredom and fear,
with the embrace of group life.

Another set of experiences concerns the susceptibility of
any community to devaluation and disruption by emergent visions
of human empowerment. Each of these visions advances a claim for
an ideal of human existence that the established forms of association
fail to realize. These novel commitments always imply a realignment
among individuals and groups, even when they fail to preach it
openly. In every case it is possible to relate much of the persuasive
force of these visions to a sense that they temper, circumvent, or
transform the conflict between the enabling conditions of self-assertion. Sometimes they explicitly claim to pave the way toward a

definitive resolution of this conflict. Even then, however, the practice of political prophecy seems to affirm what the content of the prophetic message so often denies: the irrepressible capacity of the individual spirit to break, if only a little, the shell of shared convention and established routine.

Yet another fact teaches the lesson of the final irreconcilability of the enabling conditions of self-assertion. This fact is the seduction of luxury. For here, in the love of luxury, we find a set of experiences that bind us to society while separating us from one another.

The search for luxury entices even those who have barely managed to secure the essentials of survival. It influences their images of leisure and play. It even colors the practical life of states, especially when the rejection of class prerogatives coexists with the failure to challenge the institutional contexts in which private interests get shaped and satisfied.

Three distinct elements make up the idea of luxury. First, luxury stands above and beyond the socially defined standard of survival or minimal need. Second, the luxury good is made of things that are hard to get, or is crafted by means that go beyond the normal techniques of production. Third, luxury can yield an intense pleasure unrelated to any immediate utilitarian function. Surfeit, comparative rarity, and detached enjoyment—these are the constituents of luxury. The third element towers in importance over the other two and may persist even when they are lacking.

When we try to specify further the meaning of luxury, we find that it includes different levels of experience. Though their connections are paradoxical, they nevertheless convey, when put together, a powerful message about what we can hope for in our engagements with other people.

At a first level, luxury is just what the third element of the preliminary definition indicates: straightforward enjoyment. But notice the specifically proto-human aspect of this condition of pleasure. The enjoyment presupposes no transformative relation to the world. The luxury good may well be the result of a productive transformation of nature by human skill and indeed by the very skills of the person who now enjoys the good. Or the luxury may consist in a service whose provision demands an exquisite refinement of labor that requires the laborer to transform himself. But in neither instance is the actual enjoyment of the luxury part of the process of transformation. It is more likely to be conceived and experienced as the very opposite of this process, for it is not even the consumption needed to go on surviving and working.

Moreover, the pleasure of luxury does not in itself either require or encourage involvement with other people. The delight it gives involves no transaction with their minds or sensibilities, even when experienced in their physical presence. The more intense this enjoyment, the more it suspends the awareness of time itself and thus the whole sense of engagement in the historical world in which society exists.

The twin elements of transformative practice and intersubjectivity are among those that figure most prominently in our dominant image of the contrast between the human and the animal. Their relative absence from the luxurious experience explains why this first dimension of luxury stands at, or just before, the threshold of our consciousness of humanity. Yet this explanation fails to distinguish the enjoyment of luxury from other varieties of consumption except in its degree of intensity; luxury is the consumer's orgasm.

At a second level, luxury and its attendant pleasure involve an assertion of social rank. This assertion may occur in one of two forms. It may be a display of the material accoutrements expected in a person of a certain station—neither too much nor too little, but just what the settled code of hierarchy commands. Or it may be an attempt to reassert a generalized hierarchy in societies where only limited hierarchies of role tend to be openly acknowledged. Often the material comfort gets humorously mixed up with the delight taken in the reassertion of hierarchy, to the point of bestowing a halo of pleasure upon an otherwise painful show.

The assertion of privilege, unlike the experience of pure enjoyment, has a social aspect. But it is a sociability that consists precisely in the negation of a more inclusive community. It opposes the individual as such, or the individual identified with the caste, to everyone else with whom he might have to deal. Thus, luxury as prerogative both echoes themes of luxury as enjoyment and prefigures a third, more subtle and generic side of luxury—the denial of vulnerability.

Luxury can represent a refusal of dependence upon others. The passive pleasures of luxury offer an alternative to the joys of serious involvement that the less intense contentment of ordinary consumption can only much less plausibly supply. They promise us a bright happiness without subjection to the risks and disappointments of the personal encounter.

That this extraordinary substitution never satisfies us completely and sometimes fills us with loathing are facts that result from our understanding of the actual irreplaceability of what luxury leaves out and the flawed character of what it includes. The pleasures of luxury offer no chance of personal transformation except by the strange hazards of suggestion and revulsion. Besides, the luxurious pleasure has an unmistakable element of melancholy. As the very model of sensuality without sociability, it passes quickly and leaves a void in its wake. It often reeks with intimations of death and decay.

Luxury also serves as a more direct tactical alternative to social dependence. The luxury good is frequently a means to satisfy a need that is not, but might be, fulfilled by a life in common. If the city you live in is inhumane, if it offers few occasions for unhurried sport and company, you need not care that much; you can avoid allying yourself with others to change the character of urban life as long as you can find refuge in your property. It is this same mechanism of demobilizing accommodation that in countless ways repeats itself in many more ordinary events of social life. Both aspects of the denial of vulnerability imply an acceptance of society: one form of sociability replaces another, more taxing and threatening.

A fourth level of luxury negates even this reduced degree of association. It is the suggestion of an utter and irredeemable solitude, apparent in an experience of self that cannot be translated into the categories of established social discourse. Its unworldly quality distinguishes it from the initial pulsation of proto-social enjoyment, which it resembles and restates.

There is something wonderfully ethereal about this indulgence: often the very surfeit of sensation makes you impervious to the distinctive traits of the object that sparks the pleasurable feeling. At first the specific material features of the luxurious item are submerged in the rush of sensual excitement; the delight becomes generic. But pleasure cannot easily survive this abstraction: torn apart from its moorings in particular objects and impressions, it dissolves into a flickering afterglow of contentment.

Differences between the worldly and the otherworldly seem happily irrelevant to understanding this condition. For it beckons to an integration of the person in the world—a surrender to indiscriminating nature—that frees him momentarily from his awkward social self. Other people make this experience possible; yet other individuals are what it is least about. The presence in luxury of this impulse toward breaking the bonds of selfhood throws light on the familiar affinity between material exuberance and mystical union.

Friends of republican ideas have traditionally decried luxury, for they have correctly seen in it a threat to civic life. This threat cuts far deeper than the association of luxury with hierarchy; oligarchy and republicanism have often enough come to terms with each other. Luxury's main challenge lies, instead, in its offer of a route to happiness that bypasses participation, alliance, and conflict. The individual can hope to be content even though he treats people around him as mere suppliers of pleasure.

The critics of luxury, however, have neglected to mention

that this promise of liberation from the involvements of society tells a truth as well as a lie. The lie is that luxury can ever be a fitting surrogate for personal encounter or republican involvement. The truth, however, is that the happiness of luxury is real and, in its way, irreplaceable and profound, for it rests on the tendency of some forms of individual fulfillment to disregard or subvert the attachments of society.

Consider, again, the metamorphoses of luxury. The republic may attack the luxury that consists in the overt display or underhand reassertion of privilege. It may try to encourage conditions that do not tempt people to seek in luxury a balsam for social discontents whose causes they feel powerless to transform. But the first and last aspects of luxury—the senses of proto-human enjoyment and supersession of self—cannot be cured so easily. They are rooted less in any particular social failing than in the very wealth of human possibility that underlies the accomplishments of collective effort. Political wisdom therefore will never attempt to suppress these extra-republican or anti-republican experiences. It will want to untie them as much as possible from the facts of injustice, so that the means for the enjoyment of luxury, though probably not of the luxuries now cherished, are spread about. When the delights of luxury suggest unsuspected forms of human expression and achievement, the republic will attempt to give these varieties of luxury a social interpretation that strengthens social involvements rather than destroying them. Thus, faced with the passion for luxury, the republic will coax rather than protest or prohibit, aware that it is at odds with a cagey and fickle goddess.

The lessons of luxury are retaught in the domains of art and sex, with which luxury has paradoxical relations and which it resembles in its impact on the quality of historical experience.

Even those arts that are most individualist in inspiration, performance, or message have the power to reaffirm social bonds. For art expresses and creates images of shared experience. It varies and, by varying, enlarges and sharpens the language that enables people to reflect on their collective predicament. Nevertheless, even the art that seems most intensely communal disrupts the cohesiveness of group life.

For one thing, art loosens the established sense of reality in the very course of making it more subtle. The world of meanings that it reconstitutes is never quite the one with which it started. The invention of the individual or collective artist opens a gap between the accepted reality of everyday life and the presentiment of other realities that do not fit into it. A little trace of suspicion about conventional assumptions passes into the established social world, and—who knows?—remains long dormant until in some faraway future it helps wreck the world it had seemed powerless to affect.

For another thing, the moment of aesthetic pleasure is itself subversive of society. The test case would be, say, the exaltation of a collective ritual dance, which according to certain *ingénus* submerges individual consciousness in collective emotions and reaffirms the unity and preeminence of the group. In fact, however, the more enveloping the trance-like state induced by the celebration, the greater its disruptive impact on the real texture of intersubjectivity, which is the basis and the very nature of society. The maintenance of this texture demands a constant reciprocal probing of shared or divergent perceptions and feelings. This state of active give and take is interrupted, and even denied, by the mute stare, the loss of discriminating contrast, that marks the highpoint of collective exaltation. Such a release from the strains of intersubjectivity accompanies with greater or lesser force every instance of aesthetic pleasure. Thus, art, which so often works by giving significant form to a surfeit of sensation, also recalls luxury in its gesture of release from the limits of society.

Sex has a similarly paradoxical relation to social involvement. It may represent a craving for another individual that passes quickly from the sensual to the cerebral. But as lust—untransformed by love—it may also undermine our ability to imagine the otherness of other people. This paradoxical relation of sexuality to sociability forms a major theme in the next stage of my argument.

Thus, in luxury most clearly, and in art and sex more remotely and contradictorily, we find events that break through the bonds of social life even when they seem to reinforce these ties. Each of these events suggests an experience of individuality that minimizes acceptance of a broader sociability. Each offers a release from society and a hiatus in history—a sense of time abstracted from social conflict. And each reminds us that the problem of solidarity, manifest in the polarity of the passions, can also be partly circumvented rather than partly settled.

The whole tone of historical experience is modified by the discovery of a partial escape from the active acceptance of interpersonal engagement. The force that perennially denies all society grows out of the elementary constituents of social life. This paradox—a crack in our universe—is a flaw that nothing can mend. But it is also a gracious reprieve and an opening through which we can hope to catch a glimpse of a fact that any persuasive account of a shared human identity must recognize and elucidate.

II

The personality that can live out the passions is a personality capable of self-reflection. Self-reflection or consciousness—terms used interchangeably—is the ability to move back and forth between two experiences of the self. Neither of these experiences can drive the other out, nor can the two be integrated into a single coherent scheme. Their coexistence is counterconceptual.

Consciousness is in part the sense of being the center of the world. Under this self-centered aspect of consciousness, other people are credited with a lesser measure of reality. They are shadowy analogues to your own self, targets of your perception or your striving, and points in a network of personal and social relations that extends outward from your immediate self-experience. Thus, mankind is divided into two categories: yourself and everyone else. All social distinctions that connect directly to subjective experience—such as those that contrast the members of your class or your community to outsiders—can be understood as extensions of the basic contrast between yourself and other people.

But consciousness also includes a self-objectifying aspect, according to which you are merely one of several selves and lack any privileged reality. You can overcome the partiality of your perceptual apparatus and see yourself as if from the detached, external perspective of a mind that corrects the distortions of self-centeredness. The categories of classification that enable you to make sense of your social experience can be more or less completely disengaged from any overriding contrast between yourself and other people.

Both aspects of experience are present in each episode of a fully developed life of passion. We go beyond self-centeredness whenever we draw upon the imagination of otherness: the power to recognize the singularity of others. But the alternative mode of experience—the sense of being the center—persists in the life of passion, not merely as the ravenous quality of the ego but as the relative obscurity of other people's subjective experience.

Our understanding of the world urges us to dismiss the

self-centered element in consciousness as a mistake. Because of the apparent connection between selfishness and the self-centered view, moral aspiration seems to confirm theoretical criticism. Even logic adds its bit: by treating other people as less real counterparts to the self, the self-centered aspect of consciousness seems to play fast and loose with the criteria of sameness and difference.

In our efforts to make sense of nature we may be justified in disregarding the self-centered side of consciousness so long as we recognize that theory cannot fully reshape perception. But in other endeavors—such as the practice of attributing normative force to conceptions of our shared identity—this exclusion may be dangerous. The argument of the Introduction has already suggested that, contrary to the teachings of metaphysical realism, the presuppositions of our basic practices may not be reconcilable, not at least without harm to the reasons that lead us to engage in these practices in the first place. This point may now be followed up by considering why a view of our shared identity that is meant to carry normative weight should take the self-centered element in consciousness seriously. Some of the reasons have to do with the general requirements of any attempt to ascribe prescriptive force to conceptions of personality or society, others with the particular conception of human identity defended here. Because our practices change according to what we do with them, these two types of reasons cannot be rigidly distinguished.

A view of personality or society that can support an existential project or a social vision must be one whose realization engages our most intimate concerns. Like our perceptual experiences these concerns may be influenced by the theoretical ideas we hold. But like those experiences they are not freely manipulable. A story about our shared identity may seem to be not about us if it remains silent about the many problems and paradoxes that result from our ability to move between the two aspects of consciousness.

Some moral and religious doctrines teach us to disregard the self-centered element in subjectivity so that we may better satisfy the strongest urges of the heart and give our satisfactions the stability that only freedom from illusion can ensure. But in my criticism of the ethic of fusion with the absolute and of its speculative monistic defenses (e.g., in some versions of Hindu and Buddhist metaphysics) I have already argued that such an enterprise fails on its own terms.

An existential project that takes its point of departure from a modernist reconstruction of the Christian-romantic tradition defines love rather than altruism as its organizing ideal. An ethic of altruism (like classical utilitarianism) can easily be squared with the thesis that the self-centered element in consciousness is no more than a dangerous delusion. An altruistic moral teaching insists that once this mistake has been set aside, we can devote ourselves to the characteristic moral task of combatting selfishness. But for an ethic of love, our ability to imagine one another is both crucial and precarious. Such a doctrine must reject the altruist's implicit contrast between the ease with which individuals may imagine one another and the difficulty of the struggle that they must continuously wage against selfishness. Instead, an ethic of love is more likely to give major moral significance to the very self-centeredness that appears to the theorist of altruism as no more than the combination of a perceptual bias with a moral vice. For the self-centered aspect of consciousness is nowhere more evident than in love, which represents as much a triumph of imagination as an act of self-bestowal. Only those who appreciate the constraints that an incorrigible self-centeredness imposes upon the imagination of otherness, and the power of the insights gained in the face of these constraints, can comprehend the quality of love.

This part of the essay describes characteristic turning points in the making of an individual capable of passion. This biographical genealogy of the passions suggests how the detached view of a self that resembles other selves comes to coexist with self-centeredness and how these two formative experiences are in turn changed—though never entirely displaced—by the discovery of the problem of contextuality. The aim is to amplify the central conception of passion by extending a static view into its developmental counterpart. This restatement in turn provides another occasion to show how the problem of contextuality—our need to be in particular contexts and our inability to rest content with any contexts in particular—affects the problem of solidarity—the conflict between the enabling conditions of self-assertion. The influence that the character of our relation to our contexts exercises upon our relation to one another is already prefigured by a dialectic of satisfaction and insatiability that marks every stage of the biography of passion. All moments of this dialectic repeat the significant structure if not the explicit content of the problem of contextuality.

The distinctions among the stages of self-formation discussed here have both an analytic and an empirical basis. Their analytic basis is the introduction, at each decisive moment in the early biography of the passionate self, of experiences presupposed by the general account of passion. Their empirical justification is the claim to describe actual biographical events. In what societies? In all societies in proportion as they have been transformed by the leftist and modernist commitment to jumble up the forms of work and sensibility that are available to the occupants of different social places and insofar as this jumbling up has weakened more idiosyncratic influences upon the trials of childhood and early adolescence.

———————————

At first the individual experiences no clear separation between himself and the world or between himself and others. His own experience of being the center of the world does not conflict with anything that would contradict it, for this center is also everything else. Though there may be no strong conception of identity between the self and the things around him, neither is there any firm idea of difference.

The relation of the self to his surroundings, so indistinctly separated from his own being, is here perceived and experienced primarily as desire. When it first appears, desire is a statement of incompleteness—a struggle for satiation—that cannot yet count on the help of the imagination. The imagination probes reality by conceiving its transformative variations and thereby changes the quality of desire.

In the most simple sense, imagination makes purposeful activity possible. Intentional action requires beliefs about counterfactual possibility. This requirement binds the experiences of desiring and of working upon the world so closely together that their respective characteristics can no longer be clearly distinguished. The pleasure of successful intentional action mingles with a less discriminate sense of physical satiation and changes it. For this new pleasure exhibits another happiness: the world ceases to be experienced as something merely given, through necessity or chance. Instead, it is rediscovered as a reality that imagination and will can penetrate.

Desire, not yet transformed by imagination, appears to the self under the double aspect of satiation and insatiability. For a moment desire is fulfilled. The indistinct personality basks in a glowing awareness of self-contentment. But the contented self does not yet stand apart from the surrounding world or other selves. The quality of his contentment is that of balance in a field constituted by self and world together.

Though satiation may be real, it is also brief. Another desire springs up in place of the one that has been satisfied. This ceaseless rebirth of desire, rooted in the realities of the organism and its dealings with the environment, defines insatiability. It may be called insatiability rather than simple lack of satiation because its constant reappearance already presents the self with his first formative shock: the shock of discovering that the indistinct, unified reality in which he lives is subject to recurrent disruption.

Momentary dissatisfaction is permeated by a less articulate and more relentless disquiet at the impossibility of keeping everything in the condition of dim self-contentment. The passage back and forth, from satiation to insatiability, serves as a point of departure for the whole later growth of cognitive capacities and passionate experiences. From the very start, desire suffers the anticipated influence of this later history.

Take the development of thought. Repeated unfulfillment works as the driving impulse to coordinate motor operations with one another and with ideas, and then thoughts with one another and with speech. The inability to solve given practical problems with the available set of ideas and operations requires ever-more abstract and inclusive coordinations. The effort to preserve acquired cognitive powers in the face of practical difficulties that threaten to defeat them requires that everything already gained must be occasionally reordered: stabilization demands invention. Each of these cognitive reorderings represents another step in the development of the power of the self to respond actively to reality and to change it from an oppressive realm of necessity and chance into a playing ground of will and imagination. So the torment of insatiability is associated in the life of the self with the conquest of freedom—the freedom, in this instance, of greater cognitive capability—and with a joy that the diffuse contentment of physical satiation cannot provide.

The rebirth of desire prefigures the history of passion just as it foreshadows the history of knowledge. In the effort to quiet his craving, the self turns repeatedly to another person. Already he begins to discover the differences between himself and others. Already his longing for satiation becomes confused with his search for attachment and acceptance. Already he begins to understand his insatiability as a warning that no measure of response by another person suffices to reassure him conclusively that all is well and that there is a place for him in the world.

Confronted with reemergent desire, the person discovers that what he needs always eludes his grasp and reappears as something that can be achieved only by a more basic change of circumstance. The child's repeated disappointments with every available satisfaction move him toward the idea of a satisfaction that nothing could disappoint. This ambition to make the wheel of desire stop is perhaps the first sign of the longing for an unconditional good beyond time and contingency. It imparts to the initial experience of insatiability something of the qualities of both an insight into the precariousness of the self and a rebellion against limited and relative satisfactions.

Early in his infancy the child begins to achieve a more definite experience of apartness from other people. As he discovers his isolation he acquires a new set of concerns: he stumbles into the drama of longing and jeopardy.

The people who surround the child surpass him in power. They satisfy his elementary needs. They dominate the situations in which he experiments with his capabilities and reflects upon his self. They pronounce the words with whose help he revolutionizes his activities and thoughts and reaches higher levels of abstraction in his understanding of the world. Even if they were less powerful, the mere fact of their otherness would be enough to place the child in danger.

What is the meaning of their power and their otherness? The view of his own selfhood at which he tentatively arrives—of its reality and independence—must be compatible with the clues that other people give him. Without occasional confirmation, any view loses its credibility.

Thus, the child receives from others his sense of being. Should he conclude that he lacks an independent existence and that he exists like a gleam in the eyes of other people? Or will the others give him a sign that they accept him for what he is?

Through such an acceptance they indicate to him that he has a place in the world and that, in discovering their apartness from him and his longing for them, he has not discovered a source of peril and annihilation.

The turning point in this new moment of the life of passion is the empathetic response. The child faces the other. The other embraces him. The repetition of this act represents an experience of freedom as basic as the development of the imagination. The existence of other people turns into a presence that sustains the child's sense of independent existence and gives him the conviction that in binding himself more closely to them he need not deny or dissolve himself. Through the empathetic response the world of the child's attachments—the only world there is, the world of shared actions and shared discourse—becomes the stage and medium of self-assertion. The discovery of the possibility of assertion through attachment joins with the discovery of the transforming, negating power of the imagination to constitute the root experience of freedom.

There is no clear limit to the forms that the empathetic response may take or to the people who may provide it. The assignment to the father, the mother, or others, of fixed responsibilities in providing this response merely reflects a particular version of family life in a particular society. Even within the narrow boundaries set by the recognized system of roles, the child, or the adults to whom he turns, may find unexpected paths to empathy. Whatever disappointments he suffers may be overcome much later by similar acts of love and imagination.

A new dialectic of satiation and insatiability comes into existence alongside the earlier one. Satisfaction now consists in the joy of acceptance by another person. The child's response to this joy cannot yet be understood as the passion that I shall describe as love. The full life of consciousness has not yet developed. Love draws on aspects of self-reflection that a person so unformed cannot yet have achieved. Nevertheless, this earlier episode of involvement resembles and prepares the experience of loving and of being loved.

The element of insatiability in this experience lies in the inability of any gesture of acceptance to quiet the longing and fear of the child. The reasons for this inability anticipate the dialectic of longing and jeopardy in the fully developed life of consciousness. One reason is the freedom of the personality in its acts of self-bestowal or self-disclosure. An additional reason is the gap that always remains between the longing for the other person and the act of acceptance that this other can in fact commit. Each of these points demands further analysis.

The person gives, and he takes away. No act of acceptance is for keeps. Because it comes from a living self, every such act remains subject to all the forms of distraction and change of heart. The meanings of presence and absence, speech and silence, can be altered by the subtle waverings of a dimly perceived intention. If one person's act of acceptance seems irrevocable, other people in the child's immediate world may still reject him. In the simpler experience of desire, unfulfillment brings disquiet. Conflict does the same here.

The imperfection of self-disclosure counts for as much as the revocability of self-bestowal. For reasons soon to be discussed, the whole life of passion is only imperfectly capable of being understood. Its obscurity gives every opinion about the intentions of another individual the quality of a gamble, and makes every view about how the gamble has turned out a gamble itself. More signs of acceptance are required to dispel the uncertainty of the signs that have already been given.

The freedom of self-bestowal and the obscurity of self-disclosure fail to exhaust the element of insatiability in the experience of personal encounter. The acts of acceptance may be repeated and almost unequivocal. The child nevertheless continues to crave more, to crave as someone who has not yet been given what he needs. For what does he cry out? Perhaps he has an intimation of the problem that he will confront at the next turning point in the history of passion. The others may embrace him. He may hold fast to them in a single world of mutual action and shared discourse. But this world, and his own being in it, remain subject to time and dissolution.

Though this account of the child's concern may sound absurdly refined, it describes no more than the beginning of reflection upon contingency—the discovery that things might be otherwise. The child has already caught sight of contingency in his earlier bouts with dissatisfied desire. He will later confront it more completely in the astonishing discovery of death. At the beginning, contingency means only that the paradise of satiated desire can be lost. Gradually, contingency comes to mean that the self, once and still experienced as the center of the world, and all the self's mental and passionate attachments, might be otherwise, that they might and will be nothing at all.

Something in the early history of personal encounter serves as a clue to this more drastic contingency. The child crying for the mother or father cries for more than the fulfillment of desire or the reenactment of a bond of acceptance that he may not really believe to be in jeopardy. He cries, as well, against time. He cries because he fears separation as the reminder of a loss still more terrible, which he cannot name. He cries because, left alone to himself and made aware of his dependence, he has a presentiment that everything is endangered and equivocal, that everything might vanish, or change, or turn out to be different from what it seems. If only he could think more clearly, he would not stop crying when father comes home.

To the extent that insight into this more drastic contingency already marks the early history of personal encounter, it makes for another cause of insatiability. No amount of self-bestowal and self-disclosure by another person could suffice to quiet this apprehension; no such answer could fully join issue with such a question. But neither is the response of personal acceptance entirely irrelevant to the concern. The embrace of the other is the promise of an unconditional acceptance, of an acceptance whose saving force no separation can destroy and nothing that happens to the world can cancel out. Just as the separation is feared as the omen of a more terrible disaster, so the embrace is desired as the augury of a more conclusive rescue. The combination of the relevance and the irrelevance of the answer to the question reinforces the experience of insatiability. Nothing is ever enough, but whatever happens seems like a step toward a solution.

The new dialectic of satiation and insatiability that I have described does not displace the earlier style of satisfied and unsatisfiable desire. The child still has the sense of physical pleasure and disquiet; something else gets added. But this addition changes everything: the earlier experience is invaded and poisoned by its sequel.

Precisely because physical desire and satisfaction persist alongside personal encounter, they may represent at any moment an alternative to encounter and even to the acknowledgment of separateness that the life of encounter presupposes. The possession of material things serves as an antidote to dependence upon other people. At a more primitive level, physical pleasure—providing, as it does, a different contentment—offers a way out from the exertions and the risks of encounter. Though liable to the instability provoked by the constant rebirth of desire, such pleasure is immune to the more dangerous surprises of personal rejection and separation. At the moment of most intense physical excitement, when the self revels in the luxury of the senses, even the conception of individual existence and of the individuality of things in the world may vanish in a plush aura of contentment. The psychological kinship between luxurious delight and mystical union is prefigured in the child's early experience. It is anticipated by the capacity of physical pleasure to offer a momentary escape not only from personal encounter but from the very basis of encounter in the sense of active, individual existence.

Nevertheless, individuality and attachment, once discovered, can no longer be entirely forgotten. Physical pleasure ceases to be entirely naive. It is even corrupted by its surrogate relationship to the new life of encounter. The child grasps that this life is the story of his birth as a personality and that in avoiding the risks of encounter he steps away from himself.

At the same time that the new experience of personal encounter is changed by its coexistence with the preexisting dialectic of pleasure, the latter also assumes characteristics of the former. Physical pleasure now takes on some of the redemptive significance of the act of acceptance by another person. The indefiniteness of personal longing enters into the moment of unfulfilled desire and endows it with an added element of insatiability. Each new stage of experience extends its characteristics back into what the earlier stages have already produced.

Having discovered personal encounter, the child knows individuality within a world of personal attachments and shared discourse. He knows uncertainty because he sees the lineaments of this world being constructed and destroyed, in bits and pieces, all the time. But he still sees this world as the only one that does or might exist. He does not yet fully grasp how much this knowable and seemingly permanent reality is in fact opaque and precarious. He now stands on the verge of making another discovery. This discovery will shatter the child's understanding of his circumstance and inflict on him a wound that no amount of consolation, distraction, or stupidity can entirely heal.

The next turning point in the history of the self occurs when the child discovers the utter contingency of his own being and of the world to which he belongs. The immediate inducement to this discovery is the confrontation with death.

The first awareness of death may come while the life of encounter remains in its initial defining steps. But death becomes more fully intelligible against the background of the person's more developed insight into the facts of human separateness and dependence. For it is by interacting with the full circumstance of consciousness that death acquires its distinctive meaning in the life of passion.

Consciousness, remember, is the coexistence of two experiences, each understood to be irreconcilable with the other as soon as the mind lingers over their relation. There is the experience of being the center of the world, of being more real than other people. The discovery of individuality at the previous moment in the history of passion has dispelled the sense of a single continuous reality. But the child remains imprisoned in his mind and attached to his being: he cannot conceive others as he knows himself. From the standpoint of this element in consciousness, a world without the self is no world at all. When he imagines his death the person still imagines himself present, like God watching over the wastage of time.

The other, contrasting element in the experience of consciousness is the individual's capacity to view himself as one among many, as one with access to experiences like those that others can undergo. The link between these two aspects of self-reflection rests on the most basic characteristics of thought, language, and discovery through action. To think about himself the child must both appropriate and reinvent a common discourse: the ideas and the language of the people who surround him. But the individual use of this shared language and these preexisting ideas assumes comparability in experience, even if the comparable experience amounts to nothing more than a minimally interpreted perceptual acquaintance with the natural world. There is no compulsion in reasoning or communication in talk that does not presuppose being like others and being together with them in a similar situation. The similarities may be pushed back to a minimum. No minimum, however, is minimal enough to accommodate the picture of a self unable to grant other people and their experience the reality to which he lays claim for himself and for his experience.

Again, the child must develop and test his thoughts about himself by trying them out in action among people. Whenever he takes seriously the view of himself as the center, he is soon brought up short by the resistance of opposing wills.

Now the confrontation with death and the twofold experience of self-consciousness that it presupposes have both been underway from the very beginning of the self's sentient life. A turning point occurs when the fact of self-consciousness and the awareness of death go far enough to revolutionize each other. The knowledge of death forces out into the open the conflict between the perspectives upon the self that define consciousness. At the same time, this conflict—the ability and the inability to gain distance from the experience of self-centeredness—allows the idea of death to become as real as it ever can.

When the awareness of death is added to the conviction of being only part of the whole, the quality of this conviction changes. The failure of the child and of his immediate family to hold the center of the world amounts to a more terrible decentering than he had reckoned with. So long as the intimation of death had not yet sunk in, the two contrasting elements in consciousness might seem a mere curiosity, like the equivalence of wave and particle theories of light as descriptions in twentieth-century physics. But with the discovery of death, the stakes rise. Not to be the center also means to lack all necessity, to be susceptible to instant and complete annihilation, and to see everything to which you cling stagger under the same weight.

Conversely, death gains its full value only when appreciated against the background of an experience of society in which the child can begin to analogize himself to other people and to imagine that his own life has a shape like theirs. He may not be able to picture his own annihilation without continuing to see himself as an onlooker. But he can already imagine that this disappearance might be more definitive than anything he can represent to himself.

The discovery of death is most shocking of all in a special

condition of the mind. The person sees himself as unique. The lush particularity of his life, of his attachments, of his self-reflection, comes before him. But at the same time he cannot accept any of the fixed definitions of his identity that other people may seek to impose. He knows himself to contain an indefinite fund of possible experience that no life plan can exhaust and no shared culture make intelligible. Death seems most terrible when it appears to annihilate something inexhaustibly particular, hence irreplaceable, but also infinitely productive of possibility, hence incongruous as a candidate for total annihilation.

The state of mind just described enables us better than any other to hold together in thought the two sides of the experience of consciousness. The idea of being the center of the world survives as confidence in the inexhaustibility and uniqueness of the self. It thereby gains a content that the individual can make sense of: other people might at least share in the same qualities of uniqueness and inexhaustibility. Such a state of mind may seem the privilege of an educated and discerning intellect. In less explicit form, however, it is something familiar to the child, as later to the man, whenever they feel their distinctive identities to be both real and uncertain. Thus, people become most vulnerable to the apprehension of death during the periods in childhood and adult life when a specific sense of identity is jeopardized but the limitless quality of personality becomes all the more clear. If this troubled conception of self-identity is indeed only a heightened form of the general experience of consciousness, its effects offer another confirmation of the link between the emergence of consciousness and the awareness of death.

The turning point in the history of passion that is brought about by the interaction between the awareness of death and the experience of consciousness generates still another dialectic of satiation and insatiability. The points of departure for this new experience of fulfillment and dissatisfaction are the insight into contingency and the desire for something that contingency might exempt. Both the insight and the desire constitute a tacit response to the facts that constitute this final turning point in the history of passion. The nature of the relation between the occasion and the response will become clear as the analysis progresses.

Before discovering death and entering fully into the two-sided experience of consciousness, the child imagines himself, or the world of his attachments, as an absolute frame of reference: a reality whose existence and whose evidence depend upon nothing else. This idea of an absolute frame of reference includes two elements. They can become distinct only after the emerging self has been transformed by the discovery of death and the development of consciousness. There is an element of necessity: things could not be otherwise. There is also an element of overpowering self-evidence. For the self-experience that absorbs our early attention is only barely mediated by thoughts. The truth of thoughts is always conditional because they depend in the end on certain other things being true, and the truth of these other things cannot be known for sure. Only to the limited extent that self-experience is detached from thought can it appear secure.

The awareness of death undermines the absolute center. Even that which participates most clearly in the character of an indestructible reality—the self and his immediate attachments—now begins to look like a momentary interlude. The passage of the self into the full life of consciousness, so closely linked with the discovery of death, undermines the sense of necessity and self-evidence. For it emphasizes the dependence of our acquaintance with our own selves upon collective practices and collective discourse. We may try to transfer to these social events the absolute character with which we once invested ourselves and our closest attachments. But we must then reckon with two difficulties. For one thing, the collective culture must be appropriated by acts of individual understanding. These acts constantly threaten to replace the self-evident quality of a unified and unchallenged culture with a welter of tentative and clashing opinions. For another thing, history will teach us, if only we wait long enough and think clearly enough, that we not only can but must act and reason occasionally as agents who are not bound by the constraints of established schemes of thought or forms of life. Thus, the very practice of imagination discredits the idea of an absolute frame of reference even when it is precisely such an absolute reality that we are trying to imagine.

Yet the more the person comes to understand that nothing outside himself can have the absolute character he once attributed to himself, the more he gains an incentive to renew the futile search for the self-evident and the non-contingent. For it is only because he can break the rules and overstep the boundaries of all fixed orders of society or thought that he can recognize them as not being absolute. This irrepressible capacity for transcendence and revision shows the element of truth in his initial view of himself as the necessary center of the world—the very idea that the whole development of self-consciousness has contributed to subvert. No wonder he wants to impart to the mental and social worlds that he inhabits something of the quality that he detects in himself and thereby to free himself from the need constantly to choose between the suppression of his context-transcending power and the inability to accept any specific mental or social context as a suitable and definitive home for his striving. The modernist doctrine of our relation to the contexts of our activity, discussed in the Introduction to this essay, makes this emotional and epistemological paradox explicit and suggests the senses in which it can and cannot be resolved.

Self-reflecting consciousness completes its destruction of the idea of an absolute frame of reference when it connects understanding and transformation. To understand how a part of reality works, you must grasp how it changes under different transformative pressures. Thus, the very ability to comprehend a state of affairs presupposes a capacity to see it as something that subsists only in the absence of transformative events and to imagine it as something that might be other than what it is. The focused sense of jeopardy that the idea of death generates is thereby generalized into an experience of the world that connects actuality and possibility.

This new and culminating dialectic of satiation and insatiability can be redescribed with greater psychological immediacy. A person throws himself into a set of routine activities and conventional beliefs. He fixes his desires upon tangible and identifiable rewards. He lends these aims, or the context of belief and practice within which he pursues them, the force of an uncontroversial reality and value. He pushes death back from the forefront of his awareness. The realm of action and belief that informs his desires gains an appearance of necessity and authority. The satisfaction of these desires gives him the temporary sense of having a place in the world, not just because other people accept him but because he seems to himself to have come in touch with things of unquestionable reality and value.

He has his moments of disappointment and disorientation. What matters always seems to be somewhere else. His real concerns seem to have been traduced by their particular realizations. There was something in what he really wanted that the actual having fails to provide, even if he had only set out to satisfy an apparently straightforward physical craving. These are the moments when the desire for the non-contingent appears insatiable.

This final form of the passage, back and forth, between satiation and insatiability has the same relation to the earlier two forms (physical delight and personal encounter) that the second has to the first. The earlier modes persist in their independent existence. The later addition, however, changes them. Physical happiness and personal attachment now become, among other things, defenses against questions of ultimate meaning. But the spell cast over the apprehensive mind is never complete enough to suppress altogether a disquiet whose force neither the waning of physical delight nor the accidents of personal encounter can fully explain. At the same time, the pursuit of physical satisfaction and of personal acceptance take on some of the added intensity that attends the search for the absolute frame of reference. The indefiniteness of the longing for the other had already entered into the experience of absolute pleasure. Now a poisonous trace of the relentless and unrealizable character of the desire for the unconditional passes into the search for physical satisfaction and personal acceptance. Each moment of encounter and delight becomes a provisional stand-in for the unfindable absolute. Thus, all the moments of satiation and insatiability enter into one another. This same sharing in one another's nature will turn out to characterize the relations among the distinct passions.

The person who has passed through the several stages of development narrated in the preceding pages is ready to experience the full life of passion. He may occasionally return to an earlier stage. More often, he falls into a characteristic state of division of the self. This state of division undermines the capacity for self-knowledge and self-transformation. It especially circumscribes the role of those transformative passions that enable people to accept one another more fully and to reimagine what human life can be like.

One self in this state of division surrenders to automatisms of conduct and perception. As behavior, these automatisms are habits and routines that lose any active relation to deliberate striving. As perceptions, they are a limited stock of analogies that control what the person can see and that impoverish his understanding of the actual by narrowing his insight into the possible. Under the influence of such automatisms, consciousness dims. The will is disengaged from the imagination or enslaved to an imagination spellbound by a narrow conception of possible states of existence.

The other self is able in moments of self-reflection or surprise to look at these automatisms of conduct and perception from a more detached vantage point and to deny that they exhaust the scope of personality. This power to stand apart, already implied by the nature of consciousness and by the indefinite quality of our longings, is confirmed by the threefold dialectic of satiation and insatiability. One of the most striking manifestations of the division in the self consists precisely in the passage from boredom to diversion and back again.

Thus, the self is both caught within automatisms and able occasionally to regard them from outside. Compare this division in the self to the division between what a conditional social world incorporates and what it excludes. The contained conflicts of routine politics and of normative controversy serve as a permanent reminder, within routinized social life, that society can be remade and reimagined through an escalation of practical and visionary strife.

The genesis of self-division throws light on the nature of freedom in the life of passion. The person fails to push himself into situations where his imaginative or practical relations to other people might be shaken up. He acts out of a distrust of others: of what they will do to him if his behavior and thoughts are not protected by a carapace of compulsive idiosyncracy or of submission to collective habit. Yet the effect of his action is to enslave him all the more to others by robbing him of the means to give surprise. His conduct reveals a disbelief in his own powers of self-assertion and self-transformation. This disbelief is tantamount to a failure to understand the tentative nature of any fixed version of an individual identity. The individual reduces his identity to his character and denies its transcendent and indefinite elements.

The freedom to reimagine and remake character, however, is compromised by the effects of moral fortune and confused by the constant mixture, in a normal human life, of states of division and of moments when these states seem to be overcome. To progress in self-transformation and to break the shell of character, the person must proceed through a period of heightened vulnerability. His chances for further movement do not depend upon himself alone. They also turn upon how others receive him at these times of aggravated defenselessness. If they do him in rather than accept him, his next venture into accepted vulnerability will be that much harder to undertake. No single response by another person ever constitutes an insuperable obstacle to moral invention. But the total pattern of response includes an element of pure fortune over which the striving individual has no control.

Again, ordinary experience always combines self-division and the overcoming of this division. The moment of division is a condition of diminished freedom: character and its automatisms take on a life of their own. But this contrast between freedom and constraint is always weaker than it appears. The automatisms constantly reemerge against the background of the vast spiritual sloth, the overwhelming apathy, of ordinary experience. They always contain contrasting elements. They always hit upon unexpected circumstances that may enable the person to cast them off.

Thus, the analysis of the state of division already suggests the subtle quality of freedom in the life of passion. The passions are neither free acts of will nor events that just happen to people. They are strivings in a context of troubled freedom, forever lost and regained. Just as they refer to a human reality that eludes the contrast of understanding and evaluation, so too they defeat the simple opposition of choice and compulsion, for they show on what terms and by what means this opposition may arise.

Consider now one of the most puzzling and common incidents in the life of passion—the experience of addiction or obsessional desire. The analysis of this experience calls into play the earlier ideas about the development and the division of the self. It shows how these ideas connect to one another and to their practical context.

By obsession I mean broadly any cycle of repetitive behavior from which a person feels unable to free himself. My remarks apply mainly to the instances in which both physical dependence and ideological commitment play only a subsidiary role. But these arguments apply as well to those instances in which such a commitment or dependence emerge as ultimate results of a crazed, fixed desire that preceded them. This desire may be, for example, an addiction to a particular sexual pleasure, to the accumulation of a particular good, or to the performance of a particular activity.

Addiction inclusively defined may be taken as a paradigm of obsession. So viewed, it is the most common mental disorder. It is also the most visible aspect of craziness in ordinary life. Its elucidation therefore reveals something important about the life of passion. Remember its characteristic signs.

First, it involves a state of diminished freedom. Compulsion undermines both the will and the imagination, if only by isolating the former from the latter. Second, the self feels empty when not attached to the object of its addiction; the attachment turns into a requirement of self-possession. Third, the actual condition of enjoyment fails to offer a stable contentment. Even at the height of access to the object of his desire, the addict feels something amiss and incomplete; fulfillment recedes. Fourth, the entire experience of addiction retains an element of recalcitrant obscurity. For one thing, the addict cannot really put his finger on just what he craves in the desired object or state of affairs. Any attempt to think his fascination through breaks down. For another thing, the desire is both highly directed and capable of sudden and seemingly capricious redirection. At one moment it seems fixed on a well-defined entity. At the next moment it returns to a state of indefinition or switches goals unaccountably. These traits are still only surface characteristics. Their deeper meaning is revealed when you reexamine addiction in the light of the earlier ideas about self-division and self-development.

The addictive or obsessional condition is in one sense only

an exaggeration of the automatisms of conduct or imagination that characterize the divided self. But in the normal state of consciousness these automatisms are experienced in a matter-of-fact way. They add to the apathetic quality of ordinary experience: the mute, persistent struggle to get from one chore to the next and from one perception to another. In the moment of addiction, on the contrary, there is a frenzied break with the tenor of ordinary experience.

The divided state of the self is deepened rather than overcome. While the moment of unquiet enjoyment lasts, the automatisms come to be felt as the repositories of both halves of the divided self. The addict treats the addictive (obsessional) behavior as if it were more than a localized set of automatisms from which his freer, truer, and more indefinite self can step aside. He also sees in the addiction an expression of this freer personality. It is as if the two halves of the divided self—the routinized self and the self beyond the routines, the parts of personality that character includes and the parts that it does not—had been folded one on top of the other. The repetitiveness of routine combines with the sense of a rapture that touches the vital core of personality.

The genesis of passion in self-consciousness illuminates the obsessional link between frenzy and repetition. This link calls most directly into play the final stage of the development of the self: the stage when, having learned to search for physical delight and personal acceptance, the individual sets out in quest of the non-contingent. The compulsive and agitated fixation may seem a regression to the most primitive stages of experience. But though this fixation works through repetition, the normal block to development, it calls to life the most refined and developed aspects of self-experience.

The addict behaves as if by achieving the fixed aim of his desire he could satisfy the most insatiable longings. In ordinary experience, temporary satiation passes quickly into dissatisfaction, and the reenactment of dissatisfaction constitutes the experience of insatiability. In addiction the passage back and forth between fulfillment and dissatisfaction is frozen into a single moment, just as the two halves of the divided self are superimposed upon each other. Thus, the distinctive, tormenting quality of the addictive episode is the merger of satiation and disappointment in a concentrated, prolonged episode of anguished and fixated desire. Satiation and its denial now appear joined together as a single experience.

The insatiable features of our search for personal acceptance are normally diffused through the whole life of encounter. The insatiable aspects of our quest for the non-contingent are ordinarily invested in a social world or a transcendent reality. In the moment of addiction, however, people act as if all these elements of indefinite longing could be captured and satisfied through the achievement of a particular aim. Addiction concentrates the strongest and most immeasurable aspects of desire upon a single point. But our desires do not lose their indefinite and insatiable quality by being thus displaced and fixated.

From these facts arises the anxious mixture of contentment with dissatisfaction and of repetition with frenzy. From them springs up, as well, the strange coexistence of fixation in desire with capricious changes in the direction of addictive cravings.

Addiction requires that longing be fixed so that it may bring conduct or perception under a principle of repetition. But any particular object of desire is always incommensurable with the indefinite quality of the desire itself. The arbitrariness of the tie between the desire and its object resembles the arbitrariness of the connection between the sign and the signified in a language: addiction is a language that expresses the strongest and most obscure aspects of desire in preposterous and arbitrary forms. A particular history of individual associations may explain an individual's preference for some fixations over others. But the basic reality in addiction remains the flimsiness of the link between the craving and its objects. The reflection of this flimsiness in the subjective experience of the addict is his awareness of the obscurity of his addiction.

III

The point of departure for this analysis of the passions is the effect that the modernist view of our relation to our contexts has upon the Christian-romantic conception of intersubjectivity and personal encounter. Before working out an analysis of particular passions it may be useful to restate the modernist thesis in a form that emphasizes its message about the connection between passion and society.

The first element in the modernist thesis is the belief that the passions lack a natural social context and that to assert and develop themselves they must disobey the script that every society and culture writes for them. Moreover, the absence of a single authoritative model of social arrangements deprives the emotions of an unquestionable order. For the passions, properly understood, are nothing but the more than instrumental relations among people, relations subjectively experienced, felt, and understood.

Why must the passions resist the institutions and dogmas of society? Because only through this resistance can people keep the polarity of the passions from being overtaken and concealed by the compulsive performance of predefined social roles. And only by treating one another as individuals rather than as role-occupants can they make room for the opportunities of passion.

The second element of the modernist principle is the acknowledgment of the necessity and specificity of a collective context for the life of personal encounter. Although apparently a denial of the first principle, the second thesis can be viewed more accurately as a further specification of it. Particular social and cultural orders cannot be dispensed with even though they lack the ultimate authority that would allow them to serve as blueprints for passion. Ideas and institutions, many of them inevitably specific to a society, an age, a class, or a community, inform particular passions. The very way a person feels jealousy or vanity may depend significantly upon beliefs and arrangements that he can only partially understand and only slowly transform. Indeed, the self embarks upon a futile quest when it tries to uphold passionate attachments that float above the prosaic world of social arrangements

171

and inherited ideas. Take, for example, romantic lovers who compulsively seek an exchange of pure emotion beyond social constraint. They will find that because the sentiment they treasure is incapable of admitting a social presence and fitting into a wider set of personal responsibilities and devotions it must quickly vanish without having exercised the transformative influence that the lovers expected from it. If they are self-reflective they will also discover that their conception of love bears the marks of a well-described episode in the history of their culture.

The first two elements in the modernist principle may seem, in concert, to frustrate any hope of living out passion in a way that does not pervert its most important qualities. Together, these elements appear to pose but another variant of the twin danger that threatens, divides, and disorients the project of self-affirmation: defeat through withdrawal or defeat through submission—in this case withdrawal from the claims of established society and culture or submission to these claims. Many have indeed understood the modernist principle in this fashion, as an encouragement to seek in an empty and anguished freedom the sole alternative to enslavement and illusion.

But the modernist view of passion and society includes a third component that alters the significance of the other two. This third idea is the belief that forms of social life differ in the extent to which they enable individuals to deal with one another as persons rather than as agents of collective categories of class, sex, or community, rather than as superiors and subalterns in a fixed chain of hierarchy, rather than as passive products of a collective tradition that they are powerless to revise.

The modernist shift in our received view of solidarity must be justified by its contribution to the understanding of our immediate experience of encounter and society. The consultation of experience will become easier now that the argument advances from the fundamental nature of passion and the making of the passionate self to the study of particular passions and of the life that they compose.

Viewed individually, the passions show the transmutations of our mutual need and fear. The series of these individual emotions may seem at first to constitute a table of indestructibly distinct forms of personal encounter. But as our understanding of self and society gains greater freedom from unjustifiable preconceptions about the possibilities of experience and as social life itself becomes less embedded in a protected structure of division and hierarchy, the distinctions among the passions lose their delusive clarity. Increasingly, the passions appear to be shifting and overlapping variations on the fundamental themes of love and hate, themes that in turn enter into each other. If the passions form a system, they do so less as indistinguishable elements connected by fixed relations than as amplifications of one another.

A modernist analysis of particular passions is conducted here in the antique categories of the moralists, the discourse of virtues and vices. But this willful archaism—the outward expression of an effort to treat modernism as a moment in the transformation of the Christian-romantic view of our shared identity—should not obscure the accumulated shifts in sense to which those categories have been subject. These conversions of sense simply mirror and extend the modernist reconstruction of the Christian-romantic view of solidarity and the modernist revision of the classical style of normative argument.

By one conversion of sense, each of the categories used to label a passion combines a psychological analysis with an evaluative stance. The conversation between the analysis and the stance draws upon a practice of normative judgment that emphasizes the significance of each passion for the central polarity of the passions and treats our efforts to deal with this polarity as part of our project of self-assertion.

Through another conversion of sense, the differences among the individual passions are weakened. Each passion is conceived as no more than a typical, recurrent place within the same unified experience of mutual longing and jeopardy. And each of these places suggests insights and excites motivations that invite us to occupy other places. Precisely because the distinctions among them are so fragile, an individual passion can embody the unifying polarity of the passions.

By yet another conversion of sense, the conception of passion exemplified by this discussion of typical places refuses to define passion by contrast to rational understanding or social convention. Instead, it sees the passions as the set of elementary possibilities of human connection that overflow the constraints imposed by established institutions and preconceptions. A consequence of this approach is that a theory of the passions has implications for an understanding of the mind and of society. Precisely because it can generate epistemological and political claims it does not have to apologize for its lack of an explicit epistemological or political foundation.

My study of particular passions begins with emotions that relate only obliquely to the central polarity of longing and jeopardy but that for this very reason reveal all the more clearly the forces at work in this polarity. These experiences of passion break into social life from a position at its border; they are proto-social. They seem to arise less from the give and take of encounter than from predispositions or vulnerabilities that partly preexist, envelop, or disrupt our central experiments in sociability. They interrupt the flow of ordinary social life in ways that illuminate our relation to the contexts of our action and that show how this relation influences the experience of mutual longing and jeopardy. These passions are lust and despair.

Lust and despair are proto-social in the sense that, more than any other emotions, they seem to belong to a constitution that precedes, in force and character, our life in society. Short of the physical needs of nourishment and shelter, no impulses are less likely to await a favorable environment to assert themselves. Throughout the lives of individuals and the history of societies, they reappear as destructive forces that must be tamed or exorcised if a civil order is to subsist.

Moved by lust, the person acts as a ravenous ego driven to play a role in a biological drama that overshadows social commitments. This role enables him to experience himself as a force unable to conceive society or other people except as aids or impediments to the temporary quieting of an insatiable desire. To be sure, human sexual desire has no necessary occasions or manifestations. But though this indeterminacy may allow the desire to be more deeply informed by institutional practices and shared beliefs than would otherwise be possible, it also gives lust an insistence and pervasiveness that it would otherwise lack. In fact, the roving, unfocused quality of the desire, its frequently androgynous nature, and its potentially complete disengagement from the imperatives of reproduction all explain how lust can appear as a force that eludes the grasp of culture as well as the discipline of society.

Despair is proto-social in a similar sense. It, too, appears as an experience rooted in a capability that we bring to our involvements in society. It, too, combines the sense of drivenness with a basis in the capacity that most distinguishes our constitution: our ability to stand aside from the ordinary contexts of our activity and to wonder about their status and their authority. We can despair because we can experience ourselves as masters of a freedom of reflection that immeasurably exceeds our power to imprint our immediate personal concerns upon the social and natural worlds in which we find ourselves. We can ask more questions about our social and mental contexts than we could possibly answer. That the answers we cannot give are the only ones that matter may seem simply an unfortunate by-product of our freedom to violate the rules of the social and mental worlds we construct.

These remarks already suggest a more subtle and complicated sense of the proto-social character of lust and despair. These passions threaten not only the stability and the authority of particular forms of social life and particular styles of personal existence but the fundamental claims that society and culture make upon us. They pose this more radical challenge by disturbing our imaginative capacity to put ourselves in the attitude of mind that society—any society—demands from us and that even the simplest set of personal encounters and commitments invariably require. By attacking the imaginative foundations of our social engagements they also undermine our willingness to do the endless petty chores and to make the countless unspoken sacrifices that help sustain these engagements.

Yet even in this subversive role, despair and lust can reveal truths about ourselves that any adequate conception of the life of passion must acknowledge. These truths all have to do with our unfitness for the circumstance of mutual dependence and with our capacity to act within society as if we had not been made for society, as if we had another vocation, which the constraints of discourse and practice cannot countenance. Thus, the forms of experience and vision that we may attain in moments of lust or despair represent perpetual embarrassments to all doctrines that depict us as mere products of social institutions and cultural norms. In this fact lies the special significance of these passions for modernism and for the attempt to unite the modernist conception of our relation to the contexts of our action with the Christian-romantic view of our relation to one another. The remainder of this passage deals with lust and despair as passions that combine an opposition to particular social orders, a threat to the authority of all society and culture, and a revelation of facts about our susceptibilities and our capacities that any adequate view of the self must acknowledge.

Lust is sexual attraction untransformed by love and, more generally, uninspired by the imagination of otherness. The other person figures primarily as an indistinct source of pleasure; though particular features of his body may become the objects of an obsessional concern, their attraction does not depend upon their belonging to a complex, unique personality. It soon becomes apparent that this sacrifice of distinct individuality to indiscriminate pleasure serves simply as a point of departure: the game of pleasure quickly gives way to a contest of wills, and this contest may in turn allow for a rediscovery of distinctive selfhood in the other person.

Lust attacks the most important connecting link between biology and culture. Sexuality rebels against its service to the reproduction of society and threatens to subvert the proprieties of kinship and domesticity. It turns into a free-floating and potentially disruptive force.

But what exactly does this force jeopardize? Before our own age of mass politics and world history many cultures held up an image of human coexistence that we, children of the era of partial emancipation from false necessity, have largely rejected. This image proposed a model of human coexistence that saw power, exchange, and communal allegiance as naturally and properly merged in the same personal encounters. Its program was to turn all society into a world of patrons and clients. Its conviction was that this universalized clientalism represents the sole alternative to savage social warfare and rampant egotism. Rigidified power relations became the assumed context of practical exchange. The unstable, self-regarding aspects of exchange were in turn to be moderated by the recognition of mutual loyalties that restrain each party's willingness to exact from the other—superior or subordinate—whatever circumstances allow. Though this model of human association was usually meant to apply to every area of social life, its most exemplary context of application characteristically remained the family and the immediate community. Indeed, its proponents often argued that all social relations between masters and underlings or between rulers and subjects ought to be modeled on a certain idealized pattern of family life.

Wherever this conception of the possible and desirable forms of human association commands allegiance, lust appears as a dissolving force because it disobeys the standards of the patron-client relation. But in the course of helping to destroy this relation it may also reveal the opportunity for an alternative style of coexistence. For no sooner does lust pass from the pursuit of pleasure into the contest of wills than it suggests that this contest may change the power relations in which the established forms of community and exchange are embedded.

The same point can be recast in more general terms, terms that show how a loveless experience of sexuality may exercise this destructive and constructive effect even when the ideal of patrons and clients has lost its authority. Lust always strikes a note of uncontrolled personal assertion. The sexualization of power relations resembles physical violence and collective conflict in its ability to generate connections and combinations that established institutions and ruling dogma cannot accept. The petty, comic struggles to which this sexualization gives rise easily become vehicles for the assertion of needs, and of means for the satisfaction of needs, that the existing order disregards. Thus, in the harem, taken as a metaphor for a society devoted to the quest for pleasure, conflict over the basic terms of collective life is supposed to be reduced to a minimum. (Remember Montesquieu.) Obedience masquerades as surrender to sensuality. Yet the capacity of the women to seduce the eunuchs who keep them and the master who enjoys them, and to excite their jealousy and distrust, works as a sinister and unaccountable force, capable of disorganizing even what it may be powerless to reconstruct. For our desires have an indeterminate and equivocal quality: those that cannot be entirely suppressed serve as means to assert others, more easily quashed, and the dreams that have been banished from the public world reappear in the private one. The most stubborn of these dreams and desires are those that express our longing to be accepted and to be cared for.

Thus, lust may represent an assault against a particular form of social life, an assault that helps create in the minute domain of personal encounter anticipatory images of an alternative social order. Lust may also, however, pose a more radical challenge to the imaginative foundations of social life. It may do so by diminishing our ability to imagine the otherness of other people.

The more we deny the originality of other people, the more impoverished and rigid our conception of society becomes. We see one another as the compulsive products of our forms of social life and our traditions of discourse rather than seeing these traditions and forms as partial and provisional manifestations of ourselves. Because no set of social arrangements and cultural dogmas can ever fully inform our practical and passionate connections, no degree of entrenchment of a social and cultural order against effective challenge can ever justify the imaginative denial of originality in ourselves and in others.

The extreme of this denial is our attempt to reduce others to the condition of mere occasions for the enjoyment of solitary pleasures, if indeed pleasure is not solitary by its very nature. A lesser extreme of denial is the view of other people as resistant egos in a power conflict or as strategic calculators in a system of exchange that is imagined to require only an endless flow of random desires and a stable set of neutral roles. Here you already begin to see the other person as a distinct and potentially opposing will even though you may not credit him with a more richly defined form of subjective experience. Having recognized this minimum of distinction you open yourself to the possibility of being surprised: the desired person may succeed in forcing to your attention not an isolated desire to be traded against a desire of your own but a unique personality in search of acceptance, or he may give voice to a conception of the proper terms of your material and emotional access to each other that conflicts with yours.

The radical denial of otherness and therefore of society that is implied by lust consists in the solipsistic experience of other people as mere triggers to moments of enjoyment. The origin of pleasure in the body of another person is accompanied by the ability not to imagine him as being, in any interesting sense, another person. To this extent an episode of lust provides us with a momentary experience of what it would be like for society not to exist.

But every experience of enjoyment already incorporates

something of a conflict of wills: the others must be excluded. In lust this exclusion takes on a more dramatic sense, for it is the very source of the pleasure who must be prevented from speaking and acting as the radically unique and independent individual he in fact is. Thus, if all our experiences of pleasure tend to become overlaid by the exercise of power, or of the fight about power, the superimposition is all the more inevitable in sexual life. Nowhere is this passage from pleasure-hoarding to power conflict more clearly demonstrated than in the facility with which lust takes a sadistic or a masochistic turn. Having begun with a complete absorption in our pleasures and a cultivated blindness to their source, we are soon drawn into a conflict of wills that changes the character and diminishes the force of our denial of the otherness of other people. What is now denied is the possibility of reconciling two independent selves in the same relation: you must strenuously deny either to yourself (masochism) or to the other (sadism) the condition of a self that seeks and deserves acceptance by other selves. You thereby give an unequivocally negative answer to the question posed by the central polarity of the passions—whether we can reconcile the enabling conditions of self-assertion.

The lust that has moved from naive pleasure-seeking to anxious power play sees no self-assertion that is not also isolation. As a model of personal encounter, it therefore condemns us to give up hope of changing the relation between our need to be accepted by other people and to participate together with them in shared forms of life and our need to keep and develop an independent agency. The abandonment of this hope is in turn the very core of the experience of despair; this similarity already begins to suggest how the two proto-social passions connect.

Yet this extreme instance of surrender to a despairing vision of frozen personal relations offers an opportunity for its own correction. The resisting object of a loveless desire waits for a chance to show who he is. The most insignificant interludes of awkwardness, distraction, or disappointment may serve to disclose the real individual. And when at last he makes himself heard he does so in a circumstance that emphasizes his surprising individuality all the more. For in the sexually obsessed encounter that begins by seeking in pleasure an alternative to society and then passes from an unsocial enjoyment to a stark confrontation of wills, the categories of social division and hierarchy may be placed at a greater distance than in much of ordinary experience. The object of lust may therefore appear all the more clearly, when he does appear, as the unique, unexpected individual he always is. And once you recognize the other person for the individual he is, you may be able to imagine a form of connection with him in particular—and with other people in general—that moderates the conflict between the enabling conditions of self-assertion.

Thus, lust may anticipate the dynamic of love, whose absence seemed to define its very nature. In a sexually realized love the sequence of responses includes an awareness that the other wants you in your embodied shape, and it culminates in the experience of suffusion by involuntary bodily activity, indeed by an activity oriented toward another person in his embodiment. You overcome your repugnance for the flesh of another person, and you do so in a way that confronts you in the most unequivocal fashion with your own existence as flesh. As soon as the other is shown to be more than an indistinct source of pleasure or a resistant will, the contrast between lust and love loses its force and gives way to an impulse of assertion and longing: longing for the incarnate other, assertion of the incarnate self.

The most general relevance of lust to an understanding of the self now becomes clear. Our embodiment, and the whole sensuous character of our experience that goes along with it, makes possible the imaginative disenfranchisement of the other person and the consequent petrification of the central polarity of the passions. But by making us bodies that collide and that crave one another, this incarnation also helps make it impossible for us to seal ourselves off completely from other people. We would have to be disembodied spirits to achieve either a complete isolation or a total transparency and communion.

Despair is the other proto-social passion. The central experience of despair lies in the overlaying of two events: a felt inability to reconcile our need and our fear of other people and a conviction that our basic circumstance in the world makes this reconciliation impossible. When we despair we experience the unavailability of the root freedom that consists in the ability to act upon alternate conceptions of our immediate relations to other people. Such conceptions offer to limit the conflict between the enabling conditions of self-assertion, and they promise us opportunities of attachment that serve also as occasions for the discovery and development of an independent identity. But the distinctive quality of despair is that this perceived impossibility of freedom arises less from our view of other people than from an understanding of the settings in which our personal activities are embedded, all the way from the idiosyncratic routines of relationship that betray a character to the social and natural framework of our lives. The imaginative basis of despair should be expected to appear in a specific way of experiencing blockage in our personal encounters. These distinguishing, intimate manifestations of our "imagination of disaster" are here the chief object of concern.

Note that the idea of despair circumvents the modern psychiatric distinction between ordinary sadness and clinical depression. These psychiatric conceptions describe different degrees of the same ordeal of impossibility. Even when the more severe instances of this ordeal can be traced to a discrete and predominant biological cause, the internal imaginative structure of the experience remains the same. The more serious and biologically based cases may in fact reveal more fully a conception of our situation that the moderate and psychological instances present only in truncated form. (See the Appendix to this essay.)

There is a despair of imprisonment and a despair of strangeness. Each can jeopardize our willingness to engage actively either in a particular society or in any society. When the target of despair becomes a particular social order, the criticism implicit in this despair may serve as a principle of social reconstruction. Even when despair takes the more uncompromising direction of an attack upon the very foundations of culture it teaches a lesson about our constitution and our capabilities that can exercise a constructive influence upon the reformation of character and society.

Take first the despair of imprisonment. Its most familiar mode is grief over the loss of other people and over the breaking of the bonds that united us to them. The sorrow we feel for the other's sake combines here with a sorrow we feel for ourselves. This ordinary grief passes into despair when its focus becomes a disbelief in our ability to reaffirm and reconstruct our individual identities in the absence of the relations that have been destroyed. Thus, the special quality of this despair stands out more clearly when its occasion is the disappearance of an entire complex of relations, perhaps even of a richly defined way of life.

The abandonment of faith in the capacity to survive the loss of certain relations would not become a cause of despair unless the person also obscurely felt in himself a personality that transcends these or any other relations. Many aspects of his experience testify to the basic circumstance that the modernist view of our relation to the contexts of our action has tried to illuminate: our inability to find enough room for insight, desire, and practical or passionate attachment in any of the mental and social worlds that we construct and temporarily inhabit. The individual is therefore torn between the intimation that he is more than a given series of social relations and the apprehension that he cannot survive their disappearance.

The despair of imprisonment also occurs in another, reversed, and less familiar mode. Here it becomes our experienced inability to free ourselves from a group of routines—to stand apart from them and to revise them or to reenter them on more independent and self-conscious terms. Rather than doubting his capacity to survive the disappearance of the familiar relational setting of his life, the person doubts instead his power to escape or to change this setting. But because he continues to understand the transcending power of his own self, what might otherwise have been experienced as a freely given participation begins to be felt instead as an imprisoning compulsion—a shift that emphasizes the link between compulsion and despair. In both forms of the despair of imprisonment, the force of the emotion grows out of the inability to reconcile the awareness of transcending selfhood with the recognition of the dependence of the self upon particular relations.

The quality of the prison may be attributed to an entire form of social life rather than merely to the immediate routines of a character. Even in this more general form, however, the indispensable basis of this despair remains the inability of the person to act upon the idea that his attachments can make him free. Because he imagines his situation as he does, he fails to undertake the personal experiments that might enable him to reconstruct his familiar settings or to reconstruct himself in their absence. And because he fails to undertake these experiments voluntarily, or to seize the elements of involuntary opportunity in his situation, his actual experience begins to lend a trumped-up support to his preconceptions.

Alongside the despair of imprisonment there is a despair of strangeness. The keynote to this second style of despair is the inability to make sense of the settings of our personal lives in terms that can be related to our most urgent concerns and in particular to the dynamic of mutual longing and jeopardy. This failure of connection is experienced as undermining our ability to reconcile the enabling conditions of self-assertion.

The despair of strangeness may be directed against a particular, institutionalized way of life. In every stable social order the indefinite possibilities of human association are soon exchanged for allegiance to a scheme of authoritative models of human association. This scheme allows people to understand and to elaborate a system of rights as more than tools or expressions of coercive power. In looser form it makes everyday life intelligible.

The scheme may propose the same exemplary form of

human connection for every area of social existence. (Remember the situation of the reappearing patron-client principle.) But it may also, in the manner of our own societies, assign different models of human association to different spheres of social life. Some of these models—like the modern Western ideas of private familial community or of citizenship within a democratic nation—portray forms of attachment that also serve as avenues to self-affirmation. Others, like the mixture of contractual agreement and technical hierarchy to which we abandon our workaday lives, make no such promise; their alleged justification lies in the risks of impracticality and despotism that any attempt to replace them by more morally ambitious forms of human connection is thought to entail.

Societies may therefore differ in the extent to which they recognize areas of social practice to be connected with the problem posed by the polarity of the passions. The greater the range of everyday experience that seems incapable of being translated into the language of core personal concerns, the broader the role for desperation about ordinary life. This desperation, however, invites us to imagine a reform of social arrangements that would in fact introduce more deeply into our everyday existence forms of human connection that encourage us to reimagine, and enable us to reconstruct, the relation between independent individuality and personal or communal attachment.

The subject of the despair of strangeness may grow to include social life itself, rather than any particular social order, and the place of society and culture within nature. The individual may see social life as nestled within a broader natural setting that renders illusory or insignificant our concerns of mutual longing and jeopardy while denying us any way to escape these concerns. He may, for example, reject all conceptions of social life except one that can be formulated in the language of natural science. On such a view, the vocabulary in which we deal with one another, rich as it is with the preoccupations of passion, cannot be taken seriously on its own terms. Alternatively, this more radical despair may assume the form of the belief that our human communities of sense and affect are groundless: that nothing outside them justifies the urgent concerns and the evaluative judgments that so preoccupy them. All we can do, according to this doctrine, is to pick a social and cultural world and to take this world for reality. On such a view, the natural and social settings of human activity are hostile to the sense with which we endow the life of passion, because they are incapable of supporting any sense at all.

Yet it is not necessary to draw from the perception of groundlessness—or from the discontinuity between society and nature—the conclusion reached by the despair of strangeness. After all, one of the most notorious variants of modernism does just the opposite: it infers from the idea of groundlessness an additional reason to acknowledge the evaluative sovereignty and self-sufficiency of our specific traditions. (Remember the joke about Leibniz. The optimist says: This is the best of all possible worlds. The pessimist answers: You're right.) The imaginative conception that underlies the despair of strangeness must be confirmed by a felt inability to break through the frozen character of personal relations and thereby to moderate the conflict between the bases of self-assertion.

The possibility of radicalizing despair—the despair of imprisonment or the despair of strangeness—into a break with confident engagement in a life of encounter and commitment always depends upon a troubled relation to the contexts of our action. The despair of imprisonment emphasizes the difficulty of affirming our transcendence over the particular relationships in which our individual identities are invariably entangled. The despair of strangeness depends instead upon the suspicion that we must live out our lives in circumstances that are fundamentally indifferent and even antagonistic to our most intimate aims and that make the pursuit of these aims hostage to illusion.

But whatever the imaginative emphasis the crucial point turns out to be the perceived inability to act upon the belief that the relation between our mutual jeopardy and our mutual longing might be reformed. Having attributed this inability to an ineradicable feature of our situation in the world, we then find in the resulting pattern of conduct and awareness the spurious confirmation of our initial view. Our sense of blockage in the most intimate core of personal relations engulfs ever-broader areas of our experience. We surrender to repetitious forms of behavior and perception that we are unable to recognize either as expressions of our selves or as possible objects of transformative activity. But because we can never give ourselves just compulsively even to our most unreflective compulsions we must find in a despairing conception of our circumstances an argument for our behavior. Thus the analysis of despair reveals the link between the compulsive and the saturnine elements in everyday experience. The constraint upon personal possibility and possible personal relationship is imagined as despair and lived out as unhappy repetition.

This imagined and enacted constraint represents the central element in all psychopathology. Indeed, the analysis of despair suggests the indispensable features of any successful psychotherapy that approaches mental disturbance through discourse, encounter, and action rather than through physical or pharmacological intervention. First, the main topic of such a psychotherapy must be the character of the individual's passionate attachments to other individuals and especially the problem of reconciling the enabling conditions of self-assertion. Second, the psychotherapy must seek to persuade the patient that he can reimagine his relation to other people and act upon this new conception in ways that permit self-assertion through attachment and engagement. Though a story about how the unnecessary constraint or appearance of constraint arose in the first place may be an important part of this act of persuasion, it is not a necessary part. Third, a version of the more extended possibility of personal relation must be enacted in the therapeutic setting. And the enactment must take a form that enables the patient to replicate the new style of association on a larger scale, outside that setting.

In the collective life of society we also find ourselves the relatively passive victims of institutional arrangements and imaginative preconceptions. Political emancipation from unresisting submission to these constraints advances by means that parallel those of psychotherapy. The issues addressed are now far broader than the form that the enabling conditions of self-assertion take in the life of passion. Yet the contest over factional interests depends upon background assumptions about possible alternative sets of institutional arrangements and social alliances. Men fight for their interests, Hume observed, but what their interests are is a matter of opinion. Among the most important of these interest-defining opinions are those that define the range of realizable collective contexts within which we might pursue our supposed interests. As the scope of collective conflict and of seriously considered alternatives broadens, the struggle of interests merges into a larger contest over the varieties and bases of individual and collective empowerment.

One version of this empowerment is the development of practical capabilities through socially organized problem-solving. Another version is the diminishment of the conflict between our need for other people's practical or emotional help and the justified fear of subjection that they inspire in us (a conflict that generalizes the clash between the enabling conditions of self-assertion as we find it in the life of passion). Both these varieties of empowerment require not only that social relations be jumbled up but that they be kept in a state of heightened plasticity. This condition, signaled by a softening of the contrast between context-preserving routines and context-revising disputes, is itself a mode of empowerment as well as a requirement of the other two modes, for it gives us mastery over the social settings of action. The state of heightened plasticity must be anticipated in the escalating conflicts and localized deviations that help bring it about. The partial, anticipatory realization of more empowering forms of human association, by the social movements that advocate them or the anomalous forms of current practice that exemplify them, represents the political counterpart to the therapeutic rehearsal of broader possibilities of personal connection.

In every social situation there are many small deviations from the dominant institutional and imaginative order. Some of these aberrations result from the historical superimposition of the residues of past schemes of social life, others from the need constantly to adapt a given scheme to new circumstances, others yet from the failure of any scheme fully to inform our experience of direct practical collaboration or passionate attachment. The art of persuasion that accompanies a transformative political practice consists in seizing upon these deviations. It shows how they can beat their better-established rivals at their own game, whether the game is one of practical efficiency or of fidelity to accepted ideals. And it demonstrates, more by practice than by teaching, that, once they are suitably revised, these locally successful exceptions can become new dominant principles in their own right.

In both the psychological and the political settings the enlargement of possibility may be temporarily served by a myth that appeals to false necessity. Such a myth may see an alternative, more empowering and revisable social order as the outcome of a compulsive social evolution. It may assure us that emancipation will grow out of constraint, and it may relieve its adherent of the need to describe the structure of the world that he desires. Or the falsehood may consist in a story that locates the source of constraint in localized aspects of his experience, like his early childhood life in the family. Such an account tells him that he may understand the source of his compulsions and of his despair and act upon a wider view of relational possibility in ways that nevertheless minimize the need to break with more pervasive features of his present life or his society.

But though such assurances may prove expedient in the cause of emancipation, they exact a price. Like the impostor who fools himself, the believer will not know when to stop taking them seriously. He may think himself at odds with constraints that do not in fact exist (the Marxist's preconceptions about possible class alliances, the Freudian's exhortation to confront the legacy of specific family entanglements or sexual drives). He may excuse himself from tasks that are indispensable to higher degrees of emancipation. (Thus, the Freudian fails to imagine the forms of self-assertion that might be possible beyond the boundaries of an isolated, self-regarding middle-class existence, and the Marxist fails to do the hard work of conceiving detailed institutional alternatives to the present forms of governmental and economic organization and the strategies of transition that might make them possible.) Better to have a theory of society and of the self that does not traduce its program in its arguments. Indeed, an aim of this essay is to contribute to such a theory.

This discussion of lust and despair yields an initial perspective upon the entire life of passion. The desolation of the heart has its basis in our inability to find the true image of ourselves, as living personalities or inquiring minds, in any particular set of social relations or mental constructs. If we could discover the natural context for desire and discourse—the one that accommodates all true discoveries and all worthwhile forms of human connection—we might also have a way to make ourselves transparent to one another. We would know exactly what it would be like to feel like another person in another situation. Instead of deploying tedious measures to gain an uncertain access to other minds, we would need only to analyze the built-in structure of this shared context in order to see our common nature. The canonical social order would sustain, and be sustained by, a canonical ordering of the emotions within each of us; a natural character would match a natural society. And the words by which we report our subjective experience would possess indisputable and stable meanings.

Because no such natural context exists you can subject other people to the imperialism of your images. When you experience this lack of access to another mind as a bar to changing the relation between your need of him and the jeopardy in which he (as a representative of everyone else) places you, your self-absorption becomes despair. It does so by denying you the means with which either to distinguish yourself from the immediate relational setting of your life (the despair of imprisonment) or to connect this setting to your most intimate concerns for acceptance and empowerment (the despair of strangeness). For the instrument of the connection is the same as the instrument of the distinction: engagement with other people, with people whose independent reality you are able to imagine and accept. It is the imagination of otherness that the practice of self-absorption chiefly destroys.

The fantasy of a natural context gains a second-order reality to the extent that the institutional and imaginative order of social life becomes immunized against the destabilizing effects of ordinary conflict. Because no social world can ensure the hallucinatory recognition of its own necessity and completely exclude experiments in association that violate its institutional or imaginative assumptions, no social world can guarantee us against despair. But the weaker the authority of the naturalistic claim, the less guarded against despair we become.

Lust can now be reinterpreted as the circumstance in which sexual desire expresses self-absorption rather than helping to overcome it. You do not truly experience lust—just as you do not truly experience despair—until you come, however dimly, to recognize this self-absorption for what it is. Once the acknowledgment that another person stands before you joins with the inability to imagine him concretely, and to act upon this imagination, the stage is set for the contest of wills that changes uncomplicated physical delight into the more subtle trial of lust.

The whole family of our confrontations with lust and despair makes patent the permanent disturbance of our relations to one another that results from the absence of an unconditional context of action. To retake categories advanced in the Introduction, everything happens as if the problem of contextuality had been sucked into the problem of solidarity. We are prevented from solving the latter without solving the former. This merger of the two problems—clearer here than in any other aspect of the life of passion—accounts for the extraordinary interest that these proto-social emotions hold for a modernist sensibility.

The source of the disturbance is also a basis for hope.

Because we lack a natural context, we can change both individual character and social order in ways that help us to reconcile more fully the enabling conditions of self-assertion. Because our encounters bring into question our relation to our characterological and collective settings, we can change these settings in the course of dealing, practically or passionately, with one another. We can alter not only the content but the quality of our routines, the sense in which they are routines at all.

By so doing, we can expose ourselves more completely to the dynamics of practical reason and of passion. The former opens social life to invention and recombination. The latter makes us capable of love through the same wrenching out from compulsive action and frozen vision by which it makes us susceptible to lust and despair. For if love is the very antithesis of lust and despair in its message about the compatibility between the supports of self-assertion, it resembles those emotions in its apostasy from the automatisms of society and character and in the urgency that it imparts to the ordinary events of an ordinary life.

So you can begin to see at this early stage in the analysis of particular passions the direction taken by the existential project whose foundations this essay discusses. The effort to diminish the interference between our need for acceptance and support and the danger that we pose to one another is the general form of our quest for freedom. Though the nature of this quest is nowhere clearer than in the domain of passion, the structure of the difficulty is the same as in our practical and cognitive activities. As we move into the internal description of passion we should keep this recurrent pattern in mind.

In every theater of our experience, the empowerment that comes from moderating the conflict between the conditions of self-assertion requires and produces a change in our relation to our contexts. Whether the context in question is a style of discourse and explanation, a formative institutional and imaginative framework of social life, or even an individual character, the change to be sought always has the same quality. An order must be invented that, considered from one standpoint, minimizes the obstacles to our experiments in problem-solving and in accepted vulnerability and, viewed from another perspective, multiplies the instruments and opportunities for its own revision. Such an order represents the next best thing to the unconditional context whose unavailability helps make us what we are. Its characterological form is a central concern of this inquiry; its cognitive and political versions are suggested in passing.

We face two overriding problems. One is that the requirements of self-assertion conflict. The other is that though we must settle down to particular contexts, no contexts in particular do justice to our desires and capabilities. We understand ourselves by discovering the unsuspected ways in which these two problems get implicated in each other. We empower ourselves by holding on to both sides of these dilemmas and by inventing, through forms of life and stratagems of imagination, the freedom that is possible despite their insolubility and because of their insolubility.

Hatred, vanity, jealousy, and envy all define a unique failure in our attempt to accept one another's presence in the world. Each of these passions has a center that unites its many seemingly disparate manifestations. In each case this core idea has to do with a special blockage upon the resolution of our mutual longing and jeopardy into that convergence of mutual vulnerability and mutual confirmation in being that defines the economy of love.

Hatred overshadows the ground of the vices. It involves a total rejection of the other: an abandonment of the hope that his existence might reaffirm your own. Your being is threatened and diminished by the other's mere present or past existence.

This radical incompatibility transcends any particular conflict of interests or ideals, even though it may be sparked by such conflicts and certainly will help create new ones or aggravate old ones. The perception of irreconcilability is based, instead, upon a root experience of antagonism that occurs in the realm of personality rather than in the sphere of interests or ideals. This fact provides the key to an understanding of the way hatred relates to the fundamental problem of association.

Through every encounter of his life, an individual tries to determine whether his existence as a developed person can be made compatible with the affirmation of his fellows. Hatred is just the despair of such a reconciliation, a despair transfigured by a sense of the urgency and immediacy of the matter into an active rejection of the hated person. Though the content of this rejection is likely to be peculiarly opaque, its characteristic theme is always that the very being of the hated individual represents an assault on your being. In the purer and more terrible forms of hatred the force of this assault tends to become almost independent of what the hated person in fact does or of how he actually threatens the hater's capacity to achieve his own aims.

This foreshadowing of absolute antagonism can be distinguished from the mixed and therefore weakened forms of hatred. You need other people not just as providers of goods and services but as subjects who can acknowledge you as a person with certain qualities and who can allow you to change by sharing with you opportunities for collaboration and conflict. Will you manage to gain their favor and acknowledgment only by believing as they believe and acting as they act? This is hatred in the direction of fear. Will they take advantage of your need of them to put you down? This is hatred in the direction of distrust. Will they stand for things that negate the aims by which you define yourself? This is hatred in the direction of repugnance or contempt.

Any form of social life enmeshes people in a reciprocal testing of their respective claims to be what they are as well as of their claims to particular things and roles. The encounter with another person always raises the question: Does this other existence confirm my own or merely undermine it? It is always possible to abandon hope in reconciliation. It is also always possible to treat this opposition as intolerable because it exercises a direct pressure on your personality, a pressure that, though stronger than any other force in the world save love, may carry no hint of tangible harm. Hatred is the combined realization of these two possibilities.

The experience of this urgent antagonism can be described either as a judgment or as a response in which judgment plays no part. Like any other passion, hatred never crosses the threshold at which the cognitive and the non-cognitive aspects of personality diverge.

Hatred disorganizes the perception of reality by constantly forcing conflict beyond the point of support by people's professed or justifiable stakes in particular outcomes. In the end, hatred clouds the individual's ability to define clearly the aims of his action and thus corrupts his capacity to understand himself. Above all, hatred prompts people to underestimate radically the opportunity to reconcile the enabling conditions of self-assertion.

Remember that direct personal encounter is the starting point and model of all our experiences of social life. It teaches the only lessons about what we may or may not hope for in social life that we cannot easily forget. Thus, hatred is the event in history that most tenaciously predisposes people to disbelieve in the possibility of changing the conditions that can make longing and jeopardy advance toward risk and reconciliation. The possibility of such a progression is the master key to all other possibilities of association, just as the claim to *be,* which hatred denies the hated person, underlies all more specific demands.

Vanity is the surrender of self-esteem to the opinions of other people. Each individual must wrestle with a paradox of dependence. He needs other people's acknowledgment of his being and worth if he is to develop a picture of himself, an assurance of his capabilities, and a grasp of his limitations. The easiest way to obtain this acceptance is to think as others think and to act as they act; indeed, beyond a point of tolerated deviation it is the only way. Yet the more a person delivers himself as a hostage to the views of others, the more he is seized by an apprehension of the arbitrariness of his own identity and worth, based as they then are upon the shifting and conventional preconceptions of his fellows. To assuage this fear, which touches the very center of his being, he must seek more and more the narcotic of approval. The cure worsens the disease. To be vain is to give up hope of breaking this addiction.

Like all other vices, vanity is an offshoot of hatred. It is a special and softened form of the despair of reconciliation. You come to terms with the existence of other people by making a deal with them: they lend you their approval, and you in turn guarantee them the obedience of imitation. Instead of rejecting their claim to independent existence you reject your own.

Both rejections, however, express a fundamental disbelief in the possibility of mutual vulnerability and confirmation. This disbelief implies a devaluation of the other person that is less complete than that of hatred but analogous to it: the other is reduced to the role of consensus meter and approval dispenser and thereby denied his uniqueness. Nobody becomes a servant without managing to punish his masters.

But to grasp the full force of vanity you must understand how the moral predicament to which it responds parallels the quandary of the mind in the world. Sense is ultimately parasitic upon consensus, but only ultimately. You are confirmed in the assurance of sanity by the ability to persuade other people that what you say makes sense, though it may be false. Yet these others who are to be persuaded may sometimes be a distant or future humanity rather than the actual people who surround you.

What does this power to appeal from an actual community of discourse to a hypothetical community imply for your relations to your interlocutors? It means that you can break some of the rules of sense and nevertheless continue to hope that you may be understood by the very minds whose rules you are breaking. For if distant or future people might be converted to the use of the new criteria of sense that underlie your perplexing expressions, so might these very people who stand before you. In both cases the chance of conversion rests on the power of reason to transcend the criteria of sense that it employs: it is possible to discover something true that does not yet make sense and then to formulate the rules that will make the newfound truth accessible to other minds.

Each time you try to expand the bounds of sense you run the risk of failing to persuade. If you assume this risk too often, and lose too frequently, you are deprived of the means to distinguish in yourself sanity from madness. If, however, you undertake the risk too seldom, you can discover only those truths about the world whose expression is allowed by the necessarily limited conventions of an established community of speech and perception. In any real-life situation this wholehearted acquiescence in the reigning canons of discourse never entirely prevents people from seeing and discussing experiences that those canons simply fail to accommodate. Even the plainest and shortest life is full of such subversive events.

Moreover, unless you succeed in occasionally distinguishing sense from consensus, your attitude toward knowledge will be flawed in one of two ways. You may remain unreflectively within a single universe of discourse, convinced that it covers the entire province of reason. Or you may understand the specificity of this universe and yet suppose that there is no way to break out of the shell of one established universe or another. All that is left is to choose your own world of talk and to play by its rules; the quest for sense and for truth itself becomes a matter of obedience to the conventionalism of culture. The hope of escaping the dialectic of naiveté and relativism in the life of the mind calls for something that must be an experienced achievement before it can become an argued conviction: the power of sense both to build upon consensus and to outgrow it.

The refusal to venture this reaching out of sense beyond consensus is the cognitive side of vanity. It is the temptation to surrender unreservedly to other people the criteria that govern our self-esteem as beings who know more than our assumptions allow.

Vanity does not need this cognitive parallel to affect preconceptions about reality and possibility. The quest of the vain person for prestige either reconfirms or disrupts these preconceptions. In your vanity you search out the approval of other people—less as a means to an independent objective than as an end in itself. You succeed. You are puffed up, you preen yourself, strike poses, act toward others in ways you would not have dared before—all the while more or less attentive to the ingratiation and threats of those who surround you. The chorus of applause misleads you into thinking you can go further than you can in fact. Suddenly someone calls your bluff. You are insulted, frustrated, or attacked. The balloon of self-infatuation deflates if it does not explode. You are forced back into line: made to realize that you have run afoul of the tacit standards about the conduct right or realistic in your situation.

You now have a choice. You may respond to the pain of humiliation by falling back into place and refocusing on the picture of propriety and reality that your narcissism had clouded. By accepting resolutely though dejectedly the settled code of proper behavior, you also embrace the conception of social reality and human possibility that goes with it.

But there is another, defiant response to the wreck of vanity. You may respond by confronting the links that exist between notions of propriety and differentials of power, the astonishing influence that these ties exercise over your conceptions of what can be done in or with society, and therefore also the vulnerability of these conceptions themselves to changes in the way society is ordered and people interact. These confrontations may seem a great deal to expect from so petty a setback. But as the instances of overextension and retrenchment accumulate, you are thrown off balance; at repeated but unpredictable intervals you get out of joint with the pressures of communal life.

This condition of temporary though reappearing unsettledness may tempt you to identify all the more tenaciously what should or might be with what is. But it may also predispose you to perceive how your freedom of maneuver is constrained by established routines that are at once premises about how people ought to act and assumptions about the limited number of shapes that can be given to the life of passion. The infringement of such routines provokes an outrage that is motivated by a complicated blend of ideas of right and beliefs about the normal.

The very same circumstances that uncover this tyranny of habit also expose its roots in the power that people are in fact able to bring to bear upon one another. For it is power that in the end bursts the balloon and confronts the vain man with the bitter fact of his dependence. But what power helps create, power may destroy. Thus, in being called to heel, the victim receives an intimation of the fragility of the very standards in whose name he has been brought down.

Vanity often coexists with an experience that at first seems like its very opposite. This is the holding back we call pride. The core of pride is the refusal to acknowledge—or at least the determination to act as if you did not acknowledge—your actual dependence upon other people's opinion of you. That is the sense in which pride is a vice, an impediment to the resolution of your mutual longing and fear into an experience of reciprocal vulnerability to hurt and confirmation in being. It is also the sense in which pride represents the antithesis of vanity. But common usage places this narrower conception of pride in a more ample, indistinct setting, where it straddles the territories of virtue and vice. In this more inclusive sense pride is simply a willful assertion of the reality of the self: of the worth of its projects and the depth of its freedom, against all constraint, adversity, or condemnation. The significance of this assertion of the self—its meaning as virtue or vice—depends on the specific place it occupies in a life: that is to say, on whether or not pride allows for an acceptance of vulnerability and for an ability to reconcile accepted vulnerability with self-expression and self-possession. Even this penumbral enlarge-

ment of the idea of pride will turn out to be justified by the subtle-
ties of this passion.

There is a paradoxical relation between our ordinary understanding of pride and our common observation of its role in
the life of the passion. We often see pride as the opposite of
vanity. But everyone knows that proud people are often vain.
Sometimes they show us one of these sides, sometimes the other.
Sometimes they crave approval unabashedly; sometimes they ostentatiously refuse it. Sometimes they make a spectacle of their
abasement to what other people say; sometimes, a show of asser-
tiveness in the face of common opinion.

Even when a proud man displays nothing but pride, we suspect that he covers up the traces of a secret vanity: that he does in
fact care desperately about what other people say and think of
him. This surprising element in our observations leaves its mark
on our ideas: though, when pressed, we may define vanity and
pride as the contrasting elements of a pair, we may also forget the
contrast altogether and treat them, more loosely, as the same
thing. This looseness is more than justified; it is the key to a correct understanding of pride.

Pride is the bad conscience of vanity. It *is* vanity, in the
form of a special variation. But the variation is so tightly connected to the theme, and so often trades places with it, that vanity
and pride are best treated as two aspects of the same passion.

Start with the generic idea of pride as a holding back: the
self willfully affirms its weight and worth despite the radical contingency of its presence in nature and society, the unavoidability
of its dependence upon other people, and most especially the
power of its need to be accepted by other people. Try now to pull
apart the strings of the passion, so often tied together in the most
complicated experiences of pride; only then can you find out what
it is and how it relates to vanity.

First, there is the element of denial of false vulnerability:
the tacit claim that you can do things—indeed, exist—in a way
that does not depend for its value upon other people's applause.

Your moral and material need of others does not in fact make you hostage to a consensus, so that vanity is never just an unavoidable acknowledgment of the way things are. You trust that your devotion—to your work, to your allegiances, to your principled judgment of right—will ransom you. Your withdrawal from many kinds of social relations is a device of self-expression and prudence. You refuse to give the appearance of accepting the authority of other people's opinions and you protect your commitments from the attacks or flatteries that might endanger them. Your pride may be justified: the trust in devotion as the antidote to vanity may be the ennobling element in pride, like righteous indignation in the equally confused and inclusive experience of envy.

The second element in the larger ordeal of pride is the effort to hold back from other people in order to resist vanity. You feel the seduction of vanity. You break loose of many social entanglements as part of the very process by which you assert the reality and worth of the self. But your way of breaking loose commits you drastically to compress the front on which you expose yourself to other people. By displaying so ostentatiously your autonomy, you stand aloof from others; you do not subject yourself to the risk of the equivocal, the ridiculous, the humiliating. Yet the cunning of removal is no wiser than the despairing assumptions on which it rests.

All this standing apart from entanglement produces a hardening of the self. By withdrawing from a range of morally dangerous but also promising situations, you deny yourself, to that extent, the means of self-transformation. Endured vulnerability allows you to remake character. The effort to escape from vanity by donning a coat of armor against one of the characteristic modes of vulnerability—the power that other people's opinions exercise over you—binds you all the more tightly to your character by diminishing your freedom to experiment in your personal dealings. Escaping from one form of weakness of the self you narrow down the area within which self-expression can take place and the lengths to which self-reconstruction can go. The citadel may be fortified, but it remains a citadel—with all the constraints on experience that this closure implies. You know all this; and your knowledge of it, however inarticulate, is part of your acquaintance with pride.

The crucial distinction between this element in pride and the strand described earlier lies in the nature of the flight from vanity. In one case vanity is experienced as horrible merely because it involves a form of subjection. The effort to escape subjection, born in the desire to shut off a special vulnerability, is achieved at the cost of a rigidification of character, a contraction of experience. In the other instance the holding back is animated by a sense that other people in general—or a specific group of other people—lack the authority to give or to deny you worth and reality. This sense gains strength from a devotion to another source of reality and worth. Yet in our actual experience of pride these two orientations are so often mixed together that even the keenest self-scrutiny may be unable to tell them apart.

For one thing, there is a recurrent ambiguity in the justification of pride. More often than not, the claim to be indifferent to the views that other people form of you is simply a recourse to a more impersonal but equally conventional standard of judgment: think of the pretense of the aristocrat to express in his being and his deeds the excellence of his caste. Vanity is thereby refined and disguised rather than undone.

For another thing, even the devotion that reflects a higher commitment to work and task may not suffice to counterbalance the pressure of vanity and the urge to deny this pressure through the ostentation of self-sufficiency in self-judgment. Where can a total commitment to the work at hand find support? In the inherent value of work? Even the greatest achievements may have uncertain value when originally undertaken, and even the most confident may seek out the assurances of their followers and co-religionists. With these assurances in hand, the proud hope to enter into a world of discourse that allows them to confirm, correct, and develop their sense of the valuable and the real. Or can the commitment of the proud find support in the seductive character of activity itself, quite apart from the ultimate value of its results and the opinions of other people? But no variety of self-expression, including the immersion in work, can fully wave away the problem posed by the mutually reinforcing quality of dependence upon others and possession of self. Mozart was right to ask everybody: Do you love me?

Besides, even the aloofness that reveals an affirmative devotion rather than a mere desire to escape from vanity is still an aloofness. It still narrows the range of accepted vulnerability. It therefore still fastens you down to character, unless commitment turns into the occasion for a different vulnerability. For such a change to occur, however, devotion to a task must somehow share the quality of love.

The stark denial of the desire for approval and the appeal to an independent standard do not exhaust the experience of pride. There is also in this experience an attempt to strengthen yourself against opinion without really being able to counterbalance it. The proud man suspects the futility and falsehood of his withdrawal into the citadel. There, in the midst of his gaudy demonstration of an independence purchased at so heavy a human cost, the individual still feels his weakness in the presence of other people, viewed as judges of himself. The intermittent pain of real or imagined condemnation is all the more violent because the proud person lacks a way to express his craving for acceptance and approval and because he suspects just how mendacious his denial really is and how expensive in the simplification of experience and character. He feels that in the end he can master his dependence only by denying it, yet he knows that denial is not enough.

The ordinary experience of pride involves a constant shifting among these different aspects of the passion: the partial emancipation from the immediate pressure of opinion through commitment to an independent standard of reality and worth, the willful rejection of humiliating dependence through the deliberate avoidance of the relations that might bring this dependence to the fore, and the self-consciously deceptive display of indifference to a power that is felt to be unconquerable. In this turning and twisting of the emotion, pride as pure escape becomes an unstable point of transition between pride as partial emancipation and pride as transparent lie. Part of the distinctive ordeal of pride results from the felt inability to halt the terrible anguish of these circumvolutions.

The unifying impulse amid all the variations of pride is the sense of the menace to the self posed by other people's judgment and the resolve to counter this threat by moving away from it: toward something else if possible, toward nothing at all if necessary. The others—in their character as people who look at you and make judgments about you and lay claims upon you—are a sponge soaking you up, a sieve into which you are disappearing and being dissolved. So you must hold onto a rigid point of real or pretended reality and worth to resist this dispersion of your being, this disgusting foretaste of death.

There is, here, a deficiency of love: a failure of the imagination that might allow you to recognize the power that others have over you but to empty this power of its ability to force you into subservience or flight. Love can accomplish this change by moving the decisive relations among people toward a mutual self-bestowal and self-confirmation that need not preclude moments of intense disapproval and distance. The availability of this reciprocal access, across the barriers of praise or condemnation, makes it possible to carry the burden of living in a world in which what something is worth can never be definitively separated from how other people regard its nature and value.

The relation of pride to a deficiency of love also suggests why pride has an element irreducible to the imaginative structure of hatred. If all our relations to one another cannot in fact be informed by love (though how far love can go must always remain unclear), then we must find an alternative, lesser form of self-affirmation in the face of constraint by opinion. When this form is pride as devotion, we can hardly avoid its contamination by the other, neighboring aspects of the passion. These aspects—pride as flight and pride as lying—block the advance toward the economy of love: the resolution of our unlimited mutual longing and terror into accepted risk and provisional confirmation. The withdrawal of the proud person into his own self amounts to a refusal of the risks that unavoidably accompany any attempt to change the relation between our terror and our longing.

The converse of this deficiency of love is the very same twist on hatred that lies at the root of vanity: you reject not others' claim to existence but your own. Yet here this denial turns, by a circuitous route, into its apparent opposite: the show of unconditional independence. Even as show, however, this independence avoids other people for fear of shaking and collapsing in their presence.

The antagonistic and mutually parasitic coexistence of vanity and pride can now be seen for what it is: a small-scale image of the paradigmatic failure in the life of the passions. You might say it *is* the failure, in a specific mode: the mode in which people matter to one another primarily as givers and deniers of approval. Every point in the system of the passions presents the entire system under a particular aspect: determined by the distinctive vulnerability that a person confronts and the degree to which this vulnerability is lived out as something that strengthens or destroys self-possession.

Jealousy is the perception that your ability to come to favorable terms with another person is threatened each time the desired individual becomes entangled with other people. You despair of reaching the core of the other personality; it seems constantly to recede before you and to disintegrate into a myriad of social relations over which you have no control. The best you can hope for is to stop this wastage of the other being: to keep her hiddenness to yourself even if you cannot decipher it.

It is as if this person of whom you are jealous were a treasure hidden in a casket that you were forbidden to open. Only your ability to keep others from getting near this treasure and from trying to open the casket for themselves can convince you that you have not lost it once and for all. The formative image of jealousy is always one of property or possession: the power of exclusion, which gives life to the idea of property, becomes in the realm of personal relations the second best to love.

To see how and why jealousy assumes this consoling role, consider the relation of jealousy to hate. On one definition, to hate someone is to deny that he has a place in the world (that is to say, *your* world); it is to despair of reconciling his unique existence with your own. Jealousy is based upon the perception of a lesser degree of irreconcilability—the impossibility of a mutual strengthening of the sentiment of being. As a result, only a lesser hope remains: the hope of maintaining a privileged relationship to the other person through a gesture of exclusion and domination. This gesture resembles love by acknowledging the existence of the desired person as vital to your reality and worth. But jealousy also resembles hatred in a double way.

Take first the attitude toward other people who are viewed as present or potential rivals for the person of whom you are jealous. The more imminent the rivalry, the more their existence seems incompatible with yours. This hostility may stop short of hatred only because, unlike hatred, it is fastened down to the perception of a particular harm.

A more interesting modulation of hatred appears in the attitude of the jealous man toward the desired person. In asserting a claim of possession while despairing of the possibility of deep reciprocal confirmation he tries to seize her through her place in society rather than through the individuality that transcends the role. Indeed, he wants to deny her the wealth of personal entanglements that would allow this singularity to grow and express itself more fully.

Jealousy finally delights in what was once the occasion for its anguish: the elusiveness of the person, which should be cherished as an indication of humanity—a sign of our power simultaneously to reveal and to hide ourselves—ends up prized for its own sake. It is as if you were in love with elusiveness rather than with the elusive person. This denial of living individuality shares in the character of hatred.

Thus, jealousy may be viewed either as degraded and despairing love or as faltering and confused hatred. More than any other passion it mediates between the extremes of hatred and love.

Jealousy necessarily incurs a double illusion, which produces a double failure. Each of these failures teaches people something about what they may and may not expect from one another. This lesson has the power to contradict the ruling assumptions of a culture about the possibilities of human association.

First, there is the self-defeating character of possessiveness. Jealousy is an acknowledgment that people need to be reconfirmed by one another in their basic claims of self-assertion. But the only confirmation that really counts is the one freely given by a person who is herself a rich, original, unrepeatable instance of humanity.

Jealousy strains to fulfill this need by means that frustrate its satisfaction. If jealousy had its way, the desired person would be isolated as much and for as long as possible from other people. But the more isolated she became, the more she would be denied the surprises and risks of association that might allow her to understand and develop her own distinctiveness. She would be unable to give the jealous lover the singularity that she had failed to recognize and to nourish.

Surely—you may counter—this is a fancy: no program of isolation could be so effective. Besides, the wildest jealousies are often yearnings for exclusivity that are never translated into strategies of encirclement. Even so, the impoverishment of the desired person takes place in the jealous one's mind: just as the vain person is driven to see the other as an abstract purveyor of approval and consensus, so the jealous one is tempted to see her as some-one who ought to be available as exclusive property because she cannot become available in her unadorned individuality.

The second reason why jealousy is condemned to frustra-tion is that it seeks an objective which is unattainable and miscon-ceived quite apart from the means for pursuing it. A personality lacks a core that can be captured by a single act of appropriation. Its nub of identity, intellect, and will exists in time as a receding horizon. The power of transcendence lies precisely in the never wholly suppressed capacity of the person to break through the habits and roles that encrust his existence. Time turns against jealousy: for though time hardens habit, which anesthetizes long-ing, it also shows that in the end the person always amounts to more than a mere series of moments of presence or states of being.

This coexistence of an evasive center with a shifting and discontinuous periphery confronts the jealous man with a choice between two understandings that are equally subversive of his sen-timent. If he concludes that the whole idea of a core of personality is an illusion, the best he can hope for is to master the desired per-son's shifting positions in the physical and the human world. But these places concern the jealous man only insofar as he can trace them to the personality that they seem to manifest, for it is this hidden self that both fascinates and eludes him. When, however, the jealous person accepts the existence of this transcendent center, he also affirms its inaccessibility. To be truly and insanely jealous is to believe both that the desired person has a soul and that it cannot be reached.

This dilemma can be overcome only if the jealous individ-ual manages to change his conception of the desired person. He must do more than see her from the angle of a dialectic between elusive identity and spatial or social particularity. He must exchange with her so many and so significant vulnerabilities that he is drawn into the inner circle of her experience: though unable to define or to stabilize the traits that define her identity, he gains a sense of how they express or fail to express themselves in her actions. He recognizes himself as both an author and a beneficiary of this other self. But this privileged relation presupposes a prior willingness to deal with the other as a free, transcending person, who has the power to reveal or to hide, to bestow or to deny herself. Thus, he who longs for another is in the situation of a quantum physicist who infers the existence of new particles from the energy traces that their collisions leave behind and whose discoveries transform the reality he wants to understand. To long for another in this way is to pass from jealousy to love.

As it changes into love, jealousy escapes from the alternative fixation on the elusive center and the opaque periphery of the desired person. The escape is always partial. Third people do represent a threat to my love, a threat against which there is no protection save prudence and more love. And nothing can dissipate the enigma of a real person or bridge the gap that always remains between the hidden, potential, multifarious self and its deeds in the world. We are constantly forced to discover how little we know even about the people whom we know best, and how easily we forget even those whom we love most. The whole texture of personal experience is informed by this special horror; in the midst of our greatest discoveries of others there remains the shadow of a secret, and the happiness of love carries a touch of the poison of anticipated forgetfulness.

Jealousy, like vanity, has a cognitive counterpart that highlights this ultimate impenetrability of the self. It is our difficulty in grasping the singularity of entities in the world with the abstracting and generalizing procedures of discursive thought. We seem forced to choose between two partial responses to the particularity of things. One response accepts the distortions of abstract categories in exchange for their promise of precision and power. The other solution seeks in art a way to discover and evoke general insights through the very sharpness with which we represent particular phenomena or emotions.

But there is yet another route: to acquire practical knowledge of social situations by participating in them and trying to change them. Concepts are then viewed as having no rigid boundaries; each perspective on a given situation reflects a special interest in its maintenance or change; and the accumulation of perspectives brings you closer to the particularity of the circumstance without ever exhausting its riches. This is the personal knowledge that defines one of the aspects of love.

Even in this expanded state, however, the knowledge of the other remains inescapably and radically incomplete. For the very condition that makes this knowledge possible—the passionate bond between people who have the power to reveal or to hide themselves, to reject routine and defy expectation—sets a limit to insight. All our efforts to know the world, one another, and ourselves are cursed by the pathos of particularity: our incapacity to do justice to the uniqueness of each object or event. In the knowledge of persons this pathos is overcome in some ways, but in other ways it is reaffirmed and aggravated.

Just as the failure of jealousy reveals the conditions of our insight into one another, it also suggests a principle of social criticism and social reconstruction. The epistemological and political points are closely connected though the connection becomes clear only when their shared basis in the life of passion is understood. The political counterpart to the vision of personal connection that jealousy implies may be a type of social order that deals with the problem of mutual dependence by establishing a hierarchy of the claims that individuals in particular roles and stations can make upon one another. Or it may be a style of social organization that teaches each person to seek security in a fortress of proprietary right from which he can try to minimize his dependence upon others while maximizing their dependence upon him.

Like jealousy these forms of social life promise us a fix on the problem of mutual dependence through the exercise of control and possession. But the result is the same as in jealousy itself: the constraint upon empowerment. The political form of this constraint is the limit that conflict-resistant order imposes upon the dynamics of practical empowerment and accepted vulnerability, which together represent the great forces of emancipation in social life.

The political parallel to the moral vision that overcomes jealousy is the commitment to renounce the search for possessive control in our relations with one another while reinventing forms of autonomy that neither presuppose nor produce the breakdown of reciprocity. We keep this commitment by building an institutional order that both secures people in their vital immunity against oppression and deprivation and multiplies their opportunities and reasons for engagement in conflict over the basic terms of social life. For such an endeavor to succeed, the institutional means for establishing that immunity must not create opportunities to contain this conflict and to renew through its containment the mechanisms of subjugation. A society respectful of this principle stands more fully open to a knowledge beyond jealousy.

Envy is the impulse to deny another person his advantages, whether or not he is entitled to them. It is an experience of jeopardy and longing. You undergo the other person's enjoyment of benefits that you are denied as if it represented an intolerable diminishment of your own self. You feel as if your hope lay in sharing those delights or, at the very least, in seeing the person you envy deprived of them.

The pleasures that form the object of envy always gain their attraction more or less directly from the value that an audience is thought to place upon them. This audience may be distant or future, and its standards of judgment wholly at odds with those that prevail in your immediate surroundings. Thus, you may envy a person the commission of an act that you expect to bring his name glory, though perhaps solely in the eyes of a select few, at some remote time to come. One way or another, the social confirmation of your judgment of what constitutes an advantage helps assure you that the person you envy is getting away with something worthwhile, if only an undeserved prestige. The stamp of social esteem also brings out the complicity of others in the distribution of advantages that supplies the occasion for your envy.

At the core of envy, then, is the rejection of diversity. The diversity of individuals makes for differences in the benefits to which they have access and in the way they are judged by their fellows. But the experience of diversity—and of its acknowledgment and approval by others—is indispensable to our whole experience of individuality. For this reason envy, like all the vices, ends up as an assault upon the individual existence of those against whom it is directed.

Consider the connection between envy and hatred: you view the place of the envied person in the world as a denigration of your own place. The difference is only this: when you hate, it is the being of the other person, in his naked uniqueness, that seems incompatible with yours; when you envy, this other being concerns you only insofar as he appears to enjoy an advantage. Your hostility is filtered through a socially established texture of disparities between the things people can do, the resources they have available to them, and the admiration they receive from their fellows.

Unequivocal envy must unite two elements. The envied person's enjoyment of the advantages for which he is envied must not be based on an injustice. The envier must also himself realize, however dimly and unavowedly, that his passion does not rest on any well-founded normative claim against the other person. If both these components are missing, we speak of justified indignation or the demand for justice rather than of envy.

If you begrudge someone else advantages that ought to be shared, but to which you do not realize yourself entitled, we had better call you morally confused rather than envious. Nevertheless, since you define as envy what you should view as justified indignation, you take on many of the characteristics of the envious man; your self-condemning resentment undermines your capacity to accept and appreciate many other facets of the individuality of the other person.

But what of the more familiar transitional case of envy in

which we call you envious because we believe that you want what is not your own, even though you may insist—and more or less believe—that you feel and act out of justified indignation on behalf of yourself and all those similarly placed? If we still call you envious, despite your protestations of good faith, it is because we suspect that the concern for justice is playing second fiddle to a meaner passion, or that you have culpably allowed your judgment of the relative disparities and entitlements to be corrupted by your interest in preferment. Thus, the latter half-case of envy marks the close bond between the objective and the subjective aspects of this passion. To understand just how tight the link is, start by taking two facts into account.

The first fact is that feelings of envious resentment and perceptions of disparities of advantage or entitlement color one another to the point of fading into a dense haze. Even the individual who scrutinizes himself in all good faith may find it hard to separate the threads of moral judgment, factual accuracy, and the self-propelling dynamic of personal antagonism.

Second, a special complexity is built into any attempt to settle the rights and wrongs of envy and indignation. How far does a given social order go in reinforcing these passions? Does it leave them blind, mute, and bitter? Or does it harness them to the practice of public debate and legitimate conflict about the justice and injustice of social arrangements? Precisely because even good faith will often be insufficient to draw the line between envy and justified indignation, we want institutions that will not excite the forms of envy or indignation likely to be most resistant to analysis, persuasion, and compromise. In this most bitter envy we react against what seems to be a flaunting of advantage by others—a flaunting that carries the message that they are worth everything and that we are worth nothing. But just when are we right to discern this insult to our self-respect in a situation of disparate advantage? And when are we simply misled by our envy into reading the offense into an expression of diversity against which we have no other justified complaint?

Aside from these two sets of facts, the confusion of envy

with justified indignation has a still deeper source: the intricate relation between diversity and equality. To probe this relation is to discover the larger social meaning of envy. Every diversity among individuals takes the form of a disparity between their situations—the benefits and the esteem they enjoy. By objecting to these disparities, whether or not they rest upon entitlements, envy also protests against the diversities that underlie them. We approach envy differently according to where we believe rough equality should prevail: in opportunities of advancement, in the cost of the material resources available for the satisfaction of people's wants (if not in the pleasure they draw from the resources at hand), or in specific features of their situations. Our response also depends upon the concrete scheme of forms of possible and desirable human association that commands our allegiance.

Sometimes people pretend to a geometry of moral ideas that could distinguish, once and for all, the occasions of envy from the objects of justified indignation. In fact, the persuasive authority of these deceptively precise ideas always rests upon their responsiveness to the more deeply set images of human association available to us at any given time. These images describe and prescribe for us the patterns of coexistence appropriate for the different settings of social life. Remember that in some societies this map of moral order is organized around a dominant model of human relationships to be repeated with suitable variations in every field of social life: each recurrent relationship should be a blend of contract, community, and domination. In other societies contract, community, and domination are thought to be reciprocally repellent, and a different authoritative model of association holds for each region of social life: a particular version of community for the family, another for the republic, and in between a large area surrendered to an amalgam of contractual exchange and technical hierarchy. The careful exclusion of the familial or democratic forms of association from this middle area of prosaic social life may even be viewed as a condition of their successful working in the domains that are properly theirs.

The principles that demarcate the proper limits of inequality—and therefore the boundary between envy and justified indignation—cannot be clearer or stronger than the arguments supporting the canonical schemes of possible and desirable association to which those principles at least tacitly refer. Such schemes may be tested by the range of individual and collective empowerment that they make possible or prevent. But the struggle over the schemes continues in the controversy over the tests. And even if we could settle on the standards, the value of the probe would remain limited by the restricted sense of possibility that we bring to our judgments. The models of association available to even the most radical social criticism are drawn by analogy to the limited stock of established and remembered social forms and by extension from those incongruous experiences of practical or passionate connection that fail to fit present order and dogma. The resulting contestability of our larger conceptions of possible and desirable association contaminates both our defense of equality and our definitions of its content and makes it impossible to disentangle conclusively the strands of indignation and envy. It ensures that our ideas about envy and equality, like the imaginative schemes of social life that they express, will remain vulnerable to the acid blend of envious resentment and prophetic insight.

In the ordinary circumstances of social life the half-cases of envy reappear everywhere. The genuine uncertainty of the distinction between envy and justified indignation is aggravated by contrasting delusions: the unreflective acceptance of conventional ideas about the proper forms of human association with their respective built-in standards of justice clashes with the self-serving treatment of every inferiority as an outrage.

In this state of halting moral insight the individual may sink into a characteristic anguish of invidious comparison. He moves, back and forth, between two views of each disadvantage he undergoes. It is the result of injustice: the rules of the game are unfair and rigged against him. It is the sign of failure: the rules are fair, but he has played and lost. His failure reveals a flaw in himself, and he must thank his lucky stars for not having been pushed down further. He suffers a remorseless alternation between feelings of victimization and inadequacy. The characteristic social counterpart to this rhythm of invidious comparison is the frequent hesitancy of lower classes between resentment or rebellion against their bosses or rulers and acceptance of the perceptions and ideals of the higher-ups as authoritative. This hesitancy gains a makeshift coherence from the claim that the masters have betrayed their professed standards of justice: the good old ways everyone has a right to count on.

The dynamic of invidious comparison can help destroy many of the barriers to equality in society. In so doing, it enables us better to tell envy and justified indignation apart, and to win deeper insight into the relation among love, hatred, and the acceptance of diversity.

Imagine a society in which continued mass mobilization has destroyed the stranglehold of well-defined elites over supreme power and the hierarchical and communal divisions between people have been partly, though only partly, criticized, fragmented, and effaced. Large disparities of advantage still exist: either those that inherited wealth and opportunity facilitate or those that individuals can acquire through effort and luck. In such a society men and women constantly compare their advantages to those of the people above or below them. Their comparisons do not stop at the boundaries of the classes or communities closest to their own. The advantages that measure success or failure tend to become the common coin of everyone's comparison of his situation with everyone else's. The economic, political, and moral implications reach far.

The broadening of comparison presupposes and fuels a view that sees all settled disparities of power and advantage as contingent. Robbed of their aura of naturalness and sanctity they must be seen as the result of recurrent struggles and temporary truces or of practical imperatives of collective organization. Increasingly, they must be defended, in explicit terms, if not as an integral part of a way of life that deserves defending, then as a means to the satisfaction of generally acknowledged practical needs. Since all these inequalities are now potentially available for political criticism and reformation, the inequalities left over at any given time begin to look arbitrary: a consequence of the balance of forces and prejudices. By seeming arbitrary they also seem more intolerable. Thus, even when inequalities diminish, the pain and anger caused by those that remain are likely to increase rather than diminish. The alternation of the individual between his sense of unfairness and his sense of inadequacy will now be aggravated by the expanding comparative judgments that this alternation had originally helped provoke. The contradictory beliefs that he is nothing and deserves to be everything, and that he is little and deserves to be less, inform his entire life in society.

Yet this more self-conscious confusion of envy and indignation may form part of a history of politics that clarifies the issues of envy and equality by correcting the inequalities that people cannot, in the end, justify as indispensable means to practical welfare or as irremediable features of civilized life. Over time, the recurrent destabilization of inequalities may have the effect of distinguishing envy from justified indignation. Many inequalities may be moderated or destroyed. Others may gain, for a while, a stronger claim to justification. Having survived practical and visionary assaults, they may be defended as imperatives of widely acknowledged practical needs or as features of defensible images of association.

Even in the best of cases this developing clarification would remain imperfect. The definition of practical needs would still be contestable, and its implications for work and hierarchy still uncertain. Prophetic insight into the unrealized opportunities of association would continue to be susceptible to surprising revolutions. Besides, the fight for power and authority could at any time cause inequalities more terrible than those existing before.

Imagine, nevertheless, that the subversion of unjustified inequality moves forward to its outer limits, diminishing the motives for justified indignation and depriving envy of its disguises. What then would be the concerns of envy and what would they show us about the meaning of individual diversity for love and hatred? Even then—if the material circumstances of life were thoroughly equalized, and everyone had a fair chance to find a vocation, and all power were made subject to collective choice and conflict so that renewed mobilization repeatedly cracked open the hardening structure of social life—even then, at least two objects of envy would remain.

One object would be an individual's moral fortune: his perceived capacity to love and be loved, to sustain his love through faith and hope, and prepare and protect it, and, thus, to make a home out of the world. Everything physical or social, achieved or accidental, that is seen to contribute toward this success would fall under the eyes of envy.

The other continuing target of envy would be a person's ability to make himself the vehicle of visionary revelation in art, theory, or politics, or to step forward as a leader in the midst of conflict. Though such a person still needs to be recognized, he is a privileged maker of the world in which many will live. For him, that world is forever marked by the traces of his own self. This surpassing power to set the terms of community or common discourse offers more than a partial dissolution of the externality of external reality; it has a touch of the same quality that makes moral fortune so enviable. The leader and the creator make themselves vulnerable in a world they do not control, yet from their mute or noisy struggle they emerge with a heightened experience of self-expression and self-possession. If invention is not the same as love, still it brings many of love's gifts. The envy of formative power may hardly differ much from the envy that suffers at the sight of the intimate happiness of another.

Faced with these most recalcitrant motives for envy, in a circumstance that makes envy hard to mistake for justified indignation, you undergo an experience of blockage and defeat. The diversity among people, which should have been a spur to your own freedom in self-possession, provokes instead a rage against the fullness of other beings. Their triumphs of happiness and invention seem to label you as one of the damned, unable to escape from the economy of hatred by transforming, as they did, infinite longing and jeopardy into mutual risk and confirmation. Their moral fortune seems to uncover a fate beyond good and evil that governs each person's life of passion; your modulated hatred of those whom you envy spills over, as in every variation on hate, into a hateful view of the world. Their inspired achievements appear as an irresistible and unaccountable power over you—over the conditions of your life and talk—reminding you of your emptiness and confirming you in it. Because their mere existence seems to limit your chances of being at home in the world, you experience their existence as incompatible with your own; but your awareness of incompatibility focuses on the envied only by focusing first on their advantages.

The victories of justice and the achievements of critical insight aggravate the sufferings of envy. They begin by depriving it of its excuses. Then they bring it out of its dispersion and direct it to objects of utmost concern. In this state of disappointment we are forced to confront the inevitable involvement of real individuality—and therefore of love itself—in a circumstance that permits a deep and ineradicable disparity of the advantages that count most. This disparity constantly draws us into the economy of hatred when we do not learn to absorb it in a countervailing vision of solidarity.

Love alone can correct this failure of the ability to imagine diversity and community. It invites the envious into that experience of moral fortune from which they had believed themselves excluded; if luck can rob them of the morally ambiguous gift of a quiet domestic contentment, it cannot deny them the opportunities of self-bestowal. (Even then, the element of fortune is maintained by the possibility of unrequital or estrangement.) The redeeming vision that love opens up accepts radical diversity—including the diversity of moral fortunes and creative

powers—as part of the context in which radically individual people can exist. To the extent that the dealings among people are
touched and transformed by such a faith, it is possible to love in
the presence of disparities of fortune and inspiration without condescension or resentment.

Love may carry out this work of emancipation when it takes
the envied person himself as its object—or when, in diluted, more
impersonal form, as community, it brings him into endeavors of
joint concern. Even when it has an object other than the envied
person himself, it intimates a world in which residual disparities
set up no invincible barriers to the successful passage of the self
through its trials of accepted vulnerability.

The problem of resistant envy in a situation of idealized
justice sheds light on what people must do to escape from envy
when it remains confused with justified indignation because diversity remains entwined with injustice. By one movement you throw
yourself into transformative action and reflection about the way
unjustified inequality corrupts community and collaboration.
Through your participation in conflict and controversy over inequality and diversity, you begin to pull apart, in yourself, envy
and indignation. By another movement—the movement of
love—you have, in the here and now, an experience of association
in which no disparity of advantage holds you to the descending
spiral of hatred. Through the twofold effort of this response to inequality, the facts that might have led to the self-reinforcing cycle
of envy, with its narrowing acquiescence in established constraints
on action and vision, become instead goads to the discovery of
possibilities that these constraints close off.

Faith, hope, and love do not seem to be engendered by either the internal tensions of social life, as are hatred, vanity,
jealousy, and envy, or by the limits that biological impulse and ra-

tional doubt set to social order, as are lust and despair. On the contrary, they appear as uninvited envoys from another world, resolving conflicts that seemed insoluble and breaking through frontiers that looked impassable. They have the force of surprise.

Caught in dying bodies and worldly cares, we may wonder whether we shall have time to reconcile ourselves to one another. Can the elusiveness and temporality of the self be made compatible with an experience of mutual revelation, presence, and sacrifice? Can this act of fascination and bestowal ever be more than the refinement of lust or the dissolution of the other person into a mirage of your own making? If it is an illusion, must it not suddenly disappear, leaving the lover baffled at what could have attracted him? Or else sink into a cowardly habit of grudging tolerance?

Love is the substance of these questions before it can be any particular answer to them. They are more than inquiries posed by an outside observer. Rather they exist as latent intimations in even the most intense experiences of love, just as a suggestion of atheism clings to even the strongest faith in God.

Love is an impulse toward acceptance of the other person, less in his distinctive physical and moral traits (which the lover may criticize and devalue) than in his whole individuality. The specific features of the person are never irrelevant—how else could you know him?—but they are taken as incarnations of a self that both speaks through them and transcends them. This acceptance, made in the face of the inexorably hidden and threatening being of another person, always has something of the miraculous. It is an act of grace devoid of condescension or resentment.

But the inevitability of the hiddenness and of the threat means that love cannot be pure. It must be accompanied by the presentiment of its own fragility and by at least a suggestion of defensive repugnance and inscrutability toward the other. This suggestion announces the presence of hate within love.

At its strongest, love dispenses with a convergence of interests and ideals. It sees through the spatial and social expressions of the self to the unique, living personality. Hence, it precludes neither criticism nor conflict. The independence of love from approval and consensus, however, remains limited in several ways.

It is limited even within the prototypical instances of personal love, like the full sexual union between a man and a woman. The ability to accept the other person may depend, to a dismaying degree, upon particular traits of appearance or character whose influence upon the lover seems out of all proportion to their real value as signs of the individuality of the beloved. The manifestations of the beloved easily and continuously become a screen that conceals her and reflects back to the lover the image of his own insatiability. The loved person's features of body and mind make her what she is, for they are in sum and direction, if not piece by piece, the representation of her self. If the lover's aversion to these features goes too far and deep, his love cannot survive. To be bored with another person is just to have lost, or never to have gained, a sense of how her routine presence reveals an arcane self, and boredom rather than loathing is the most common ruin of love.

As we move out from these exemplary instances of personal love to ties of love within larger groups, the need for shared aims and mutual esteem increases. No sharp break separates total love between man and woman from love among friends, and ultimately from love within a broader group, though often we prefer to speak only of friendship in the second case and of sympathy, loyalty, or solidarity in the third.

The vitality of communal affection depends upon an allegiance that makes up for the unavoidable attenuation of love in a wider social setting. The required allegiance is the commitment to the communal venture as, in some measure, an end in itself, quite apart from the specific goals that it furthers. This loyalty is misunderstood or perverted when it is mistaken for an infatuation with a hypostasized collective entity. Such an infatuation degrades the experience of collaboration into the idolatry of an artificial personality, the group itself. The most complete communal experiences are those that most resemble love: the sharing of aims is complemented by a net of personal attachments that spreads outward from each individual, without perhaps ever embracing all or most of the other members of the group. The awareness of common purposes eventually becomes inseparable from the sense of close involvements with particular individuals.

To put the matter this way is to recognize that within a larger group love necessarily weakens. The multiplicity of personal encounters, the impossibility of choosing group partners by the criterion of love, and the importance of carrying out tasks that help justify the existence of the group and allow it to survive and prosper—all this accounts for the weakening. The smaller the role of love in communal life, the greater the need for consensus about the shared goals of the common enterprise as well as for punctilious rights-consciousness among the members. The participants must at least view one another as capable of contributing to the joint enterprise. If both attachment and consensus fail, the group slides toward the example of the self-interested bargain: people deal with one another as means to one another's ends, exchanging and then departing.

There is a more radical imperfection in love. To understand this flaw you must reconnect the analysis of love with the root facts of infinite mutual fear and longing. Love exists when you experience the existence of the other person as a confirmation of your own. The acceptance of his otherness in its individuality helps you discover and strengthen your own distinctive being. Through the affirmation of the other, you enter more fully into the possession of your self.

This is more than a matter of wishing it so. The mere experience of longing for another, and the readiness for self-bestowal, cannot make this mutual confirmation come true. What will the other person do in the face of this longing and self-bestowal? No matter what he does, and even if he has the same experience in reverse, nothing could either justify conclusively the belief that the existence of the other reaffirms your own or safeguard you definitively from the anguish of continued longing and the danger of later failure.

That wishing it so does not suffice is shown by the many ways in which love may be destroyed. Though love need not disappear instantly in the face of a rebuff, neither is it likely to survive indefinite unrequital. More generally, the heightened vulnerability that love both requires and creates may become at any moment the occasion for suffering a hurt. And love may enter into a losing contest with the economy of hate as the vices take root in other areas of a life. The impossibility of conclusive vindication adds to the reality of the risk. Like all passions, love brings together a predisposition to action and a view of the conditions for reconciling self-affirmation and attachment. Nothing in the world can provide this view with a definitive justification.

As predisposition and as belief, love refers to a background intimation about the ultimate possibilities of relations among people: the belief that you can act toward another person in a way that treats him as a source of sustenance just because he is who he is. You offer him an exposed self ready to receive a similar sign of radical acceptance. But the world as we find it passes no unequivocal judgment upon the realism of this intimation. We lose the thread of our emotions and reflections, we withdraw into our selves, out of disenchantment, boredom, and worldly care, and at last we die before we have had a chance to find out for sure. For this reason the renewal of love in a world that neither validates nor refutes its realism depends upon other events and opportunities in the life of passion.

Because love is so difficult and because we must suspend judgment about the realism of its suggestions, we need additional ways to affirm the reality of others without giving in to the logic of lust and despair or the economy of hatred. Sometimes we find this alternative in fellow-feeling or sympathy, which, strengthened by collective standards of decency, carries diluted love beyond intimacy. Fellow-feeling teaches us to see in each existence a person struggling under a weight of his own. Sometimes we find the antidote in an art form like the novel that shows us how an understanding and acceptance of others in their otherness can outlive the disillusions and disappointments of the world.

This general conception of love, of its possibilities, limits, and dangers, can be restated as a hierarchy of forms of love, increasingly disengaged from illusion about the beloved and about the nature of love itself. The higher you climb in this hierarchy the less does the ardor of the emotion depend upon the extent of a distortion. As love frees itself from illusion, it also becomes less susceptible to sudden disenchantment and more capable of surviving in the face of everyday reality. The reconciliation of self-assertion and attachment becomes fuller because love reaches the beloved more intimately and becomes less dependent upon the image repertoire of the lover. Thus, this hierarchy describes a movement away from narcissism and passivity toward a condition in which the acceptance of otherness accompanies the discovery of the extraordinary within the ordinary.

At the lowest level of the hierarchy love appears in one of several closely related forms. All have in common the predominance of a compulsion that makes the actual reality of the other person almost entirely irrelevant except insofar as she happens to satisfy the very limited though often highly indeterminate requirements that preoccupy each of these varieties of love. Thus, the lover may be obsessed with discrete physical or psychological qualities of the beloved. These qualities may respond to an image of need and desire that his past experience imposes upon him and over which he has lost active control. Or he may fall in love having been moved primarily by the reigning social opinion about what he should do and whom he should find desirable. The tyrannical image emerges then from society rather than biography. But its effect remains the same: to turn what might have been the exemplary experience of freedom and realism into frenzied automatism and illusion.

Higher on this hierarchy of forms of love stands the love that desires the beloved as the expression of what the lover is not: the darkened, unrealized, and hence supremely valuable part of the lover's self. To possess her is to cure the mutilation of his own self and to compensate, at last, for all those aspects of experience that deny him the sense of being the center of the world. Even the

most immediate physical attraction becomes suffused by the longing for the unfinished self. This is love as the sickness for the ideal.
It differs from the cruder forms of love in its search for self-
completion and transformation and in its willingness to establish a
closer imaginative connection between the actual personality of
the beloved and the ideal sought by the lover. But it resembles
those other versions of love in its subordination of the real other
person to a vision of the lover's own needs.

Here is the love described by high Romantic myth, the love
that tries to turn the beloved into the redeemer. The search for
such a love becomes all the more enticing in a society whose
authoritative culture accustoms people to seek in love a salvation
beyond the merger of sensuality and tenderness while encourag-
ing disbelief in other possibilities of divine or secular redemption.

A yet higher love presupposes no idealization. The
beloved, beneficiary of a dependence that is also an exercise of autonomy, can be seen as just an ordinary person, though a uniquely
individual one. Here the acceptance of the otherness of another
person and the confrontation with common human reality reach
their high point. For this very reason the beloved cannot be mistaken for a redeemer whose saving power is in direct proportion
to her lack of individual characteristics. The acceptance of the
other is recognized to remain both limited and precarious.

Each step in the hierarchy of forms of love represents a
double advance over the previous one: an additional move away
from narcissism and illusion and toward the acceptance of the
beloved in her defective, ambiguous, original reality. It is
therefore not surprising that the relation of understanding to love
should change in the course of this progression.

At the lowest levels understanding destroys what is taken
for love. To see the dependence of infatuation upon a biograph-
ically determined image or a socially authoritative opinion is to undermine the attachment. With the coming of insight nothing
remains but manipulation. You manipulate the other person by al-
ternately disclosing your revised view of the bond so as to frighten

her into submission and concealing this change so as to renew her hope. You may even manipulate yourself. Thus you may expose yourself to experiences that reinvigorate the image or the opinion. You may trick yourself into finding in the shared tasks, the endless puzzles, and the surviving dependencies of parenthood and communal life the more realistic substitute for the childish infatuation you have overcome, as if a spiritless community could compensate for the emptiness left by a solipsistic, compulsive, and bygone experience of longing.

At the upper reaches of this hierarchy of attachment, however, insight becomes the preserver rather than the destroyer of love, something that does not jeopardize love and that love cannot do without. The unentranced vision of the flesh and the heart—the dying, tremulous flesh, the secretive, divided heart—need not destroy such a love. There will nevertheless be moments of spiritual inertia, of despair, anger, and conflict, and of disappointment at the disproportion between yearning and circumstance. At such times you will be tempted to make up for the stagger of love with a weaker, more benevolent recurrence of the manipulation that accompanies a love more tainted by illusion. It then requires moral intelligence to resist this temptation. You resist it out of an awareness of the perils of narcissism and solipsism that attend a carefully plotted strategic fiction meant to do the work of an encounter without a ready script.

To elaborate the conception of love described in the preceding pages and to understand more fully what this passion teaches us about passion in general, you must now distinguish between the two registers of love—the sexual and the sexless—and see how they connect. In the sexual register, the primordial base of personal love is the demand for the body of the beloved—a demand marked not by the exclusionary concern that distinguishes jealousy but by an unthinking and relentless, though intermittent, craving. In personal love, this violent demand—violent because it threatens the minimal conditions of civility and apartness—is overlaid and transformed by an element of gentleness: gentleness toward the other body and, in the end, toward the incarnate person.

The violence and the gentleness are so often and so strongly connected that the distinction between lust and sexual love can be hardly more than a contrast of predominant directions. (To define lust as pure violence without any touch of gentleness, even the gentleness that appears as remorse or hesitation, would restrict lust to the most extreme perversions.) We hope that the gentleness will last and that it will transfigure the violence. It never entirely does. In sexual love, a person experiences himself as embodied and therefore as part of nature. He also recognizes himself as standing in need of other bodies, who are both parts of nature and persons like himself. That the tenderness and violence in sexual love are so commonly linked does not mean that they join harmoniously. The more strongly love is lived out in sexual terms and the less its sexual expressions are contained and transformed by a rich and stable context of social life, or by an artistic imagination, the less likely it becomes that the tenderness will change the violence.

The sexless register of love is revealed most clearly in a relatively sexless love between people unconnected by the complicating tie of family intimacy (parents and children, brothers and sisters). Its elemental basis is the experience of desiring the freedom of another, the wish to give another person to himself. It is the stance of haughty spirit in its sacrificial and creative pose.

At first this may seem to be the highest assertion of humanity—an experience of freedom in the giving of freedom, a will that the other be on his own without anything asked in return, not even gratitude. In fact, however, such a love strikes a crude relation to the other person, a relation that cannot empower either the beloved or the lover. The reason for this limit is that this sacrificial love seals itself off from danger and places itself on a higher plane of benevolence and self-denial. It does not offer the beloved the opportunity to confirm and reinvent himself through involvement with another imagination and will, nor does it enable the lover to achieve this experience himself. Such a love treats mutual confirmation as a project that can be willed into reality without being lived out and risked. It falsifies the condition of spirit by masking the force of a person's need for other people.

Nevertheless, in the sexless register of personal love the awareness of the need for the other often ends up overtaking the diligent, protective will for his good. The spirit sets out as a proud and self-sufficient demiurge and returns humbled and shaken by its yearning. It yearns not for the simple act of gratitude but for the more complicated act of presence and response by the person it loves. (Thus, the believer insists that the love that God has for his human creatures would be unintelligible to us if we did not attribute to Him a need for man and experience our longing for Him through His longing for us.) But the refusal of self, the avoidance of love on equal terms, is never completely overcome in sexless love if only because the total weight of fragility is not carried to its utmost so long as the body is not thrown into the gift of self and into the desire for the presence of the other.

Now, by a series of remarks about these two registers of love and their relation, it may be possible to identify the varieties of sexual and sexless love that matter most to the general project of a theory of the passions: to squeeze the doctrine of every element of sentimentality and to see what remains, for this residue will be the truth about passion as love.

Both sexual and sexless love are forever on the verge of descending to the same minimalist concern. This concern is the ungentle demand for the other's body or the forceful will to the other's good. In each case the special subjective quality of this request is the recognition of a loss, of something missing. The lover is in unrest, unable to remain content with himself. But in turning to the beloved he remains preoccupied with his own insatiability: his attention is directed to the craving of the body or to the exercise of the creative and sacrificial will. In the minimal version of sexual love, the other person becomes the compliant or resistant body. In the minimal variant of sexless love, the other person is the intended beneficiary, held at a distance and kept, by the sacrificial posture of his benefactor, from embracing and embarrassing him. In both instances the beloved fails to be seen as a being with social imagination, that is, with the power to invent fictions about attachments and to act these fictions out.

The reality of the other person is only more fully accepted to the extent that craving is overtaken by gentleness, and sacrificial will by the awareness of need. The appearance of tenderness in lust or sexual love requires an ability to imagine the beloved and to discern his experience of the encounter. The pathos of need in sexless love implies a willingness not just to want the other's good but to subject yourself to the unforeseeable and unsettling demands of his love and of your recognition of your need for it. Only then, in sexless love, does the other person become more than the occasion for sacrifice and the stationary target of beneficent will; he becomes a center of movement in his own right.

Take each of these two registers of love when neither has been transformed by the discovery of the other register. They then show a parallel subjective quality. Sexual and sexless love may even coexist: one as an overtone of the other (as in the relationship between the orator and the crowd). But in no ready way can they come together and be experienced as related elements of a single encounter. They move toward different ends and seek incompatible things in the beloved. From the standpoint of the violent element of demand for the other's body in sexual love, the benevolent and demiurgic attitude of sexless love is an irrelevancy or an interference. From the perspective of this attitude, the sexual demand is a profanation, the spoiling of a protective stance by a selfish desire.

The merger of the sexual and the sexless becomes conceivable only when tenderness enters into the craving for the body and the creative will comes to terms with its need for the beloved. Then the touching of the other's body, in demand and gentleness, can be experienced as a deepening of the recognition of need. Then the simultaneous desire for the good of the beloved and the recognition of longing can be lived out as an extension of the experience of craving and tenderness toward the body. The discovery of the other—the acceptance of him as a person with will and imagination—is the only ground on which sexual and sexless love can converge, however partially and precariously.

There is nothing to choose between sexual and sexless love as pictures of human encounter. Neither of them does better than the other in offering opportunities to imagine the beloved and to reconcile the enabling conditions of self-assertion. But each is capable of moving toward the discovery of the otherness of the other person. This discovery may in turn enable it to achieve what it needs in order to join with its sexual or sexless counterpart. Though this combined sexless and sexual love may go no further than its constituents in resolving the fundamental conflict between longing and jeopardy, it involves the person more inclusively in whatever resolution it does achieve. When you view as a limiting case the more inclusive love that results from this convergence, you can begin to understand the paradoxes of this master passion.

The sexual and the sexless enter into a subtle confrontation even at the very moment when they seem to be confirming each other. The body, in assertion or tenderness, makes its own demands. The spirit, as imagination and will, drives forward to a wider arena of response and attachment, ready to forgo the bodily encounter. The sexual element in love fights against the attempt to smother it in a drama of ambitious moral effort, of sacrifice and disclosure. The sexless element rebels against the comedy, the artlessness, and the eventual decay of the sexual.

Moreover, both sexual and sexless love testify to the fragility of our power to acknowledge the reality of the other person. This acknowledgment runs against the more immediate reality of one's own self: the forceful demands of one's body and the imprisoned character of one's subjectivity. Precisely because the other person cannot be fully as real as the self, the sexual or sexless relation to him remains subject to the double law of indifference and distraction. Distraction is the volatile seizing on isolated features of the other—his body, character, situation, or experience. It changes the passion by narrowing its focus and corrupting its ardor. In the isolated traits of the beloved that serve as the objects of his fascination, the distracted lover discerns a secret meaning, a private value, intelligible only in the light of his own past and vulnerabilities. Indifference is the waning of the power to imagine the other: the giving up of the added effort, of the heightened availability, required to recognize his originality. Through indifference and distraction the transforming elements in sexual or sexless love fall away, and the sexual and the sexless forms in love also lose the ability to cross into each other.

There is never any assurance about the precise point at which love stands along this chain of transformations. Because love makes claims on every aspect of the personality rather than on the isolated faculties of intelligence and because its instability is rooted in the defining conditions of the self rather than in some flaw of effort, our insights into love always seem too limited or too late. When you think that you are advancing toward the discovery of the other, you may in fact be sliding back, through distraction, into an image of your own suffering. When you believe you have handed yourself over to a heartless lust or a haughty benevolence, you may in fact have discovered in the ruin of your autarky the saving presence of the beloved. So this passion is a miracle-maker of deception and self-deception and of discovery in the disguise of illusion.

The love whose sexual and sexless forms I have described takes hold against two backgrounds: a metaphysical groping that extends the significance of love while threatening its stability, and a kindred emotion that broadens the reach of love while helping to secure the psychological conditions that enable it to exist.

The metaphysical concern represents the most subtle and sublime element in the psychology of love. This concern becomes evident only when all these transformations of sexual and sexless attachment are placed in the larger setting of man's relationship to nature. The personality suffers a horror at the prospect, or the memory, of a complete sinking into nature. It is the vision of man's own being—body and mind—placed in a world of vegetable and animal life that forever moves through decay and renewal. This is the world of death and fertility without consciousness. The inexpressible disquiet at total merger into this universe of nature leaves traces that go all the way from children's fear of animals, and from the terror that the lushness and strangeness of a jungle can excite, to man's stubborn insistence on finding in himself an element of the demonic or the angelic. For the angelic and the demonic signify that which is not embodied, the holy or the evil lifted from its corporeal state.

This fear of total immersion into nature almost never appears with the full range of its potential strength, for it is normally counterbalanced and purged by an experience of the isolation of consciousness. At first this separation is experienced in relation to other minds; it is from them that, as you begin to form an idea of your own self, you feel at first cut off. But then this arrest within a distinctive world of subjectivity is generalized to our relationship to all of nature.

The ordeal of isolation is an event coeval in everyone's life with the birth of self-reflection. Only from the vantage point offered by this ordeal can you long for unification with nature and feel the demonic and the angelic in yourself. Only on these terms can the idea of a sinking into nature be purged of its horror, until you are even able to view with detachment the inclusion of your life into a natural order. Still, some people have moments of intense imaginative experience when the dissolution of consciousness into nature strikes them as an immediately terrifying reality, more terrible because so much more richly defined than the blank idea of death.

At these moments it takes artistic imagination or mystical vision to rescue them from their fright. Art presents natural reality as a realm of transformative variations recognizably similar to those that consciousness acknowledges in its internal life. Mystical insight takes nature as a theater in which a drama of universal spirit is being played out; for the mystic, the same spirit in which mankind participates underlies the luxuriance of nature and turns all its variations into a parable. Thus the threatening strangeness of nature may be mastered through the imagination of art and the dramatization of physical reality. Through this mastery a more serene contemplation of our place in nature becomes possible.

These larger anxieties and aspirations inform the psychology of love. We are struck by the flaws in sexual love, this most complete experience of entrance into our own bodies: the ambivalence of violence and tenderness and the dimming of consciousness that may attend the bodily encounter. We are taken aback by the precariousness of the merger of sexual and sexless love, a merger that seems to be our one best hope of fully bringing the body and, through it, our whole natural condition into the life of personal relation.

Nevertheless, all these limitations constitute the reverse side of the condition of subjectivity. Even in sexual love the self-reflective experience of consciousness denies us lasting contentment, torments us with the ambiguities of tenderness and violence, and surrounds our encounters with loneliness and our delight with sadness. Yet this very awareness that we are cut off, because we are conscious, enables us to accept without horror our embodiment and its great triumph in sexual love.

Love relies upon a passion that might be equated with sexless love if it did not possess certain distinctive features. These traits give it a more general scope and a unique place in the whole life of passion. This passion—the second background to love, alongside the metaphysical anxiety just discussed—is sometimes called fellow feeling, benevolence, sympathy, or compassion. Moralists have often put it at the center of their conceptions of human nature. In many ways it serves as the enabling passion—less a passion than the moral capability supporting the entire life of passion. Its relationship to particular episodes in this life remains enigmatic.

A person is approached by a suffering stranger who asks for help. He responds not just with alacrity but with the emotion described as sympathy. His response includes the desire for the good of the other. Yet it is both more and less than sexless love.

The subjective experience that holds the foreground in compassion is a connection established among several types of response. There is the acknowledgment of commonality with the other person. But it is a mistake to treat this acknowledgment as a simple matter of identification with another: attributing to him the sufferings or joys that you might undergo in similar circumstances. Such an approach would explain the impulse to help the other and to participate in his experience only by explaining away this impulse as an oblique self-reference and a tacit narcissism.

Sympathy includes a recognition of comic incongruity: the incongruity between the state that someone is in, whether of weakness and suffering or strength and elation, and the deeper conditions of selfhood that combine embodiment and finitude with a longing for the unconditional. If the person benefited by sympathy is in distress—thrown into a demeaning or destructive condition—you nevertheless recognize in him the same individual who sooner or later demands to shatter and revise the contexts of his activity and who sooner or later succeeds: the individual who loved most completely, and struggled against the limits of reason, and produced masterpieces of art, and who, even in the midst of very ordinary life, was found on closer inspection to be not so ordinary after all. He is not man as hero, or saint, or genius, but rather he is greater than these because he is everyman.

Suppose now that he is the very opposite of someone in the situation of incongruous distress. He is, for example, the young person triumphantly besieging the world and eliciting, through his razzle-dazzle insistence, your blessing and encouragement. Sympathy then sees the gap between this headlong aspiration and the real circumstance of the self in the world, a circumstance subject to happenstance, disappointment, and illusion.

We constantly present to one another the image of a dissonance between what in the end we cannot avoid being—embodied, contextual, and turning toward the uncontextual—and what through chance, ambition, and failure we occasionally and apparently become. This incongruity between what we seem to be and to want, on the one hand, and what happens to us and what we make of ourselves, on the other, recounts the master tale of humanity. It summarizes all our other misadventures and accomplishments.

When you stumble across the person who arouses your sympathy, he appears before you in his dual nature. He is a unique individual in a concrete situation. He is also someone who embodies the great comic sorrow and hope of everyman, thrown into a world to which he does not fully belong and in which he does not entirely fit. For an instant, everyman and the concrete individual are bundled together in the sight of a third person who looks at them, or at him.

This third person sees himself as both involved in the same predicament as the everyman-other and removed from it. Because he is removed, he is able to give his assent, his encouragement, his silent benediction, or his tangible help. This intervention signifies more than a roundabout gift to himself. Because he is involved, his gift amounts to something more than a sacrifice. It stands protected against condescension.

Now, there are two ways to understand the spirit of the gift. In one sense it is a prefigurement or an attenuated modulation of love. In another, more fundamental and revealing sense it is a response by the imagination and the will to the incongruous situation of the everyman-other. This response acknowledges that the life of passion, which is the life of longing and jeopardy, binds people together. It also recognizes that this life can be simultaneously tenacious and self-knowing only when transformed by the offer and the acceptance of sustaining mutual involvement.

So here the will and the imagination, in seeking out a particular individual in a particular situation, also reaffirm the very ground of passion and the dynamic of its progressive transformation. In the course of a lifetime of passion, the self finds a chance in these episodes of loving-kindness to assert through action the formative and transformative principle of all passion. No wonder that sympathy, the highest ennobling experience of association, is also the overriding creative force in any art that deals with persons in relation. Sympathy, when radical enough, fuses with detachment, and the greatest literary artist is the one whose representation of life in art carries out this merger most fully.

Outside art, the enactment of the ground of all passion in a single encounter is only a passing episode, though one that can be repeated. Sympathy is not an enduring scheme of benevolence, protection, and sacrifice. When the initial sympathetic encounter gives way to a lasting mutual involvement, sympathy gets entangled in all the paradoxes of sexless love. The tendency of benevolence to be overtaken in this way by the more ambiguous experience of sexless love is accelerated by a striking feature of the psychology of sympathy: the ease with which the object of the benevolence is confused in the mind of the sympathizer with an image of someone important to him in his prior experience. Thus, the stranger in trouble evokes the picture of a father or brother; or the young man about to plunge into a course of ambitious striving, an image of your past self. When the person who excites the sympathy has no long-standing relation to you, the confusion between him and the image becomes all the easier. The sexless love (or narcissism) felt toward the person held in the image is transformed by memory, nostalgia, and remorse and by the superimposition of this image upon the concrete individual standing before you. Then the double game of illusion begins: the gift to the other is part of a hidden settling of accounts with the resurgent image. The settling of accounts is kept from reaching an impasse of pain and powerlessness by its diversion to the figure of the other whose needs or presence seem to lift some of the weight of your past.

Faith, like hope, occupies a place of its own within the larger economy of love. Even if we give a purely secular interpretation to faith, we can distinguish two elements in it. The first and most basic of these is the willingness to open yourself up to another person or to place yourself in his hands. The second element is the more familiar, cognitive jump: characteristically, you do not know how to justify this hazard of personal openness and vulnerability. If someone challenged you to show that you were justified in undertaking the risk, you could not do so.

The person who has faith in another is not blind to what the other person does, but these deeds remain subordinate to the acceptance of an individual. The normal criteria of evidence are set partly aside because the urge to a knowledge that can be shared matters less than the quest for personal insight and reconciliation. Both strands in faith are included within the ruling theologies of the monotheistic salvation religions. To have faith in God is to put oneself in His hands, with nothing to go on but the ambiguous signs of His presence in the world and of His intervention in history. Each of the two elements of faith internalizes the other. In this personal context faith ceases to exist if the risk fails to include an enlarged acceptance of another person, with its sequel of inescapably hazardous reliance upon him, or if the expanded dependence is perceived as merely a better or worse gamble.

Every act of love implies an act of faith. The lover must suspend the defensive aloofness that marks so much of his experience in society. He must run the risk of being rebuffed or disappointed. He must expose himself to perilous emotion and ridiculous gesture. The risk is all the greater and more difficult to warrant because it is not directly related to any expectation of the capacity of the beloved to execute specific tasks. It is at most an expectation of the happiness and fulfillment of love itself, which, as the most surprising of passions, is the one most likely to confound our designs.

The reference to risk remains legitimate although love may often seem an overmastering impulse in which deliberate choice plays little part. For the stronger the love, the more it involves a turning of the whole being—reason and will, mind and body— toward another. In portraying this turn as an assumption of risk, we must steal from the language of cognition to describe an event that takes place at a point of our experience that remains foreign to the contrast of impulse and understanding.

Consider the transformations of faith first in the primary, personal setting of the emotions and then in the more impersonal cases where the immediate object of faith becomes an institution or an endeavor, as when someone is said to have faith in the constitution of his republic or in his calling as a poet.

The willingness to risk putting yourself in the hands of another beyond the limits of rational justification—the pure acceptance of vulnerability—easily passes into a form of spiritual corruption. The essence of the corruption is the turning of the occasions of vulnerability into devices of dependency, withdrawal, and self-delusion. This change occurs through a double failure, of love and intelligence.

One instance of this reversal of the human meaning of faith is surrender to the entanglement of community in exchange and in domination. Thus, trust deprived of reciprocity, untouched by love, and projected into a situation of rigid inequality becomes subservience to power. The power order does in fact gain features of exchange and mutual allegiance that transform it into something more than an outright structure of coercion. On this narrow ground the self builds illusions that excuse it from fighting over its circumstances and reimagining its possibilities. People may take the pretense to community and exchange at its word. They may dismiss their acquiescence in permanent dependency as if it were only a slight twist on the demands of love and friendship.

In this way a deep and lasting perversion takes place: ideas of accepted vulnerability and dependency become so tied up in each other that the rejection of the latter leads to a rebellion against the former. The psychological experience of openness to the other becomes subtly tainted by the fear of subjection. Once a liberating force, this fear becomes instead a mere impediment to novel attachments.

Faith in others sometimes becomes a reason to retreat into

the core community, of a family or a circle of friends, as a citadel against history and society. The possibility of relations of trust within such a haven is affirmed by contrast to the impossibility of trust outside it. A heightened vulnerability within the magic circle becomes the pretext for a strategy of remorseless defense outside it. The result is a secret wastage of the experience of trust within the secluded area itself. The mutual giving of self takes on an obsessional intensity, an intensity fuelled by the fear of being left alone and defenseless in a brutal world. Under the pressure of this anxiety, people's apprehensive clinging to one another overshadows and corrodes the reality of trust.

These instances of corruption of the faith that we have in one another are special cases of a more general event. We use our ability to enchant others, and to be enchanted by them, to cast a spell on ourselves. The life of trust and vulnerability becomes a way to forget not only power and history but limitation and death. In this way the meaning of human community is reduced to a gathering of the condemned in wait for the execution day, a conspiracy of chatter and of silence against the terror of their situation and the evil in their hearts. At the very summit of reciprocal openness and reliance people discover that they have turned one another into magic ciphers and instruments of evasion. Having changed the inner significance of faith they cross into the area of instrumental relations that lie outside the ground of passion.

Love and intelligence are the forces that oppose these failures and illusions. Love does this less by any final purification of personal faith—for it generates illusions and failures of its own—than by its focus upon another living personality. The other person twists and turns in the net of hierarchy and dependence. He is shown to be as dangerous as the outside world that you were trying to escape. He rebels against the role of bringer of forgetfulness to which you try to reduce him. Intelligence carries out a similar task by giving you the ideas with which to grasp what is distinctive to faith and to tear away the deceptions so paradoxically connected to its liberating work.

Faith may attach itself to a more impersonal context: to activities and institutions. The quality of giving the self to another in a way that lifts defenses is now conferred on a more impersonal endeavor. As a result, the nature of the accepted vulnerability becomes more diffuse. It is still the risk of hurt from others, both the people involved in the same endeavor and the ones who remain hostile or indifferent to it. But it is also the danger of unwanted and unexpected self-transformation and of final disappointment in the venture.

The sign of this more impersonal faith is the breakaway from the undercurrent of boredom and diversion in everyday life and the discovery, in an activity or an institution, of a human reality that fascinates the imagination and enhances the will through a higher measure of self-reflection and self-justification. The endeavors that serve as the objects of faith belong to a mode of action and vision that tries to slough off whatever is merely given, opaque, and unguided by a masterful impulse. Nevertheless, this faith is no privilege of high inspiration: in one tamed form or another it is even more common than personal faith.

This experience of faith as ardor and dedication need not arise from any actual psychological revision of faith as commitment to another person. Impersonal faith is nevertheless subsidiary to personal faith: only the comparison with the latter enables us to separate the elements of truth and illusion in the former and to understand its internal transformations. For though this faith in people is no more common in an ordinary life than the faith in activities and institutions, it approaches more closely the central polarity of the passions.

The truth of faith as dedication is that activities and institutions provide the context of material and moral opportunity in which all acts of self-expression and reconciliation, and therefore of endured vulnerability, can take place. These apparently impersonal objects of faith carry the traces of a larger community that includes the dead and the unborn. They therefore free human life from some of the smallness and blindness of its concerns.

There is nevertheless a danger of illusion in the workings of this impersonal faith, a deception more basic and universal than the particular defects of each institution or activity. The heart of the illusion is the failure to bear in mind the relativity of the context that provides impersonal faith with its object. In the banal and the inspired versions of faith this failure takes sharply different forms while keeping its basic unity. In the ordinary devotion to a scheme of human coexistence it is the inability to see that this scheme represents only a temporary and partial experiment in associative and expressive possibility. The emotion becomes attached to a fragmentary form of social life rather than to the faculties and realities that this form temporarily embodies. This replacement of faith represents the precise counterpart in the life of passion to the exemplary defeat of political will and imagination, the surrender to a conditional social world and the implied denial of its conditionality.

The inspired forms of devotion seem at first to belong to another world. They presuppose a sharp break with the structures of ordinary social life, and they define themselves by opposition to the pieties of ordinary people. This is what we face in the visionary claim of the political prophet, the discoverer, and the creator. However, once we have understood the internal dynamic and ambiguity of this experience, we see that in both its spiritual power and its human danger it differs less from the banal expressions of impersonal faith than at first appears.

The sensible individual and the refined skeptic agree in looking upon the person touched by this high devotion as something between an idiot and an outlaw. They can see nothing that would make it worthwhile to abandon the sweetness and safety of available arrangements and to betray—for betrayal is what visionary insight amounts to—an established form of life. However, their attitude differs in this respect: the repressed religious emotion of the ordinary person can be fired by the human possibility that he sees embodied in the visionary, whereas the cultivated, disillusioned individual has barred himself more carefully against this response and allowed his apprehension to dwindle into a distaste.

A central question for liberal political doctrine is: What should sensible people do to protect themselves from the zealots in their midst? But for an understanding of faith the reverse question is the interesting one: What should he, the man of faith, do to the faithless people around him? He perceives the superstitious character of their faithlessness. In failing to see reality or value beyond the setting of received practice and opinion in which they find themselves, they slide into the reification of that setting, and mistake opinions for objective truths and practices for natural forms of society. They worship a world from which all strangeness has fled, other than the strangeness intermittently revealed to them in the suffering of their hearts.

When he sees through this illusion, the faithful person becomes susceptible to another danger at a higher level of spiritual insight. He may fail to see what is extraordinary though hidden in the ordinary life, its contained and silent devotions, its struggle with each day's relentless demands, and its sheer delight in life and self, however dimmed by habit and preconception. At the same time he may cease to recognize the limited and provisional quality of his own insights and experiences. He may forget that the power to go beyond a context is never the power to reach a supra-contextual reality and value.

In his views of himself and others, he loses his hold on the unity of passion. Having lost it he is punished, even at the height of his accomplishment. He is punished by the superstitious attitude that he now begins to display toward his own discoveries as he forgets their contextual limits and repeats, at a higher visionary level, what he so scornfully condemned in his fellows.

He is rescued from these failures by sympathy and intelligence. Sympathy enables him to experience the analogies of experience. Intelligence allows him to raise this experience into the light of ideas that help clear his insights from pride and deception.

The visionary ardor and modest sacrificial piety that together exemplify impersonal faith can therefore best be understood as a crossfire between the faith people put in one another and their fitful yearning for the absolute or the supra-contextual. For each of these moments of commitment has something of the quality of risking yourself in an encounter and something of the quality of seeing beyond the transience and arbitrariness of faithless drudgery. The constant turning of this iconoclastic impulse into an idolatry that reverses the sense of the impulse is a source of unfathomable grief and cruel delusion in the life of passion. But it is also a reminder that our longing for the unconditional confirms our inability fully to attain it in the realm of human striving and knowledge. The denial of either the longing or the unattainability makes us less than human and undercuts the transformation of faith by sympathy and intelligence.

Hope, like faith, represents an extension and deepening of love. It is the acknowledgment of more openness in a situation than the situation easily reveals: openness above all to the possibility of attachments that are also opportunities for self-assertion, openness to our chances of resolving the problem of solidarity in a way more promising to our freedom. The hopeful person does not merely envisage this possibility; he acts upon it now. He loosens the hold that the routines of society or character exercise over his imagination of personal relations and therefore over these relations themselves.

Hope must already be motivated by love, at least by the generalized and minimal form of love that is sympathy. A person's hope in turn enables him to undertake the experimental lifting of defenses that love requires. Hope, however, is more than a cause or a consequence of love; it is love—love from the standpoint of our ability to downgrade the influence of past and present structures and compulsions, and to act in the present as if we were already driven toward a future marked more fully by the type of encounter between self and self that love most fully exemplifies.

A theological account of secular hope might broaden its

meaning without reversing its sense. When the adherent to the religious mode of this tradition of thinking about personality hopes in his God, he conceives the possibility that his distinctive selfhood might survive in this confrontation with God. He reads in the ciphers of God's presence in the world the message of the openness of history. He sees in each successful event of mutual acceptance among people the annunciation of his final encounter with God and of his communion, in God, with his fellows. He rejoices in the signs that society can become a more fitting home for the context-breaking self. Yet he does so without supposing that any social order can ever provide a definitive context.

You can now see how much hope differs from mere expectation. It has a specific theme, the freedom at stake in the polarity of the passions. It is a predisposition to action rather than merely a foretaste of pleasure. It instantiates a conceived future rather than merely looking to it. Its anticipatory power accounts for the special quality of exaltation that accompanies it.

Hope confronts an apparent dilemma. If the moment of happiness and perfection is always thought to lie in the future, hope degenerates into an ever-frustrated yearning that, convinced of its own futility, eventually becomes a reverie of escape rather than a device of transformation. If, however, the hopeful person settles upon a particular ordering of practical and passionate human relations as the sole object for his hope, he both fools himself and destroys the basis for further hope. His experiments in attachment become once again hostage to a rigid structure of character or society, and he ends up placing his hope in the very things that limit his opportunities for self-transformation.

The definition of hope anticipates the solution to this dilemma. The experience of a hopeful person is already colored by his sense of a future in which the enabling conditions of self-assertion would be more fully reconciled. It is less that he feels improvement to be imminent or inevitable or that the traces of a higher order within a lower one compensate for the defects of the latter, than that he draws guidance and ardor from the elements of his present situation that reveal its capacity for moving toward a greater reconciliation of the polarity of the passions. Hope, like art, is a promise of happiness that sharpens rather than blunts our sense of the incomplete and the unredeemed.

The proposed solution to the dilemma of hope may seem a mere play on words. Yet it merely draws out schematically the implications of certain substantive theses that have performed a central role throughout this argument about personality: that the structures of society and the routines of character never fully inform our practical and passionate dealings with one another, that we can find in the resulting anomalies of personal experience and collective practice elements for the construction of countermodels to existing personal or collective order, that the countermodels on which we have reason to act now are the ones that promise to empower us more fully, and that among the varieties of empowerment for which we strive is the one that results from diminishing the conflict between the implications of our mutual jeopardy and the consequences of our mutual dependence, between the imperative of engagement and the perils of oppression and depersonalization.

Hope, like faith, loses its integrity whenever it breaks its connection to a change in the character of relations among people. Thus, for example, people may then put their hope in a program of social reconstruction that promises to create a more favorable context for their experiments in empowerment. This hope will gradually become utopian dogma as soon as its votaries lose sight of its tentative, experimental justification. The utopian dogma may in turn inspire a mode of conduct in the present that is the very opposite of what hope requires.

People may even find a source of hope in an activity of play, art, or inquiry that enables them to achieve a greater measure of detachment from their present compulsive routines and thereby makes it easier for them to reimagine the life of encounter. But they will be quickly disappointed if they expect this activity to provide a surrogate for the dangers and opportunities of accepted vulnerability. Not even the spectacle of a vaster reality excuses us from the need to imagine an alternative human world and to imagine it in a way that enables us to act in the present as if this alternative had already begun to emerge and its anticipated norms had already begun to bind us.

What, then, can be said, in general, about the relationship between epiphanies of faith, hope, and love in individual lives and the authority commanded by reigning social organizations and political beliefs?

No social situation can preclude these epiphanies or determine the place and time of their happening. Cultures and collectivities differ, however, in their hospitality to these unruly occurrences, in their selection of the areas of social life that they recognize as appropriate to the assertion of faith, hope, and love, and in their willingness to draw political inferences from these revelatory events. To what extent are people able or willing to take risks with one another's conduct by making themselves vulnerable? To what extent, conversely, does their distrust lead them to avoid vulnerability by holding one another to rules or by supervising their subordinates? Insofar as vulnerability exists, is it reciprocal or is it asymmetrical and therefore, perhaps, an aid to the maintenance of a system of domination?

It is in the interstices of mutual vulnerability that the experiences of faith, hope, and love have the best chance of taking hold. An institutionalized condition of shared vulnerability already represents, if only in a pale and distorted way, the net of actual involvements and potential reconciliations that is implied in the higher virtues. The availability of these institutionalized arrangements means that faith, hope, and love have that much less distance to cover before they can gain a grip on a slice of ordinary existence. Trust, like distrust, feeds upon itself; and trust is the common coin of the greater virtues, the normal perimeter of their transforming work, and the atmosphere in which they ordinarily flourish.

The reverse effect of faith, hope, and love upon the habits, prejudices, and hierarchies of established society is an offshoot of the inability of any system to limit the settings in which these passions appear or the means by which they exercise their influence. An episode of faithful and hopeful love occurs when least expected and then repeats itself under countless diluted and disguised forms: at one time an awkward gesture of solidarity among the downtrodden; at another a strange, more perfect example of reconciliation, lodging itself stubbornly as a cyst in a foreign social body. In all these instances the ability to draw political inspiration from the event depends upon the qualities of visionary intelligence and of patient and hopeful availability discussed in the concluding passage of this essay. But if it is true that only these qualities contribute most directly to the making of critical ideas and movements, the raw material of the effort remains the human experience opened up by the transforming passions.

These passions provide an ironic perspective upon established societies and cultures. For every form of social life relies on partly unexamined assumptions about both the ways in which and the extent to which the enabling conditions of self-assertion can be reconciled. These premises are subject to assault on both fronts: they may have underestimated the virulence and versatility of our malevolence or they may have exaggerated the redemptive power of the transforming virtues.

A double progression marks the career of the passions that rigidify and aggravate the antagonism between the conditions of self-assertion. First comes the escalation of distrust. As the conviction grows that hatred, vanity, jealousy, and envy abound, vigilance devours trust. In this climate of increasing menace, precaution, and control, suspicion and hostility proliferate, helping the vices extend their influence and justifying additional restraints. The second element in the progression is the dynamism of domination. The rule-like constraints and the stratagems of surveillance that make up for the disappearance of trust help transitory advantage congeal into conflict-proof privilege. They do so both because they ordinarily require a hierarchy of authority and because they inevitably circumscribe destabilizing controversy. This twofold descent has no natural stopping point. It halts only when it hits against the limits imposed by the ability of the group to satisfy the minimal felt needs of its members, the capacity to survive in the struggle with other groups, or the hope that social life can be put on another and better footing.

For their part, faith, hope, and love may act upon our premises about society and our shared identity in two contrasting ways. Our experiences of partial reconciliation of the enabling conditions of self-assertion may nestle in the corners of the existing system of domination, softening its crudities without changing its substance. Alternatively, these experiences serve as starting points for challenges to this system in the name of a bolder vision of human possibility.

The strategy of compromise puts least initial strain on the transforming passions. But this strategy recapitulates the paralyzing distinction between private and public life. When love, faith, and hope fail to make a mark upon their social surroundings, they must sooner or later be tainted by their service to domination. At any given moment it will be unclear to what extent the promise of reconciliation is a cover-up for the reality of subservience. Because vulnerabilities are unevenly distributed and because people sense this unequal distribution even when they are not wholly conscious of it, the social opportunities for the exercise of the transforming passions may be drastically reduced. Eventually, the equivocation about servility and solidarity finds its way into every area of social life, from friendship or sexual love to the protestations of loyalty to party and country. Thus, the acceptance of power offers these passions a sham and dangerous peace.

When the strategy of attack on the established system of

social division and hierarchy prevails, faith, hope, and love are threatened in a much more direct way. It then becomes necessary to engage in practical or imaginative struggle. This fighting means conflict with the real people whose perceived interests and identities are shaped by the attacked system.

Yet only the willingness occasionally to run the risk of defiance and conflict allows the transforming passions to extend their redemptive influence and preserve their integrity. The better they succeed in this enterprise, the more they broaden the area in which people are willing to expose themselves to surprise in their relations to one another and in their attitudes toward the development of their own talents.

Here, then, is the chief difference in the way that the two directions of the life of passion disrupt our established view of the real and the possible in society. The cycle of hatred, vanity, jealousy, and envy increasingly constricts the realm of human freedom until the cycle is broken by a force external to itself. The career of faith, hope, and love, however, may decisively enlarge the area of social life in which human reconciliation can take hold and human freedom can be acknowledged.

Whenever this tentative enlargement of reconciliation and freedom occurs, the transforming passions reach the height of their power. We then know, less as an abstract idea than as a living experience, that every form of social life is at best a transitory approach to a higher image of solidarity and freedom, an essay in the possibilities of humanity. Our insight into self and society advances because our confidence in the clarity of the distinction between the practicable and the visionary is shaken.

IV

The loving and the hateful passions lack any natural point of balance: their relative influence over an individual's core experiences of relationship and identity may advance or retreat. Moreover, the passions remain obscure to those who undergo them. People understand passion through encounter. But each new encounter alters the subject matter of interpretation and allows for alternative readings. From each new moment of love or hate you can draw different inferences for the sustaining habits of personal or collective existence. The dynamism and ambivalence of the emotions mean that each passionate event can quickly change into its apparent opposite. Every breakthrough toward an experience of greater reconciliation between the enabling conditions of self-assertion takes place in circumstances of heightened vulnerability and self-revelation. In these circumstances all bets are off. Sudden disappointment, despair, and fear may turn the self in another direction, away from the route of self-assertion and reconciliation on which it seems to have embarked. An intense episode of hatred may break apart a set of routines of submission, self-deception, and self-suppression that imprisons the self within a frozen character and an immovable vision.

There are powers and dispositions that enable you to confront these uncertainties and to press forward, in their face, toward the truth about the predicament of mutual longing and jeopardy that the transformative passions vindicate. These dispositions and powers help the person find the structure of conduct and vision that can drive him to a repeated acceptance of vulnerability and sustain him in the face of the ensuing dangers. They do not differ fundamentally from the capacities that enable people to search for the social ideal amid the uncertainties and ravages of history. Their closest parallels in the traditional moralistic writing on human nature are the wise and worldly-wise virtues of courage, moderation, prudence, and fairness.

The way we grasp the point of such virtues, however, changes drastically according to which of two perspectives we adopt. It is one thing to see these norms of conduct as the self-sustaining anchor of the moral life. They then stand for the highest ideal that we can reasonably try to attain in a world where no major advance toward reconciliation and self-expression is possible and where self-assertion must ultimately turn into the display of a heartless natural power. Our overriding moral ambition must then become to restrain or to ennoble this self-assertion—though why, if this is all the world amounts to, should we want to do so? It is another matter to value these qualities as the shield and spur of a more drastic shift in moral experience: the shift manifest in love, hope, and faith. This second perspective forbids us to take any ordinary virtue as a good in itself. The authority of every such virtue, indeed its meaning, will depend upon its relation in context to the possibilities of human connection that the transforming passions enlarge.

The path of advance toward these passions may require you to act in foolhardy and preposterous ways. For when you conceive the life of passion in the manner described, you refuse to see yourself as the custodian of a patrimony not to be squandered or as the guardian of defenses not to be lowered. You understand that the redemptive impulse—the impulse to change the relation between longing and jeopardy—lives in danger of dying within a coat of spiritual armor. You do not forget that the provisional, partial structures of habit and vision that sustain, guide, and protect you must be periodically shattered and remade, in renewed acts of accepted vulnerability, so that you may remain in touch with the personal realities that count most. You have taken to heart the negativistic, remorseless, and impish answer that traditional religious insight gives to the question: Where is wisdom to be found? Not among the wise, that's for sure.

On such a view, the clear-eyed virtues of moderation, prudence, courage, and fairness can best be seen as incidents to the transforming passions. Our received picture of these virtues must be torn apart. Their place in our ideal and descriptive account of personality may be taken by categories that are more abstract and indeterminate, in part because, like every other element in this analysis of passion, they join a psychological account to an evaluative stance. I choose for this purpose the ideas of visionary intelligence and of hopeful and patient availability.

Through the transforming experiences of faith, hope, and love or through the countervailing experiences of the hateful passions, you make discoveries about the relation between the enabling conditions of self-assertion. Visionary intelligence is the capacity to think through the implications of these discoveries for the tenor of ordinary personal and collective existence. The privileged moments of self-expression and reconciliation cannot embrace the entire life of an individual, nor can they penetrate all social existence. Even on their own ground they remain precarious, as the earlier discussion of love was meant to show. A special insight must identify the possible spin-offs of these moments: the changed forms that can endure and take hold of a larger part of personal and collective existence. At the same time this insight must find the ordinary, enduring dispositions in personal activity and in social arrangements that can resist the cycle of hatred and distrust.

The labor of visionary intelligence is a work of moral realism. This realism distinguishes itself by its refusal to make exaggerated and impractical demands upon self and society. The usual effect of efforts to satisfy such demands is to turn moral aspiration into a sentimental fluff thrown over the harsh facts of weakness and compromise. But this realism also sets itself apart by its refusal to mistake personal or collective possibility for the established routines of a personal or a collective experience. Such routines must always be placed within a larger setting of unrealized opportunity. It is for the definition of this setting that we need a social theory free from the illusions of false necessity, whether they be functionalist or evolutionary, materialist or cultural in temper.

To maintain this spirit of realism, visionary intelligence must accomplish two overlapping tasks. It must find the collective equivalents to the inherently personal experiences of love, faith, and hope. It must also discover the structures—more or less habitual dispositions and more or less institutionalized arrangements —that can preserve in ordinary existence something of what life momentarily becomes under the influence of the higher passions. Though the first task constitutes an aspect of the second, each repays discussion in its own right.

The transforming passions show us what it is like for the enabling conditions of self-assertion to be more fully reconciled. They raise ordinary, profane existence to a higher order of power and free it for the moment from its meanness. Set to work by this experience, the visionary intelligence must ask itself which imaginative plan and practical ordering of social life can capture and enact a touch of this heightened possibility of human connection. In asking this it also asks how these imaginative and practical structures can best acknowledge the force and resist the triumph of the hateful passions. To these questions there are never direct or uncontroversial answers.

Different schemes of human association can supply plausible, alternative collective equivalents to an experience of human connection from which the shadow of a flat conflict between the conditions of empowerment has been lifted. Many social visions rigidly exclude from much of ordinary social life the fuller personal connections represented by the transforming passions. This exclusion may be justified by an appeal to practical requirements whose satisfaction supposedly enables more perfect forms of human association to flourish in narrower areas of social existence. The visionary intelligence refuses to accept such justifications at face value; it seeks to reimagine and redesign social life in ways that bring prosaic social existence a little closer to the quality of our best moments of mutual acceptance.

Consider, for example, the past societies in which a single model of human association was proposed, like a theme and variations, for every area of social life, from the relation between a ruler and his subjects to that between a master and his servant, or a father and his son. This paradigmatic form of human association was often thought to specify a style of coexistence that would bring together in the same relations communal attachment, unequal exchange, and the ties of domination and dependence. Unequal exchange and potentially violent dominion would be cleansed and ennobled by the acknowledgment of mutual duties of loyalty.

The exercise of dominion in any of its forms destroys the climate of mutual vulnerability. Deprived of this climate, the transforming passions and the human truth to which they testify become accessible only in distorted fashion when accessible at all. Each gesture of acceptance and attachment is confused with the effort to manipulate another person or to excuse the abdication of your own freedom. The struggle to preserve, to manage, and to conceal this structure of rule and subjection enmeshes the attachment in a series of puns about love and power. The sincere or feigned self-restraint of the superior and the craven, half-resentful loyalty of the subaltern both aggravate and temper the dilemmas of sexless love: they aggravate it by the tangible force of dominion and temper it by the relative weakening of the passion. Faced with an authoritative image of human association that insists upon the rightful merger of attachment, exchange, and dominion, the visionary intelligence sees another reality. It infers from the ordinary experience of passion the subversive influence of power upon love and therefore upon the communal attachments that represent weaker counterparts to love.

Community is sometimes understood as a circumstance of restraint upon the play of self-interest or as a condition in which shared interests and values prevail to the exclusion of conflict. But the analysis of the passions shows that all such definitions of community are superficial or subsidiary. Though they intend to describe a deep bond of union among people, they stop short of the strongest connections. The adherence to shared values and interests remains more a partnership for the advance of a common cause than an act of radical mutual acceptance. The survival of such a partnership characteristically depends upon continued antagonism to outsiders and continued allegiance to certain ideas. In the better community, union outlasts conflict, and conflict drives people into a deeper reciprocal involvement until at last they feel responsible for one another's fate. A far-reaching restraint on the play of self-interest can exist in a situation in which the parties remain distant from each other and in which their ties mean little more than the unwillingness to treat one another as mere instruments or obstacles. These varieties of community represent truncated versions of a more basic idea: precisely the idea of heightened mutual vulnerability that serves as the ground of the transforming passions.

But how can the visionary imagination derive such insights from the life of passion when the experience of this life is unavoidably shaped by reigning ideas and institutions? In all the societies in which visionary intelligence must carry out the task of imagining the practical, collective parallels to the achievements of the transforming passions, even the most intimate encounters between men and women, or parents and children, are marked by the puns of love and power. Nevertheless, the events of passion always do move beyond the limits imposed on them by established institutions and ideas. The life of passion undergoes variations, and conceals insights, that have no place in the professed dogmas about society and self. Whenever a social world is pulled apart by escalating practical or visionary conflict, our imagination of the possible and desirable forms of social life returns to the lessons of passion. Though society informs these lessons it does not inform them entirely. The unshaped part—the deviations, the anomalies, the surprises—provides the visionary imagination with the materials for subversive insight. These materials never remain inaccessible even when the practical and imaginative order of society seems to have become unbreakable and unquestionable.

The search for the collective equivalents to personal discoveries represents an element in a larger program, the program of defining the habits of collective or personal existence that favor the recurrence of the transforming passions. Because it is realistic, the visionary imagination understands that the life of an individual cannot consist in an uninterrupted flow of transforming passions nor the life of a people in an endless series of practical and imaginative conflicts that keep society in a condition of permanent indefinition. But what should the moment of rest be like? To a greater or lesser extent it may keep the qualities that distinguish the moment of transformation. A visionary intelligence seeks the social order that multiplies in ordinary life the occasions for the practical and imaginative collective activity from which that order arose in the first place. It wants to soften the contrast between the times when society is broken open to aggravated conflict and the times when it closes in upon itself. The visionary intelligence proposes to make the latter more closely resemble the former. When it addresses itself to personality and character (which is the routinized order of personality), it tries to develop the dispositions that preserve in ordinary activity and perception the more intense at-riskness of the self and its greater openness to an alien presence—qualities that mark the transforming passions. The immediate moral and psychological basis of this attitude must be found in the analysis of another stabilizing virtue: patient and hopeful availability.

This virtue establishes a link between the transforming experiences of faith, hope, or love, on one side, and the simple attachment to life, on the other. More generally, it describes a response to the contextual quality of our actions, a response that acknowledges rather than traduces the polarity of the passions.

This availability implies an immense gusto of attachment, venture, and existence, a delight in the surprises and opportunities of life, and a readiness to treat personal or collective structures of vision and action as realities that are not for keeps. Hopefully and patiently available, the person combines two experiences of his situation. He throws himself into it—all the way—taking its attachments for real and refusing even for a moment to regard himself, however unfortunate his circumstances, as a permanent exile from a golden world. But at the same time, he treats any particular aspect of this world as something that already is, or might or should be, up for grabs. On his lips is always the question: What will happen next? And in his heart the assurance: You haven't seen anything yet.

The most elementary ground of the whole system of passion is the brute quality of attachment to ordinary existence: the dogged clinging to life and established relations no matter what the hardships. At the most simple, unreflective, and undeveloped level, this attachment is merely the inertial effort to meet the responsibilities of the day. It is the holding on to existence and its demands, as devotions turn into loss and as life slides away into death. It is the dim, dazed, fabulously somnambulant atmosphere for much of ordinary existence. So long as immediate physical needs remain in command of people's concerns, this crepuscular tenacity may absorb a large part of effort and reflection. But as soon as the pressure of these inescapable needs begins to relax, this root involvement can move in other directions. Through progressive transformations it may at last become the patient and hopeful availability of which I now speak. Consider the alternative changes that this simple vitality can undergo.

The elementary attachment to life and its daily demands may define itself ever more clearly as an apathetic and defensive submission to the habitual contexts of your activity: both your character and your station become confused with your very self. You lose all sense of possible distance from them or from the larger situation in which they exist. The struggle to sustain them against the ruins of time, misfortune, and failure absorbs all your attention. When not actively defending station and character, you fall back exhausted into the torpor of the original dim attachment to life, a torpor that now appears to be less punishing than the occasional, more anxious intervals of uncertain effort and unforeseen pressure. Existence dwindles into the play of boredom and diversion.

An alternative route that the elementary attachment to life can follow is the heightening of the sense of experienced human power. It is the brio and panache, the sheer vibrant life, of a personality that acts as master of its own world. Sometimes this quality shows itself in the joy with which people defy established personal habits or collective arrangements and perceptions, or even ordinary physical limits. Sometimes it appears in the partial, acid substitute for this defiance: the ability to lord it over other people. The capacity to impose terms upon other people's activities is always a small-scale, contained, and distorted version of the larger, freer power to re-create the terms of collective existence. But even if the rapture of capability takes the more generous form, it has about it something cruel and remorseless, something that is superhuman without being divine. The will and the imagination set themselves on a course of collision with the physical, cognitive, and spiritual limits to life. They act as if they were the masters of a world they do not in fact possess more than a little. These votaries of splendor refuse to acknowledge the implications of contextuality. They worship in themselves and in others the manifestation of a structure-breaking power, and they subordinate to this worship all judgments and attachments.

But there is yet another direction that the original, dim attachment to life may pursue. Like the display of magnificence, it rejects the fatalism of apathy. But unlike this display, it alters and restrains the quest for mastery over the particular social and mental worlds we inhabit. It does so for the sake of a certain vision of the relation between love and empowerment, a vision that this entire essay has been devoted to describe. The apostles of magnificent action sometimes mistake this other view for a gospel of pathetic self-abasement and surrender. But its true nature appears in a response to the basic facts of existence. This response makes use of moral dispositions that together constitute the greatest qualities of the heart.

You find yourself set down in particular social and mental worlds. These worlds have all the characteristics that the modernist doctrine or our relation to our contexts has illuminated. The modes of discourse and explanation available to you never exhaust the possibilities of understanding and communication. You may at any moment make discoveries or inventions that cannot be validated, verified, permitted, or even conceived within any one of these ways of thinking and talking. Having made such inventions or discoveries, you may construct retrospectively the form of thought or discourse that can show its sense. Similarly, the established scheme of human association never exhausts the opportunity to establish practical or passionate attachments that promise more fully to empower us in many of the senses of empowerment earlier distinguished. The course of life in society generates disguised and undeveloped intimations of personal and collective possibilities that the established social world seems to exclude. The direct, passionate relations among individuals always contain more than is envisaged by the reigning imaginative scheme of human association or the established practical plan of social division and hierarchy. The routine politics of bargain and privilege, endlessly fought out within the limits of an entrenched practical and imaginative order, can escalate at any moment into conflicts that shake up this order. The practical imperative to recombine and to renew institutional arrangements for the sake of worldly success generates an unceasing flow of half-voluntary, localized social experiments that suggest, when they do not favor or demand, more far-reaching transformations. What is true about the revision of thought and society holds as well for self-transformation. The constant pressure of distraction and temptation, and the surprises of involuntary remembrance and emotion, longing and dreaming, present to you the signs of all the selves that your hardened character seems to have stamped out forever. Part of the sympathy and horror that you experience in your dealings with others comes from your recognition that unmanifest and unacknowledged parts of yourself are realized in the people you encounter.

So you know in all these ways that, though it is your fate to live within conditional worlds, you also have the power to break outside them. When you do that, however, you do not reach the unconditional: the thought beyond limiting method and language, the society beyond limiting practical and imaginative structure, the personality beyond limiting character. You can, nevertheless, work toward a situation that keeps alive the power to break the limits: to think thoughts that shatter the available canon of reason and discourse, to experiment with forms of collective life that the established practical and imaginative order of society locks out or puts down, to reach out toward the person beyond the character. And you can therefore also hope to change the sense of contextuality: to create the thought, society, and character that lessen the distinction between incorporated realities and excluded opportunities and that hold themselves more fully open to the recombinant forces of passion and problem-solving.

An all-embracing frame of reference is what we cannot have. But we can develop a freedom that has a twofold relation to the dream of finding the absolute context, the context that would give us our true image and our definitive home. This freedom has the same source as the basic circumstance of contextuality that makes the dream impossible to realize. At the same time, however, it constitutes the attainable element in that impractical longing. The idea of this freedom offers us a vision of empowerment that touches every aspect of our experience and takes on more specific forms when applied to thought, society, or character.

Thought, within and outside science, advances by overthrowing the tyranny of immediate experience. The more powerful it becomes, the better it is able to absorb actuality into a more articulate and inclusive appreciation of possibility and to override the choice between a narrow sense of necessity and an empty conception of contingency. Our thinking is never more successful than when it can treat facts as special cases of a broader counterfactual realm from which they come and to which they may return. To understand how something works is to grasp the occasions and varieties of its possible transformation. To see only what is there to be seen is to understand nothing at all.

The science of our day has given this idea a support in the nature of physical reality by suggesting that all the regularities of nature are relative to a specific degree of energy just as the order of society depends upon the interruption and containment of conflict. At increasing levels of temperature and density the distinctions of the observable world break down one by one, and its deeper symmetries are revealed, if they exist. Thus, science does the unfinished work of higher energy just as social theory does the work of unfinished conflict.

The thought that can relieve its subject matter of a dumb and impenetrable facticity steadily acquires certain characteristics of its own. It devalues the fixity of genres and forswears the commitment to privileged methods or representations—those whose privilege consists in their insensitivity to changes in our empirical beliefs. It becomes less and less a closed system of inferential rules or stable presuppositions and more and more a machine for making discoveries that require the retrospective addition of new rules or new presuppositions. In these ways it comes to embody the qualities that it attributes to the reality under study and to subsume itself without paradox in the world for which it accounts.

Society improves by laying its practical and imaginative order ever more open to correction.* To each feature of the social structure of hierarchy and division and of the imaginative vision of right human association there should correspond an activity that can bring it into question and open it up to renewed collective conflict and decision. The more available such activities become in the ordinary course of social life, the weaker the sense in which the practical and imaginative order of society exists at all. For this order does not subsist in the same way as the structure of a physical object nor does it survive just because people hold certain beliefs about its nature, justification, and possible reform. It exists in the absence of the practical or imaginative activities that might reconstruct it. The more entrenched against recurrent transformative activity the basic structure of society becomes, the sharper the

---

*For a more extended discussion of the legal and institutional implications of this ideal and of the ways in which it may be defended, see my "The Critical Legal Studies Movement," 96 Harvard Law Review 561 (1983).

contrast between two moments of social life: the long, quiet, hallucinatory periods when major arrangements gain their delusive halo of naturalness and necessity and the shorter intervals when society returns, through practical and visionary fighting, to indefinition. As opportunities to revise institutions multiply, the gap between these two conditions of social life shortens; each bears some characteristics of the other. The convergence of both these moments has a practical and a spiritual significance. Together, these two aspects of the convergence help show why the breaking open of structure to politics should count as a regulative ideal.

An element in the ability to develop practical collective capabilities is the readiness to recombine and reconstruct the institutional arrangements within which practical activities take place. The content of this thesis may be defined by contrast to both the narrower economic conception of rationality and the Marxist view of the favoring social circumstances of repeated material progress. The economic idea of rationality as the free recombination of the factors of production within a given institutional context must be extended to the free recombination of the elements that define such a context. The Marxist view of the recurrent shattering of a mode of production for the sake of the development of productive forces must be generalized into a view of innovation. Collective invention for the sake of worldly success requires an ability to shift at frequent intervals, and at many different levels, between the relative stability of vested rights and the accelerated movement of revised institutional positions. Both the economic notion of rationality and the Marxist view of material progress can best be understood and justified as special cases of a more general insight. Political economy limits the reach of this insight either by distinguishing arbitrarily between the recombination of the factors of production and the remaking of their institutional context or by supposing unjustifiably that this context has a natural form. Marxist doctrine limits the reach of this insight by alloying it with necessitarian ideas about society and history (the sequence of modes of production, each with a coherent logic of its own).

The opening up of the practical and imaginative order of society to a principle of accelerated revision, to conflict and deliberation, has a spiritual as well as a practical significance. The ties of dependence and the pressure of depersonalization draw their force from an institutional and imaginative ordering of social life that has gained immunity to the disturbances of our ordinary activity. But we can create institutions and conceptions that go ever further in denying such an immunity to themselves and to the routines that they help shape. By such means, we can break through the false necessities that enmesh exchange and production in rigid hierarchies and that hold each individual's experiments in association and self-expression within frozen social forms. We thereby lessen the conflict between the enabling conditions of self-assertion. We prevent society from resembling nature, or history from turning into fate. And we keep ourselves in the state of permanent searching, and therefore of uncompromising and undeceived self-respect, that nearly amounts to a secular salvation.

The person becomes better by laying his character—the ridigified version of his self—open to revision. We should desire that a social order perpetuate in its routine institutions and activities something of the experience of remaking and reimagining society that marks the times when practical and visionary struggle escalates. So, too, we should want that a character include the disposition to change through repeated subjection to moments of heightened vulnerability, moments whose avoidance allowed the character to form in the first instance. And just as we prize the plasticity of social life for the sake of the experiments in practical problem-solving and passionate attachment that it encourages, so we value plasticity in character for the corresponding forms of empowerment that it makes possible. Our experiments in accepted vulnerability represent the individual equivalent to the escalation of context-respecting quarrels into context-revising disputes.

Among these experiments, those that involve a repeated subjection to the central incidents in the life of passion occupy a special place. But none of these incidents are privileged over others: though nothing can entirely replace the tests and discoveries of personal intimacy, the pursuit of a task in the world offers another way to throw the character up for grabs, another refusal of the vain attempt to hedge bets against time. Even within the realm of personal encounter, the commitment to this repeated hazard of self-transformation does not always imply a willingness to destabilize attachments. It all depends. Thus, for example, one reason to view a marriage as indissoluble is that this commitment enables husband and wife to accept and experience conflict without fearing every disagreement as a possible cause of separation. And conflict within a union informed by both sexual and sexless love is one of the devices that may allow an experiment in accepted vulnerability to go on.

The basic facts about contexts and context-breaking and the ideals which these facts help support may now be joined to earlier remarks about the primacy of the personal in the imagination of society. These combined ideas suggest a deeper interpretation of patient and hopeful availability as a distinctive enhancement of the primitive, tenacious hold on life. Here, as elsewhere, the most penetrating view of passion directly links our basic circumstances and our most urgent concerns.

The more a person possesses the quality of patient and hopeful vulnerability, the less he treats the social world he is in as merely a wretched purgatory that separates him from true value and true reality. He sees his attachments and his circumstance as the contextual facts that they are. He does not confuse them with the unconditional insight and satisfaction for which he continues to yearn, wildly or softly, clearly or dimly, so long as he retains his humanity. He looks beyond his present contexts and recognizes in the very devices of their continuance the instruments of their possible transformation, not just into different contexts but into contexts of a different type.

For all this, he is hopeful and, being hopeful, available. But he does not conduct himself as an outcast, nor is he always in a rush to be someone else and somewhere else. For the people in his world fascinate him, and with some of them he is in love. The quality of the personal gets shaped through the conditional, constraining force of impersonal institutions and ideas. But it is still there, and it has the marks of something less provisional and less imperfect than itself.

The life of passion confirms this context-transcending quality of the personal. Though informed by the practical and imaginative order of each social world, the range of encounter spills over the limits of this order. Nevertheless, we hold on to this life-giving quality of the personal and of personal attachment only by periodically destroying and remaking the social and individual routines into which personal relations constantly descend.

What we see in the world as a whole that corresponds to the entrancement of personality is the spectacle of being, being as something beyond the discrete forms it provisionally takes and the discrete representations of these forms that we temporarily entertain. This is more than a superficial analogy. Our most credible experience of a foundational reality is our experience of the quality of the personal. It is only through a generalization which is also a gamble that we may see in the world as a whole the same context-transcending quality that we rightly attribute in society to the experience of personality and to the creation of practical or passionate attachments. Someone who makes this gamble may show toward all nature a measure of the patient and hopeful availability that he shows more understandably toward people. He sees all the transmutations of the world as conditional. But he detects in them the signs of a reality that they do not exhaust. Such a person is no fugitive in the world. When, however, he attributes to his insight into nature the intimate comprehension that he can hope for in his experience of the personal, he fools himself about the power of the mind and the nature of intellectual objectivity. And whenever he seeks in science and in the vision of impersonal being a refuge from the disappointments and dangers of personal intimacy, he risks the withering of his own self.

The attitude toward being-in-a-context that I have described under the name of patient and hopeful availability appears most purely and intensely in the alliance of ardor with gentleness. To be ardent and to be gentle—this is the moral perfection that we all desire for ourselves when we manage to be wise without being wordly-wise. Whenever we discern an element of this combination in ourselves or in others, we sense in it the presence of something that escapes the meanness and dimness of ordinary existence, something that might count as the badge of spiritual nobility if anything could.

Ardor is a transformation and enhancement of the primitive attachment to life and its demands. It is the enhancement that consists in the experienced conviction that your life touches facts that do not depend for their reality and value upon the survival and authority of particular social or mental worlds. Only two facts are like this: primarily the experience of personality and derivatively the spectacle of being. To be truly ardent is to be moved by concerns that transcend the clash of immediate interests. But it is also to judge and to experience these concerns—ideas, institutions, programs—as more or less flawed embodiments of personality or being. Only when ardor takes this direction can it join with gentleness.

Gentleness, in this setting, is just another name for sympathy. It is to see and to treat the other as a person always precariously and incongruously caught in finite and conditional worlds and situations, character and body, and thus entangled in circumstances disproportionate to the context-transcending capabilities of the self. What saves this disposition from condescending pity is the certainty that you share the predicament you identify in the other. To call it gentleness is to bring out the special quality of the ardor with which it combines and to emphasize how it differs from the display of magnificence. The vibrancy of engagement in life connects with an inability to treat other people as passive objects or convenient instruments of self-assertion. Whenever ardor becomes detached from its reference to personality or being, whenever it takes particular ideas, institutions, or states of affairs as its ultimate aims, it passes into the fanaticism of idolatry. For we call idolatry the effort to treat something finite and conditional as if it were unconditional and infinite.

Gentleness and ardor correspond to qualities that many cultures and many institutionally enforced role systems have identified as the distinctive virtues of the man and the woman. The woman is cast as the expert in the nuance of personality. She has insight into the primacy of personal encounter as the basic human reality from which all the more institutionalized forms of association emerge. She treats the institutional arrangements and the reigning dogmas of society at a discount, identifying in the concrete ways they are manipulated the personal demands that they ostentatiously conceal: the desire to be cared for and to be assured a place in the world, the fear of rejection and the denial of loss, the perpetual transformation of all advantages and accidents into symbols of the relations between people. She reads the elusive heart and sees through the revealing and obscuring film of words and deeds. Her *esprit de finesse* is the reverse side of her expertise in personality. Once she has mastered this ability, however, she can apply it even to the impersonal world, not because she interprets nature animistically but because she possesses the secret of art, which is depth without abstraction, achieved through detail pursued to the point of obsession.

The man, by contrast, lives in the tumult of history. He is more ready to affirm personality through a contest of wills that repeatedly mixes up noble and base motives. His worldliness passes quickly into the devotion to intangible ends, precisely because his personal ambitions so quickly assume a more impersonal form. If you define the political standpoint narrowly as the attention to the impersonal ideas and practices that set the terms of personal relationship, the man knows that politics is fate. No wonder he is more inclined to think abstractly, for abstraction is another aspect of the power of the impersonal, that is to say, of the influence that our mental and institutional contexts exercise over our practical and passionate dealings.

Even in the societies in which people uphold this polemical contrast most fiercely, it never exhaustively describes the experienced differences between men and women. Some of each excel in the qualities that, on the ruling view, more naturally belong to the other. But those who want to join gentleness to ardor in the fashion of the view developed here turn these embarrassing deviations into deliberate experiments. They neither disregard the sexual difference nor envisage any definitive, harmonious integration of the two styles of experience with which it has been traditionally associated. They nevertheless reject the surrender of the division of the sexes to this mutilating antithesis and put in place of this antagonism the ideal of the psychologically androgynous person. They seek the forms of insight and experience that can arise only through the joining of what the stereotype divides and through the new oppositions that the new combinations make possible.

More generally, the alliance of ardor and gentleness brings out the distinctive psychological meaning of the attempt to reconcile the ideals of love and empowerment that have had so troubled a relation in the history of our major tradition of thinking about personality. To be, in this sense, both ardent and gentle is to act in the spirit of one who affirms the primacy of the problem of solidarity but understands this problem from the perspective of a modernist view of our power to escape, reimagine, and revise the settings of our action.

Those who are ardent and gentle have learned how to be in the world without being entirely of it. They know and feel themselves not fully imprisoned within their context, but not because they have mistaken it for the absolute. Theirs is the only happiness that rests on no illusion and requires no indifference.

Appendix:

A Program for Late Twentieth-Century Psychiatry

Presented as the William C. Menninger Memorial Convocation Lecture at the 133rd annual meeting of the American Psychiatric Association, San Francisco, May 3–9, 1980. Published in the American Journal of Psychiatry, 139:2, February 1982, pp. 155–164.

Psychiatry as a science can no longer progress without confronting certain basic theoretical problems that it has habitually minimized or dismissed. The effort to recognize these problems requires a reconsideration of the basic explanatory structure of psychiatry: psychiatry's image of the relationship between biological and psychological accounts, its background conception of the fundamental reality of passion and subjectivity, and even its tacit assumptions about what it means to explain something. Consider what is most interesting and most disheartening about psychiatry as a science today.

The Denial and the Trivialization of Disarray

Two or three problems stand at the center of contemporary psychiatry. One set of issues has to do with the advance of biochemically based explanations and therapies and their uncertain relationship to psychological models and diagnostic categories. A second cluster centers on the disturbing, systematic indeterminacy of the psychological models themselves. By indeterminacy I mean the startling fact that explanations and treatments supported by apparently clashing assumptions often seem to work equally well or equally badly. It is possible to distinguish from this problem of indeterminacy still a third zone of puzzlement: an odd feature of psychiatry's relation to its subject matter. Psychiatrists deal with the human passions. (I use the concept of passion in a sense that includes the areas covered by current usage of the terms "affect" or "emotion" but that is meant to incorporate a broader field of reference. This field will be defined more precisely at a later stage in my argument.) Psychiatry has never entirely abandoned the principle that the understanding of mental illness and the analysis of the ordinary emotions and the ordinary consciousness bear on each other. Yet it has failed to develop a view of the passions that is anything other than the shadow of its particular conjectures about insanity, its therapeutic strategies, and its diagnostic vocabulary.

By understanding the scientific riddles and opportunities that lie at the heart of each of these sets of questions, psychiatry could grasp their relation to one another and begin to reorganize itself as a science. Instead, its current tendency is to hesitate between two unwise responses toward its own major problems. There is the attitude of obsessional sectarianism that fixes on one well-established perspective—biochemical, Freudian, or whatever—and then disregards or downplays the insights that are not readily assimilable to it. Alternatively, there is the posture of flaccid eclecticism that treats the plurality of explanatory models less as an unsettling and instructive predicament than as the customary price of excessive scientific ambition. The first response hides from the riddles. The second trivializes them. Each amounts to both a theoretical and a moral failure.

Nothing harms science more than the denial or the trivialization of enigma. By holding the explanatory failures of psychiatric science squarely before our eyes, we are also able to discover the element of valid insight in even the most extreme and least careful attacks on contemporary psychiatry: to make even his most confused and unforgiving critics into sources of inspiration is a scientist's dream.

From this point on, my argument will proceed by four steps. First, I shall suggest that the achievements and opportunities of biological psychiatry can—indeed should—be viewed in a way very different from the manner in which we have grown accustomed to seeing them, in a way that lends new force to the ancient idea of the unitary character of mental illness. Second, I shall argue that the disintegration of the dominant psychological and specifically Freudian theories in psychiatry has gone much further than we like to think. The starting point for an analysis of the psyche must be a sustained reflection on the significance of the indeterminacy of the psychological models available to us and a redefinition of these models as special cases of a more general theory of passion. The third part of my discussion will make the claim that the development of biological and psychological psychiatry along the lines I will have sketched suggests the elements of a unitary program for scientific psychiatry. The execution of this program can alone enable psychiatrists to solve the crucial explanatory and therapeutic problems that must increasingly concern them. In the fourth stage of my argument I shall briefly place this program in a larger context of modernist culture and contemporary politics.

What I need from you is an imaginative effort to recapture the strangeness of puzzles and ideas on which you have spent a lifetime of study and struggle. The effort will be all the more exacting because my comments are unavoidably hacked down to a barebone of argument, example, and refinement. The act of intellectual and moral availability that I ask of you demands, in miniature, all the decisive qualities of the scientific mind: its detachment, its remorselessness, and its magnanimity.

The Biological Program

Take first the background of biological conceptions in modern psychiatry. For all the divergence among theoretical schools, there is a fund of ideas about the relationship between biological and psychological explanation that are shared by seemingly incompatible schools of thought. As new discoveries are made in brain pathology, neurophysiology, and psychopharmacology, their significance is more or less assimilated to this underlying view. Crudely put, it goes like this. The better we understand the organic substratum of mental illness, the more accurately we can trace the relation between specific physical events in, say, neuroregulation and specific mental diseases already known to us. This relation provides us with the key to the deep causation of the disease and to the specifically effective therapy. On

one view—a view to which Freud himself kept returning—
psychological accounts and therapies are a holding action until the
explanatory and therapeutic triumph of biochemistry. Opinions
may differ only on whether that day is already at hand. On
another view, which behavior and learning theorists have often
defended, there is a fundamental difference between biologically
based mental diseases, like senile dementia or porphyria, to
which the medical model applies exclusively, and other behavioral anomalies, to which it does not apply at all. Not only biological explanations but all accounts that invoke the unconscious
may be irrelevant to these latter disorders.

There are two aspects of this hidden stock of ideas that immediately disturb the unceremonious critic. One of them is the
tendency to hold the diagnostic descriptions constant: to assume
that the biological explanations will show stable relations to familiar diagnostic categories although these categories were formulated with totally different theoretical aims and assumptions. The
other strange fact is the habit of viewing the interaction of biological and psychological explanations in an exclusionary and
reductionist way. People forget that even in physical science the
premise of the ultimate reducibility of one level of explanation to
another is less a fact about the world than a programmatic slogan.
The premise becomes all the more dubious when consciousness is
at issue. The variety of possible ways in which a psychological dynamic might work upon a relatively indeterminate biological condition, and change it, gets repeatedly slighted.

These disquiets create the intellectual opportunity to
suggest that the progress and prospects of biological psychiatry
can be reinterpreted from the standpoint of three central ideas.
Together, these conceptions would define an alternative approach
to the significance of biological explanation for scientific psychiatry. This approach is at least as compatible with the available experimental evidence as the reservoir of assumed conceptions I described earlier, and much clearer, simpler, and more
fruitful.

The first idea is the distinction among different levels and senses in which biological phenomena can be active in mental disease. A great deal of recent psychopharmacological research—precisely the kind that seems to reveal fixed relations between identifiable organic deficiencies and particular mental diseases—focuses on events that can just as well be given a narrow interpretation. It deals with the immediate biochemical correlates of a syndrome, correlates that may already prove to be effects as well as causes of a psychological episode. These biochemical events are perhaps rather late and superficial counterparts to a more basic process by which the person as organism becomes susceptible to a chain of psychological events leading up to the well-known psychoses. It is remarkable that even many of the mental diseases with a strict organic foundation—like the psychotic pellagra studied by Llopis—seem to manifest, in the course of their development, a large part of the symptoms displayed in the classical psychoses.

The significance of this similarity is masked by an unacknowledged, pseudoscientific prejudice. We expect there to be an immediate and well-defined homology between the causes of a disorder and its manifestation in the structure of conduct and cognition. A mental illness with a specifically organic base is supposed to differ clearly from one in which psychodynamic factors are paramount. But the principle of homology may apply only at a level far deeper than we suspect. The parallelism between the organically based and the other psychoses suggests that the organic and the mental are involved in each other to an astonishing degree and in a manner to which the reduction of the mental to the organic cannot do justice.

The same set of mental experiences always presents itself to us as the result of two sets of factors: one, physical; the other, psychodynamic. Any disorder or therapy that begins with one of these factors will immediately have effects upon the other. At opposite poles of the field of mental pathology, one or the other of these elements may dwindle in importance. But in the broad middle range they coexist. If the principle of homology still applies, it must hold at a deeper level of causation, to which our current conceptions of the mental and the organic may prove equally foreign.

The significance of this formulation is to save us from pretending to understand what we in fact ignore: the final connection between the organic and the mental. It allows us to recognize remarkable facts, like the symptomatic analogies between the organically based psychoses and the other mental disorders. It keeps us from misinterpreting the occasional success of a physical or psychodynamic approach as an indication of the ultimate relationship between the mental and the organic. This argument has an implication that must now be brought out as the second idea in the biological program.

The implication is that the unitary conception of mental illness should be revived and reconstructed. Among the many assumptions that biological and Freudian psychiatrists have shared is Kraepelin's principle of the specificity of the psychoses. Since the late nineteenth century, the advocates of a unitary view—like Llopis himself, or Karl Menninger, or Adolf Meyer in his later writings—have always been condemned, on this point, to a marginal position. But things are not what they seem: the heart is going out of the anti-unitary position. The diagnostic classification becomes a brittle shell as it is increasingly emptied of its original theoretical content in order to be immunized against disconcerting facts. The seriousness with which the diagnostic vocabulary is still taken today turns Kraepelin on his head: the master would never have admitted that the classification could be anything more than shorthand for a particular theoretical view, with its supporting climate of interpreted facts.

The larger significance of biological research for psychiatry may—paradoxically—turn out to be the vindication of the unitary character of mental life and of the recurrent patterns by which it falls apart or regenerates itself. But in order to make the unitary conception of mental illness part of a unitary program for psychiatry you need to dissociate it from the reductionist organic bias that it had during its mid-nineteenth-century heyday and never completely lost in the hands of its later defenders. This bias was the assumption that the biological correlates to be discovered are the sufficient cause of all major mental illness.

Once we free the conception of the unitary mental disease from its reductionist prejudice, we can also give it a more subtle meaning. It signifies less the belief in a single mental disorder than an awareness that almost all symptomatic differences are unstable, shallow, and circumstantial. They disclose more or less partial and more or less severe aspects of themes that recur throughout the entire field of mental pathology. (I shall later offer a summary description of these themes.) The physical and psychodynamic processes that generate mental disorder achieve a provisional symptomatic definition only fairly late in their development. This remark brings me to the third idea in the biological program.

The study of the biochemical triggers, residues, and counterparts of mental disease is no substitute for the analysis of the internal world of the imagination and, above all, of the imagination of selfhood and relationship, whose crisis constitutes the heart of the psychotic event. The interesting difference is the one that separates the very few diseases in which the biological defect almost automatically provokes the disintegration of the imaginative realm of relationship and selfhood from the much more common ones—perhaps all the classical psychoses—in which the organic facts are mediated and redirected by a personal drama. It is precisely because of this mediation and reciprocal influence that the disintegration of consciousness is likely to be more partial in the classical psychoses: in them consciousness falls apart only at its weakest point.

From this there arises a striking and counterintuitive theoretical possibility: just as psychological theories discover facts about the normal from the study of the anomalous so we can learn about the more common, less organic mental diseases from the rarer, more directly organic ones. In these diseases, the biological mechanisms are cruder and more overt. The trials of a consciousness in trouble appear more fully. It is as if the organism had turned the self into a puppet and, like a demonic puppeteer, forced it to enact the entire script of its downfall.

The three elements of the biological program have an intimate relation to one another. In fact, properly understood they form a single view. The first idea—the conception of a unified symptomatology and a double causation of mental disorders—develops into the third idea—the study of the less organic through the more organic. The development proceeds through the mediation of the second idea—the rejection of false determinacy in the diagnostic classification. This is in turn only a corollary of the first idea.

The Psychological Program

The Problem of Indeterminacy

Now let me shift the ground of my discussion quite suddenly to the criticism of psychological explanations in psychiatry. The focus of my remarks will be the significance for psychiatry of its extraordinary encounter with Freud's theory. Once the heretical doctrine had been incorporated into the mainstream of orthodoxy, it began to change and dissolve in ways that remain misunderstood. A reflection on this experience can reveal another point of growth and opportunity for psychiatry.

The great scandal in the use of psychological models—Freudian or not—in contemporary psychiatry is what I have called their indeterminacy. By indeterminacy I mean the overabundance of plausible but only ambiguously successful responses to the same explanatory or therapeutic problems. There are just too many alternative explanations and treatments based on too many incompatible pictures of what is in fact the case. The variety of meaningful interpretations in turn puts pressure against the diagnostic categories. It makes them seem more or less arbitrary.

First, there is the indeterminacy of the explanatory stories that can be told to and about a particular patient—and told in a way that makes sense not only to the psychiatrist or psychoanalyst but to the patient himself. The same biographical material can be retrospectively interpreted, and even occasionally foreseen, through accounts that invoke the Freudian oedipal conflicts, or through an analysis of reinforcement episodes that produced a rigid pattern of inference and habit with respect to particular issues of perception and conduct, or through a larger set of moral ideas about the growth of the self on the testing ground of vulnerability to hurt, loss, and disappointment.

Then there is the indeterminacy of the therapies. Strategies of discourse and relationship based upon very different psychodynamic models, and embodied in very different styles of practice, often turn out to be startlingly comparable in their effect or lack of effect.

Finally, there is the indeterminacy in the empirical referents of the underlying psychological theories themselves. It is shocking, for example, to discover that many of the central propositions of behavior or learning theory and of Freudian psychology can be mapped onto each other, if the content of learning processes and reinforcement mechanisms is defined in certain ways. It is possible to suggest alternative persuasive stories in therapeutic discourse about a particular psychotic episode. It is even possible to take a large range of mental facts and give them, systematically, alternative causal explanations.

The full extent of this multisided indeterminacy is constantly understated and repressed in modern psychiatry. There is more to the repression than an uncritical commitment to a particular theory; there is also the intimation of a dilemma. Either you avert your gaze from the indeterminacy or—so it seems—you are led to an unqualified relativism and left with nothing but the hard core of biological explanation.

The problem of indeterminacy has nevertheless had a far-reaching influence upon the use that psychiatry makes of psychological models in general and of Freudian ideas in particular. Compare, for example, Freud's analysis of melancholia or anxiety with the superficially similar treatment of these experiences in standard textbooks and monographs admittedly influenced by Freud's ideas. In his system, these affects were part of a tight explanatory structure: they were the specific results of specific episodes in the history of repression, as narrated in *Mourning and Melancholia* or in the convolutions of his writings about anxiety. In the neo-Freudian psychiatry, they tend, instead, to become more or less generic ego affects.

The whole explanatory scheme has undergone a subtle but remarkable change. The first key element of this new theoretical scheme is the idea of the psyche as an equilibrium system engaged in transactions between external stress and internal instinctual or unconscious demands. The second element is the hypothesis that a defect in psychological development amounts essentially to a failure of plasticity in the psyche—a routinized pattern of perception and conduct with respect to a crucial source of conflict like dependency or sexuality. The third element is the notion that some added internal or external stress calls the bluff on the pattern and upsets the equilibrium. Anxiety and depression count as the signs of this forcing of the limits.

This emergent picture differs greatly from Freud's. It changes the sense of the entire Freudian vocabulary. It is an oblique response to the problem of indeterminacy. Because it is indirect, it is also inadequate: it fails to acknowledge the depth of its own rupture with the ideas from which it grew and to develop a theoretical system and practice with which to look the embarrassments of indeterminacy in the face.

This loosening in the determinacy of psychodynamic explanations, which the relativization of Freud's ideas exemplifies, has an even more dramatic consequence. The whole conception of a psychodynamic psychiatry rests on the belief in a stable middle ground between organically based mental disorders and the ordinary experience of suffering. The middle ground is the one studied by people who, though they may not deal in chemistry, claim to draw upon the fabulous authority of science rather than the general moral wisdom of mankind. The enlargement of the psychodynamic models under the pressure of the indeterminacy problem and the simultaneous advance of insight into organic factors in mental disease have the effect of weakening the hold on the middle ground. The practitioners of psychodynamic models, such as the neo-Freudian theorists of the self, find themselves often enough dealing with people whose complaints of despair, confusion, and apathy seem indistinguishable from the subject matter of Rousseau's *Emile* or a thousand other meditations on the making of a self.

The defenders of a reductionist, biological psychiatry see in this situation a chance to move in for the kill. Those who resist their claims in the name of a psychodynamic psychiatry hold on to the middle ground all the more fiercely. They do so against mounting odds.

Both groups, however, are mistaken. The destruction of the middle ground will not produce the consequences that the reductionists desire and that their enemies fear. Why this is so will become clear only after my earlier argument about the mental and the organic has been combined with views that I shall now develop.

Indeterminacy and the Appeal to a Foundational View of Passion and Imagination

To confront the problem of indeterminacy in its full dimension, consider another still larger and more speculative issue: the nature of passion (affect, emotion, and more), which is to say the nature of the reality with which psychiatry deals insofar as it is more than a branch of biology. For this is the way thought develops: it tears through the distinction between the technical and the philosophical to gain partial and temporary respite from the paralyzing effect of its own presuppositions.

It seems strange but it is true that though psychiatry is about the human passions it has no conception of passion at all, except derivatively from some other formative idea. In fact, like all modern thought, it has always depended for its image of passion upon two ruling contrasts. One view contrasts passion to reason; another, to social convention. Each of these traditions of thought suggests a different perspective upon what madness ultimately means. In one case, it is passion that gets out of hand, rebels against reason, and causes a loss of the sense of reality. In the other case, it is emotion that detaches itself from its normal objects in society, rises up against the demands of an established form of social life, and goes from maladjustment to complete social antagonism or paralysis. In either case, the paradigmatic reality lies somewhere other than in passion itself—in reason or social convention. Passion, or madness as the rebellion of passion, is the black box that holds whatever opposes these exemplary forces. Many of the humanistic attacks on modern psychology and psychiatry can in fact be understood as a half-conscious polemic with these images of passion, whose hidden, guiding presence in the ruling theories the critics rightly intuit.

I shall not try to show the many disadvantages that each of these conceptions has as the starting point for a psychological psychiatry. Instead, I shall suggest the possibility of a view that puts passion at the center and that describes it in relation to itself rather than to a contrasting reality. At least, such a view has the virtue of providing a perspective on the whole life of passion that does not prejudge its relation to the claims that society and external reality make upon the will and the imagination.

Among the elements of an alternative account of passion might be the following. The ground of passion—the area of life within which passion moves—is the domain of experience in which people count for one another as more than means or obstacles to the realization of practical ends. The other person is surrounded by an aura, as if each episode of passionate encounter raised, and provisionally answered, the basic questions: Is there a place for me in the world, or am I one too many? What is to become of the relationship between my longing for other people and the way they jeopardize me? What is my possible relationship to my own distinctive identity and character? Is it given to me as a fate? Can I either reject it or transform it?

Within such a conception, passion means everything that falls under the current psychiatric usage of the terms "affect" or "emotion." But it means a great deal more as well: the enactment of possible forms of experience within the key setting of the personal. The experience of passion is located at the point where distinctions between desire (wanting something from the other person) and knowledge (viewing him and oneself in a certain way) collapse. Together with collective experiments in the organization of work and power, it is the substratum from which more articulate images of society are drawn. It is the liquid form into which these images melt back at times of heightened practical or visionary strife.

Two formative themes run through the vicissitudes of the passions. There is the theme of human association: the struggle to find a way to experience relationship with others as something that confirms the person in his own being rather than as an outright assault on his distinctive identity. In fact, all the vices described in classical moral doctrine, starting from the root experience of hatred, can be understood as different forms and degrees of failure in the achievement of a solution to the problem of longing and jeopardy. And then there is the theme of identity and character: the capacity to enter into your own character while recognizing it, at any given time, as a partial, provisional, and transformable version of your own self. It is not something fragile or alien. Nor is it an irrevocable fate that rules you once and for all.

Each of these themes presents itelf under a dual aspect. It is a problem of freedom and will: the power progressively to extend our intimate sense of relationship and identity, whose collapse represents the paradigmatic experience of blockage and loss. It is also a matter of reality and imagination: the ability to conceive the life of relationship and identity as something that, like physical reality itself, is intelligible only insofar as it is capable of changing. The life of passion amounts to a continuous exercise in the ability to imagine identity and association, by imagining their transformative variations. The struggle for reality can never be separated from the idea and the experience of transformation, particularly of the transformation of the facts that define the continuity and the apartness of the self.

The link between the derangement of passion—identity and relationship—and the disorder of perception and cognition is one of the most seductive problems in psychiatry. All I can do here is to indicate summarily how the two sets of problems might fit together within the kind of theory for which I am arguing. The subversion of understanding, like the disturbance of passion, presents variations on a small number of themes. These themes run throughout the whole field of mental illness, whatever the relative role of psychodynamic and physical factors. Here again, different disorders show different faces. But the more deeply we penetrate into the clinical material, the more clearly we see that these are faces of the same thing.

One way to characterize the central principle in the disorganization of perception and reasoning is to say that it consists in a waning of the capacity to distinguish sameness and difference. The cumulative loss of this capacity deprives the self of the power to deal transformatively with the world, whether by thought or by action. Things appear simultaneously merged and isolated in ways that depart from ordinary reasoning and perception without enlarging the reconstructive power of the imagination.

The decline of the ability to grasp sameness and difference, assertion and negation, is connected in several ways with limits to the understanding and the experience of possibility. The capacity to identify facts, and to characterize them as the same or different, always turns upon an insight into counterfactual possibilities: to know what would happen to things under alternative circumstances of change-inducing pressure. The destruction of insight into counterfactual possibility in turn always connects with the weakening of a person's ability to imagine himself as standing in a practical, transformative relation to the world around him, and, most immediately, to the people with whom he deals.

The crisis in the power to establish sameness and difference reconfirms the loss of freedom. It does so by circumscribing the reach of the imagination: the faculty of conceiving of things neither as rigid nor as randomly mutable but as transformed through conflict and contradiction. Thus, the effects of the crisis are only superficially similar to those of creative insight in science, art, or religion. Such insight disorganizes conventional views of sameness and difference by expanding the sense of possible transformation and the power of the mind to represent and to enact possibility.

The privileged realm for the experience of possibility is precisely the relationship of individuals to one another and to their characters; in the inner life of mental disease, the disturbances of passion have a priority over the derangements of perception and knowledge. The life of passion is the school of freedom.

The Diagnostic and Explanatory Implications

Now, some such elementary picture of passion and imagination does not depend upon an underlying contrast to reason or social convention. Moreover, it can be developed into a very concrete set of ideas about particular turning points in mental life. All I shall do here is to point out the implications that such a development might have for two crucial issues in psychological psychiatry: the basis of the diagnostic categories and the stubborn puzzles of indeterminacy.

The classical psychoses ring the changes on the problems of identity or character and relationship or association as they present themselves to the will and the imagination. The less arbitrary diagnostic categories may turn out to be the ones that play out a particular aspect of the central history of passion. Various schizoid and paranoid states and other affective disorders focus on the simultaneous failure of relationship and apartness; dissociative hysteria, on the resistance to the acceptance of continuing identity; and obsessive-compulsive tendencies, on the reverse of this resistance, which is the denial of experiment and plasticity in the life of the self. The deeper forms of paranoia and schizophrenia bring together the failures of relationship and identity. But they do so with a difference: in what we are used to describing as paranoia, the will struggles to inhabit an imaginative world in which identity and relationship are possible. In outright schizophrenia this world has dwindled into a more terrible state of dissolution.

Such an approach to the diagnostic categories leads to a multiple relativization. It effaces the rigidity of the distinctions among the psychoses, between the only mediately organic psychoses and the so-called psychoneuroses, and, most importantly, between all these mental phenomena and the ordinary life of passion. Our general moral insight and our psychiatric discoveries are relevant to each other. One of the aims of a theory of the passions must be to construct the basic analytic language that enables us to translate one of these sets of ideas into the other.

This underlying theory would also have implications for the problem of indeterminacy. There is perhaps an escape from the dilemma of unrepentant single vision and despairing agnosticism in our attitude toward the stories and theories of contemporary psychiatry. It is the hypothesis that insofar as these available warring views are correct and effective, they will turn out to be special cases or partial descriptions of the more fundamental account given in the theory of the passions. The only reason for legitimate substantive divergence would be a consequence of the special way in which the problems of identity and relationship manifest themselves in each society or historical period. For example, the perspicacity of Freud's developmental psychology, on this view, has to do with the extent to which the sexual psychodramas on which it fastens represent in miniature the life of passion. The least successful elements in Freud's theory result from its mistaking of the localized variations for the deeper themes and from its failure to grasp the extent to which its account is oriented to a certain historically bounded experience of social and family life.

The work of theory in this area must be to show how the more general view of passion generates more limited and concrete explanations that apply in the presence of well-defined boundary conditions. Many specific explanatory or therapeutic proposals would be excluded by the general view. This exclusion is what, in the end, would make the theory testable.

The Therapeutic Implication

The approach I have outlined has a general therapeutic implication: all the forms of discourse and action with the power to enhance the will and the imagination as they direct themselves to the core facts of identity and relationships may be effective forms of non-pharmacological psychotherapy. The unification of theory may be directly proportional to the diversification of therapy. The psychotherapies would be successful to the extent that they shared in the power of art to emancipate the imagination and the will.

Every non-physical therapy with a chance to succeed over a broad range of psychiatric practice contains three elements. The first element is the enactment of a larger set of possibilities in the experience of identity and relationship and in the neighboring realm of perception and reasoning. This enactment is made possible by the convergent influence of two more elements. One of them is the patient's acceptance of increased vulnerability to his therapist. Trust must be given and won. The enlargement of the life of identity and relationship must be prefigured in the therapeutic setting. The other additional element is an explanatory story that enables the patient to make sense of the connection between his present condition of straitened constraint and the larger set of possibilities of passion and perception that the psychodynamic therapy wants to make available to him. This story may—but it need not—be cast in the form of a biographical argument about how the situation of constraint arose.

The Freudian analytic technique can then be understood as only a special case of this universe of possible therapies. Read "working through" for enactment, "transference" for trust, and "analysis" for explanatory story. All such special cases will appeal to stories based on psychodynamic theories that are themselves only special cases of the general account of passion and perception.

The crucial theoretical and therapeutic problems lie concealed in the last of the three elements I listed. An assumption that underlies almost all psychological therapies, including the Freudian, is the existence of a close tie between the success of a therapeutic strategy and the objective truth of the explanatory stories that it deploys. But this assumption is manifestly false, so long as we define success as the restoration of the patient to normal functioning within his society. The story with the best chance of success, in this sense, is the one that combines a truth with a lie. (Every agnostic psychiatrist knows this when he talks about religion. But he forgets it when he talks about himself.) The truth is the existence of a real connection between the stories that are told and the general history of passion and imagination. Sheer make-believe will not work unless it expresses, at least metaphorically, something that is in fact the case. The lie is the passage of this true insight through a prism that filters out whatever understandings of the history of passion and perception would be most likely to subvert willing participation in established society and culture.

Here is a simplified example, which takes a narrow focus the better to elucidate the argument just made. Imagine a society in which public and private life are felt to be more or less starkly separated and in which the most probing experiences are, for most people, reserved to the intimate realm of private experience. In such a society, it will be convenient for the explanatory stories to narrate family and childhood psychodramas. Such stories will encourage the patient to enact possibilities in ways that make it easy for him to insert himself into a social world that sharply contrasts the public and the private realms.

Now suppose a therapy that rejected the alloy of falsehood in the amalgam of explanatory ideas. It would deliberately offer alternative kinds of explanatory stories (and not just alternative stories of the same kind) in order to expose the necessarily hypothetical and partial quality of each. It would relate every concrete psychological constraint to the most basic problems of identity and relationship and of the insight into counterfactual possibility. It would do all this in a way that drove home the contingent and transformable character of the social and cultural settings of personal experience. Such a psychotherapy would be more than a special case within a universe of possible therapies; it would be the general case itself turned into a therapeutic approach. Its aim would be less to restore the patient to effective presence within an established order than to enlarge his realm of possible understanding and experience, to enlarge it even beyond what his society and culture could readily countenance.

To gain freedom of insight and action in a more remote context, often at the price of ineptitude in an immediate one, is a definition of genius. The psychotherapy that takes this freedom as its goal wants to heal the self by making it share somehow in the accomplishment of genius. But this is not the road to happy, stable, or resigned living. Truth gets people in trouble. The only practical problem with self-deception is that some people don't know when to stop. For them you have the *Diagnostic and Statistical Manual.*

The conception of a psychotherapy that refuses to stay within the realm of the special case has a close though hidden connection to my earlier remarks about the mental and the organic. Explanatory stories compatible with the fluidity of nosological distinctions must be able to relate particular mental disorders to the unitary inner life of passion and imagination.

The project of such a psychotherapy also has an important parallelism to the idea of transformative political mobilization, even though it lacks any particular political direction of its own. For every exercise in transformative politics must appeal to forms of human association that the present order of society excludes. It must build movements and organizations that present, in their internal structure, an image of the future that it intends to establish.

What a Psychiatrist Should Be

By placing my earlier remarks about the relation between the organic and the mental alongside my later discussion of the indeterminacy problem, it is possible to arrive at a view of what a psychiatrist ought to be. Three sets of concerns must join to guide his activity. First, he should be a person committed to studying and treating the disorders of passion and perception in their unitary inner life. These disorders are defined by their subversive effect upon the representation and enactment of possibility—a criterion with only an oblique relation to the restoration of adaptive ease and normal function. Given this way of looking at things, no rigid distinction exists between the analysis of the ordinary consciousness and the approach to mental pathology. The element of madness in ordinary thought and conduct consists precisely in the arbitrary constraint on possible experience and possible insight that every stable social world and every settled mode of discourse impose. Second, the psychiatrist should be somebody interested in the relative roles of physical and psychodynamic factors in mental disorders. He may approach explanation and therapy more from one of these angles than from the other. But he would be a fool to mistake occasional explanatory and therapeutic success for a revelation of general truth. He should understand that proximate causation can take the form of parallel factors that converge at some still undefined limit. Third, insofar as he is a scientist, he should define it as part of his concern to work toward an understanding of this limit: to find out how the unitary life of passion and perception comes to be so deeply imprinted on the organism that a disturbance at one level so regularly produces repercussions at the other.

The Unitary Program in a Nutshell

The overall structure of my argument should now be clear. There are two decisive elements in the program that scientific psychiatry must carry out in order to correct itself and to advance beyond its present hesitancy between a blinding sectarianism and a dazed eclecticism.

The biological aspect of the program demands the reorientation of theory and research beyond immediate psychopharmacological effects. It proposes the revival and reinterpretation of the unitary view of the core mental diseases as an interruptable chain reaction or progression of episodes that encompass the entire universe of imagination and will, of identity and relationship. It suggests the use of the more strictly organic mental diseases as material in which to study not only the biochemical triggering mechanisms and correlates but even the imaginative world of those psychoses whose relationship to the organism is more reciprocal and mediated.

The psychological aspect of the program is the open

confrontation with the problem of indeterminacy in all its forms, the redefinition and revision of available psychological models as special cases of a more general theory of the passions, the use of this theory to compare the internal experience of the psychoses with the ordinary experiences of identity and relationship, and the overthrow of the traditions of thinking about mind that appeal to a derivative and undeveloped view of passion, as a foil to rational understanding or social convention.

The biological and psychological aspects of the program confirm each other. Both of them presuppose a reconstruction of our understanding of the relationship between the organic and the mental and the refusal to reify a superstitious view of the hypothetico-deductive method and to imitate the internal organization of other sciences, in other domains. Both of them work toward a picture of the deep unity of mental phenomena as a realm of transactions between the mind and the organism, the imagination and the will, passion and imagination, transactions that address the fundamental conditions of personality. On these two bases a new generation of psychiatrists must reestablish the foundations of psychiatry.

Let me now summarily place my argument within two larger settings: a context of culture and a context of politics.

The Contexts of Culture and Politics

One of the most important events in the history of modern culture was the development of a revolutionary view of human nature by the great artists, and especially the great writers, of the early twentieth century. Compared with this modernist view of the self, earlier images of man look shoddy and unconvincing. Modernism, however, allows us to regain the deeper meaning of insights into human nature that lie buried in the teachings of the great world religions. The premodernist views of man characteristically alternate between sentimentality and cynicism, between the classical moralizing doctrines of the virtues and the vices and the cynical counterattack of a Machiavelli or a Hobbes. We find this mélange between a superficial sentimentality and an equally superficial cynicism reproduced even in the work of so radical a thinker as Marx. It is a blend that unhappily continues to support much of contemporary social theory.

The conquests of cultural modernism in its investigation of the self include the following three ideas. First, modernism discovered that the passions have no natural structure of social hierarchy and convention, contrary to what the moral and political doctrines of most of the great civilizations have preached. The world of face-to-face relations contains in undefined form all the possible schemes of human association; in it we can always find inspiration for resistance to the claim that each society tacitly makes to be the natural or the necessary or the best possible ordering of human relationships. Second, modernism insisted on the relativity, the ambivalence, and the dynamism of the passions: the presence of love in hatred and hatred in love, of virtue in vice and vice in virtue, the experimental and surprising quality of the life of passion, forcing us at every moment into a transvaluation of our moral preconceptions without inevitably leading us into moral agnosticism. Third, modernism emphasized lust and despair as passions that not only undermine particular ties and beliefs but that call into question the claims of culture and society to self-sufficiency and authority.

This modernist investigation of the self failed to produce the vision of a reconstructed society or to inspire a social theory that could match and develop, in the language of discursive thought, the understandings available as art. When the criticism of bourgeois society fell apart into separate and incommunicable halves—leftism and modernism—both parts suffered. They suffered in the effectiveness of their practice as well as in the truth of their ideas. Insofar as psychiatry carries out the program described here, it will be helping to find as theory and science what we know only as art; to transform cultural modernism into theoretical accomplishment.

There is another setting in which the execution of that program can be viewed: the context of politics.

An unmistakable and unsettling fact about modern psychiatry, and especially about psychotherapy, is that it flourishes in the rich countries of the contemporary Western world, where politics are a narrow exercise in bargaining and drift, where the possibility that society might be deeply transformed through collective action is made to look like a revolutionary reverie, where permanent cultural revolution coexists with permanent political deadlock, and where the privileged devote themselves to the expensive, selfish, and impotent cultivation of subjectivity. In these societies, a large part of the structure of social life that is effectively withdrawn from the scope of democratic politics is handed over to the professions and treated as a matter of technical necessity or scientific expertise.

The effort to expand the scope of democratic politics, to restore society to collective conflict and collective imagination, must encompass, in these countries, an attempt to demystify professional expertise. In the case of the economics and legal professions, this means showing how their fundamental controversies are the same contestable issues of social fact and social ideal that lie at the heart of moral and political debates in the contemporary world. In the case of psychiatry, the implication is more subtle.

We stand at a point in world history where everything that is most constructive in political thought depends upon attempts to weave political schemes of social life together with visions of associative possibility rooted in the elementary experiences of personality. The mode of thought responsible for the maintenance of this linkage has always been something analogous to what we in the West know as classical humanism. But we are no longer able to credit this stately moral wisdom with political authority, given its tacit and unargued conservatism, its non-empirical and non-experimental character, and, above all, its superficial, rigid view of the passions and of their relation to society.

It is part of the mission of psychiatry to force us to acknowledge that the mold of classical humanism is broken forever and to help us fashion a less illusory alternative. To do this, psychiatry need not compromise with political and moral interests beyond its ken. It must carry out a theoretical program that, like the one outlined here, grows out of its internal development as a science. In so doing, it will have to acknowledge—with all the implications this has for the practical exercise of authority—that there are no clear-cut and permanent frontiers between psychiatric and non-psychiatric discourse.

The reconstruction of psychiatry along the lines suggested calls for familiarity with a vast amount of clinical material joined to a mastery of the most diverse traditions of social thought, the patient shrewdness of scientific disbelief and discovery drawn into the service of visionary insight. Seen against its wider background of culture and politics, it is both an intricate scientific achievement and a high spiritual task. It exacts from those who undertake it cold and cunning ardor.

To help it in its labors, psychiatry has an advantage that other sciences lack. Its fate and failures as a science are paralleled by the experiences of the living person with whom, in madness or sanity, it deals. All human activities mirror one another in their most basic elements: from the activities by which people uphold or surrender a world of identity and relationship to those by which they invent a bold theory about that very same world, regaining as science what they have first undergone as life.

A time comes when this science falls apart. It has either too few or too many answers. Its puzzles can be solved in too many alternative ways, and none of these has the power to exclude the others. Its theory and its practice are subject to a mounting tide of outsiders' criticism. Will the science retreat into a stockade and anxiously hold its critics at bay as it tries to forget its own fragility? Or will it renounce what it has in order to recreate it, seeking instruction everywhere and reassurance nowhere?

A time comes when the person begins to stagger under the weight of his own selfhood. The torn and tenacious heart swings between the unresisting body and the uncompromising mind. At last, he stumbles and cries out. Will he give up hope of being both together with other people and apart from them, and of having a character that is his very own and yet incomplete and transformable? Or will he subject himself, again and again, to experiments in vulnerability to hurt by others and to the risks of deliberate action? Experiments that empower the will and the imagination and renew the life of relationship and identity.

In the practice of science, as in the ordeal of the self, there is no rescue by immunity. Salvation through the acceptance of vulnerability is the only kind of salvation there really is.

Roberto Mangabeira Unger teaches law and social theory at Harvard University. He is the author of *Knowledge and Politics* and *Law in Modern Society* (both, The Free Press) and other philosophical, political, and legal writings. His forthcoming *Politics* (Cambridge University Press) presents, in several books, a general social theory and a program for social reconstruction. An active participant in the politics of his native Brazil, he has devoted himself to the development of a democratic leftist party and directed a governmental organization that assists homeless and needy children.